TRAVELER'S GUIDE TO

CAMPING MEXICO'S BAJA

Explore Baja and Puerto Peñasco With Your RV Or Tent

Mike and Terri
Church

Rolling HOMES PRESS

ROLLING HOMES PRESS

Published by
Rolling Homes Press
P.O. Box 2099
Kirkland, WA 98083-2099

www.rollinghomes.com

Printed in the United States of America
First Printing 2001

Publisher's Cataloging in Publication

Church, Mike.
  Traveler's guide to camping Mexico's Baja : explore Baja
and Puerto Peñasco with your RV or tent / Mike and Terri Church.
  p.cm.
  Includes index.
  Preassigned LCCN: 00-92956
  ISBN 0-9652968-5-7

  1. Baja California (Mexico : State)–Guidebooks. 2. Recreational vehicles–
Mexico–Baja California (State)–Guidebooks. 3. Camp sites, facilities, etc.–
Mexico–Baja California (State)–Guidebooks. 4. Recreation areas–Mexico–Baja
California (State)–Guidebooks. I. Church, Terri. II. Title.

F1246.2.C48 2001   917.2′204836–dc21

*This book is dedicated
to three very good friends*

**Sophie, Sarah, and Mark
Aoki-Fordham**

Other Books by Mike and Terri Church
and
Rolling Homes Press

Traveler's Guide To
Alaskan Camping

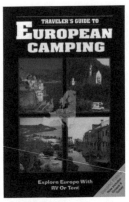

Traveler's Guide To
European Camping

Traveler's Guide To
Mexican Camping

RV Adventures in the
Pacific Northwest

A brief summary of the above books is provided on pages 222 and 223

When traveling by RV the most complete and up-to-date information on RV parks is always important. To provide our readers with the most current and accurate information available we maintain a website which lists all known updates and changes to information listed in our books. Just go to our website at www.rollinghomes.com and click on the *Book Additions and Corrections* button to review the most current information.

WARNING, DISCLOSURE, AND COMMUNICATION WITH THE AUTHORS AND PUBLISHERS

Half the fun of travel is the unexpected, and self-guided camping travel can produce much in the way of unexpected pleasures, and also complications and problems. This book is designed to increase the pleasures of Baja camping and reduce the number of unexpected problems you may encounter. You can help ensure a smooth trip by doing additional advance research, planning ahead, and exercising caution when appropriate. There can be no guarantee that your trip will be trouble free.

Although the authors and publisher have done their best to ensure that the information presented in this book was correct at the time of publication they do not assume and hereby disclaim any liability to any party for any loss or damage caused by errors, omissions, or any other cause.

In a book like this it is inevitable that there will be omissions or mistakes, especially as things do change over time. If you find inaccuracies we would like to hear about them so that they can be corrected in future editions. We would also like to hear about your enjoyable experiences. If you come upon an outstanding campground or destination please let us know, those kinds of things may also find their way to future versions of the guide or to our internet site. You can reach us by mail at:

Rolling Homes Press
P.O. Box 2099
Kirkland, WA 98083-2099

You can also communicate with us by sending an e-mail through our web site at:

www.rollinghomes.com

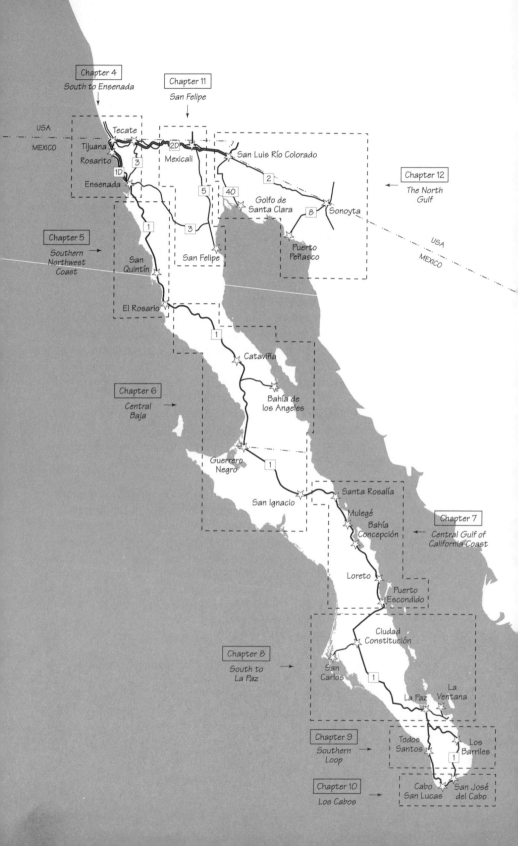

Chapter 4
South to Ensenada

Chapter 11
San Felipe

Chapter 12
The North Gulf

Chapter 5
Southern Northwest Coast

Chapter 6
Central Baja

Chapter 7
Central Gulf of California Coast

Chapter 8
South to La Paz

Chapter 9
Southern Loop

Chapter 10
Los Cabos

USA
MEXICO

Tecate
Tijuana
Rosarito
1D
Ensenada
2D
Mexicali
San Luis Río Colorado

3
5
40
Golfo de Santa Clara
8
Sonoyta

USA
MEXICO

1
San Quintín
3
San Felipe
Puerto Peñasco

El Rosario

1
Cataviña

Bahía de los Angeles

Guerrero Negro
1
San Ignacio
Santa Rosalía
Mulegé
Bahía Concepción

Loreto
Puerto Escondido

Ciudad Constitución

San Carlos
1
La Paz
La Ventana

Todos Santos
Los Barriles
1

Cabo San Lucas
San José del Cabo

TABLE OF CONTENTS

PREFACE 10

CHAPTER 1
WHY CAMP THE BAJA PENINSULA? 13

CHAPTER 2
DETAILS, DETAILS, DETAILS 18

CHAPTER 3
HOW TO USE THE DESTINATION CHAPTERS 39

CHAPTER 4
SOUTH TO ENSENADA 44
    Introduction 45
    The Routes, Towns, and Campgrounds
        Tijuana 48
        Tijuana to Rosarito 50
        Rosarito 53
        Rosarito to Ensenada 54
        Ensenada 60
        Tecate 67
        Tecate to Ensenada 70

CHAPTER 5
SOUTHERN NORTHWEST COAST 72
    Introduction 73
    The Routes, Towns, and Campgrounds
        Ensenada to San Quintín 78
        San Quintín 81
        San Quintín to El Rosario 85
        El Rosario 85

CHAPTER 6
CENTRAL BAJA 88
    Introduction 89
    The Routes, Towns, and Campgrounds
        El Rosario to Cataviña 95

Cataviña 96
Cataviña to Guerrero Negro 98
Guerrero Negro 100
Side Trip to Bahía de los Angeles 103
Bahía de los Angeles 104
Guerrero Negro to San Ignacio 108
San Ignacio 110

CHAPTER 7

CENTRAL GULF OF CALIFORNIA COAST 112
Introduction 113
The Routes, Towns, and Campgrounds
San Ignacio to Santa Rosalía 117
Santa Rosalía 118
Santa Rosalía to Mulegé 120
Mulegé 122
Mulegé to Bahía Concepción 125
Bahía Concepción 125
Bahía Concepción to Loreto 131
Loreto 131
Loreto to Puerto Escondido 135
Puerto Escondido 136

CHAPTER 8

SOUTH TO LA PAZ 138
Introduction 139
The Routes, Towns, and Campgrounds
Puerto Escondido to Ciudad Constitución 142
Ciudad Constitución 142
Side Trip to Puerto San Carlos 145
Puerto San Carlos 145
Ciudad Constitución to La Paz 147
La Paz 148
Side Trip to La Ventana 153
La Ventana 153

CHAPTER 9

SOUTHERN LOOP 156
Introduction 157
The Routes, Towns, and Campgrounds
La Paz to Todos Santos 161
Todos Santos 161
Todos Santos to Cabo San Lucas 163
La Paz to Los Barriles 164
Los Barriles 165
Los Barriles to San José del Cabo 168

CHAPTER 10
Los Cabos 170
    Introduction 171
    The Routes, Towns, and Campgrounds
        Cabo San Lucas.. 174
        Cabo San Lucas to San José del Cabo 176
        San José del Cabo 179

CHAPTER 11
San Felipe 182
    Introduction 183
    The Routes, Towns, and Campgrounds
        Mexicali 185
        Mexicali to San Felipe 186
        San Felipe.. 188

CHAPTER 12
Puerto Peñasco (Rocky Point) and Golfo de Santa Clara 198
    Introduction 199
    The Routes, Towns, and Campgrounds
        Sonoyta, Sonora and Lukeville, Arizona 202
        Lukeville/Sonoyta Crossing to Puerto Peñasco 203
        Puerto Peñasco 205
        San Luis Río Colorado, Sonora and San
           Luis, Arizona 212
        San Luis Río Colorado to Golfo de Santa Clara 212
        Golfo de Santa Clara 213

Index...216

PREFACE

Traveler's Guide to Camping Mexico's Baja is our fifth guidebook for campers. The titles of the others are *Traveler's Guide to European Camping, Traveler's Guide to Alaskan Camping, Traveler's Guide to Mexican Camping* and *RV Adventures in the Pacific Northwest.*

Like all of our books this one is a guidebook written specifically for camping travelers. As a camper you don't need the same information as a fly-in visitor. You don't care much about hotels, restaurants, and airline schedules, but you need to know what campgrounds are near, how to drive right to them without making wrong turns, and where to buy supplies. We want our book to be the one that you keep up front where it's handy, the one you refer to over and over because it contains what you need to know in a convenient format.

This book builds on the information included in *Traveler's Guide to Mexican Camping*. While that book covered the campgrounds of the Baja pretty thoroughly, it seemed to us that many travelers to the peninsula didn't really need the mainland information that is part of that book. Not only do they not need it, but they probably would rather not pay for it! It seemed to make sense to publish a subset of the Mexico book and offer it for a much lower price.

So that's pretty much what we have done. All of the Baja information that is in *Traveler's Guide to Mexican Camping* is included in this book. If you only plan to visit the Baja you don't need the larger book. We've also added a lot more Baja information to the book. We spent about one hundred pages talking about the region in the Mexico book, this new book has more than twice that number of pages. The information is all updated, we've visited every campground again. There are many more campgrounds, more maps, and more supplementary information.

This book also includes information about two destinations in northwest Sonora. The reason we've included this information is that these two locations offer many of the same attractions to RVers that the Baja does. They're just to the east of the Baja, close to the border, have great weather, and offer lots of outdoor attractions. If you haven't been to Mexico before give Puerto Peñasco or Golfo de Santa Clara a try. Once you get your feet wet you might opt for a trip down the Baja or even one to mainland Mexico.

Updating the information and expanding the book has been a lot of fun. The Baja is one of our favorite camping destinations, we enjoy it more each time we visit. The peninsula is a Mexican jewel that is easily available to anyone with an RV and a sense of adventure. We hope to see you there!

BAJA

Top Row Left: Fishing pangas on the beach in La Playa
Top Row Right: Beachside camping at Bahía Concepción
Bottom Row Left: Mission in San Ignacio
Bottom Row Right: The Baja's own Cirio cactus

CHAPTER

. . . . 1

WHY CAMP THE BAJA PENINSULA?

The border between the U.S. and Mexico's Baja Peninsula is like no other border on earth. It divides two countries with huge contrasts in culture, language, wealth, lifestyle, political systems, topography, and climate. Mexico is a fascinating place to visit and we think that driving your own rig and staying in campgrounds is the best way to do it. We hope that with this book in hand you will think so too.

People from north of the border have been exploring the Baja for years. The trip became much easier in 1973 when the paved Transpeninsular highway was built. Today this paved two-lane road leads to unparalleled camping opportunities.

Probably the largest number of folks who visit the Baja do so as fly-in tourists bound for the Los Cabos area at the end of the peninsula. There they find huge hotels, beaches, golf, fishing, and a bit of Mexican culture. That may be the easiest way to visit, it certainly is the most expensive. You can visit Los Cabos too, but as a camping traveler you'll also see the rest of the peninsula as you drive south, and you'll probably find you like it better.

While not really on the road to Los Cabos, Puerto Peñasco and San Felipe offer an easy introduction to Mexico. Both have easy to use border stations and good roads leading to seaside resorts that cater to the RV crowd. These are small, friendly towns that are easy to get around. There is a tradeoff, of course. Neither has great fishing and neither (so far) has a golf course. They do have great winter weather, decent prices, campsites along the beach, miles of back roads to explore with your four-wheeler, grocery stores, restaurants, and crafts markets. If you have any doubts about heading into Mexico these two towns can help you get your feet wet.

The west coast of the Baja near the California border, from Rosarito Beach south to Ensenada, is more of a weekend destination for folks from California than a long-term RVing destination. That's a simplification, many people have permanently-located rigs in this area. Others bring their rigs south for a month or two. The attractions here are bigger Mexican cities; lots of top-quality shopping, restaurants, and entertainment; golf; and decent fishing. Access isn't quite as easy as San Felipe or Puerto Peñasco because Tijuana is a bit of a roadblock, but you can finesse your way through the city or do an end run around it by crossing at Tecate. We explain how to do either in a later chapter. You should be aware that unlike the rest of the Baja, this area is more popular as a summer destination than a winter one because winter weather is cool.

For those interested in desert flora and fauna the Baja between El Rosario and Santa Rosalía is a fascinating place. For over 300 miles (480 km) the road winds its way through a variety of desert terrain with a wealth of cactus species and rock gardens perfect for photography. There's even a sight offered nowhere else on earth - desert whales! During January through March you can visit the California gray whale nursery lagoons and actually closely approach the whales with government-supervised small boat tour operators. Another unusual attraction of the area is the cave paintings left by ancient Baja inhabitants.

If your real dream is to boondock in your RV on a quiet beach next to tropical waters there are many places you can go on the Baja. Many great camping beaches are located along the Gulf of California between Santa Rosalía and Puerto Escondido. Lots of people go no farther south, they're perfectly satisfied to stay on one beautiful beach for the entire season.

Fishermen love the Baja. Both coasts offer great fishing. Some places require heavy open-water boats so you either have to bring a big boat from north of the border or charter. In other places a small car-top aluminum boat or an inflatable will give you access to plenty of fish. Or you can fish right off the beach. There are many places to go if you want to find excellent fishing, some favorites are the East Cape near Los Barriles, the Loreto area, and Los Cabos.

Are you looking for a winter destination offering a comfortable full-hookup campground with the services of a larger city, lots to do, and great weather? Consider La Paz. It has a population of about 180,000, large supermarkets, airline service, and five campgrounds with full hookups, many with swimming pools. Los Cabos is only a day trip from La Paz. For a smaller town to use as a winter base try Todos Santos, it has a beachside campground with full hookups, a quiet artsy atmosphere, and both La Paz and Los Cabos are nearby.

A Possible Itinerary

Probably the best way to actually show you what Baja has to offer is to outline a tour down the peninsula. This is a seventeen day tour, that's the bare minimum, better would be a month.

The 1,060 mile (1,731 km) long Mex 1 stretches the entire length of the Baja Peninsula, from Tijuana in the north to Cabo San Lucas at the far southern cape. The two-lane highway gives access to some of the most remote and interesting country in the world including lots of desert and miles and miles of deserted beaches.

This proposed itinerary takes 17 days and allows you to see the entire length of the peninsula. There are layover days at Guerrero Negro, Bahía Concepción, La Paz, and Cabo San Lucas. Many travel days require only a morning of driving leaving lots of time to relax and explore.

The most tempting modification to this itinerary will be to spend more time at each stop. There are also many additional stopover points along this route, just take a look through this book. Finally, it is possible to take a ferry from either La Paz or Santa Rosalía to the Mexican west coast where you can head north for home or head south for more fun. If you plan to do that don't forget to take our book *Traveler's Guide to Mexican Camping* along.

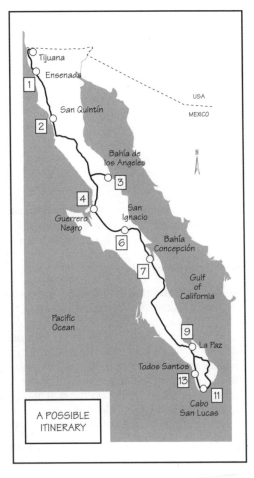

🚐 **Day 1 - Tijuana to Ensenada, 67 miles (108 km), 1.5 hours driving time** - This first day you cross the border at Tijuana. You probably won't even have to stop when entering Mexico because vehicle permits aren't required on the Baja. There's a four-lane toll road that follows the coast all the way to Ensenada. Once you arrive you will park and visit the *Migración* (Immigration) office near the entrance to town to get the tourist permits that are required since you will be in Mexico over 72 hours. You completed the drive to Ensenada before noon so there's plenty of time to look around town and pick up some groceries at one of the large modern supermarkets. Instead of spending the night at a campground in town you decide to stay at the beautiful Estero Beach Hotel/Resort campground beside the ocean a few miles south of Ensenada. You can celebrate your arrival in Mexico by having dinner at the excellent hotel restaurant.

🚐 **Day 2 - Ensenada to San Quintín, 122 miles (197 km), 4 hours driving time** - This will be another short day so there's really no hurry to get started. Once on the road you pass through rolling hills with the countryside getting dryer as you head south. At San Quintín you have a choice of campgrounds, try the Old Mill Trailer Park if you want full hookups and a restaurant or maybe the El Pabellón to sample a simple ejido-run campground with miles of windswept beach out front.

🚐 **Day 3 - San Quintín to Bahía de los Angeles - 219 miles (353 km), 6.25 hours driving time** - This is a longer day's drive so get a fairly early start. You'll want to stop and explore the cactus and rock fields in the Cataviña area before leaving Mex 1 and driving east on a paved but rough road to Bahía de los Angeles for your first glimpse of the Gulf of California. There's not a lot to the town itself, perhaps this is a good opportunity to head north of town and boondock along the water. If you have a small boat you might give the fishing a try. This is also great kayaking water.

Day 4 - Bahía de los Angeles to Guerrero Negro - 121 miles (195 km), 3.75 hours driving time - Today's destination is back on the other side of the peninsula, the salt-producing company town of Guerrero Negro. You'll spend two nights here because you want to visit the California gray whale nursery lagoon (Scammon's Lagoon) south of town. Spend the first night at the Malarrimo RV Park and visit their well-known restaurant. The second night you can spend at the primitive camping area right next to the lagoon after a day on the lagoon with the whales.

Day 6 - Guerrero Negro to San Ignacio - 89 miles (144 km), 2.25 hours driving time - San Ignacio is a true date-palm oasis in the middle of desert country. There's a new campground here, the Rice and Beans Oasis. It has an excellent restaurant. Don't forget to visit the plaza at the center of town to visit the cave art museum and the old mission church.

Day 7 - San Ignacio to Bahía Concepción, 95 miles (153 km), 2.5 hours driving time - Today, once again, you return to the Gulf of California side of the peninsula. You'll pass two interesting towns en route, Santa Rosalía and Mulegé. Neither has much room for big rigs so don't drive into either of these little towns. At Santa Rosalía you might leave your rig along the highway and take a stroll to see the Eiffel-designed metal-framed church. You'll probably have a chance to explore Mulegé later since it is quite close to the evening's destination at Bahía Concepción. Many people decide to end their journey at this point and go no further since the ocean-side camping along beautiful Bahía Concepción is many folk's idea of camping paradise. We'll assume you'll be strong and only stay for two nights.

Day 9 - Bahía Concepción to La Paz, 291 miles (469 km), 8.25 hours driving time - Since you are all rested up after that time along the bahía you decide to get an early start and blast on through all the way to La Paz. Don't forget to drive into Loreto for a quick look around, this was the first permanent Spanish settlement on the peninsula. You'll have to ignore the golf course too, even though you'll see people teeing off as you pass.

You will find your progress along the coast to be quite scenic but slow, especially as you climb up and over the Sierra de la Giganta, but for a long stretch on the plains to the west the roads are flat and straight allowing you to make good time. A late arrival in La Paz is not a problem because there are lots of campgrounds to choose from. You can take it easy the next day and explore the city.

Day 11- La Paz to Cabo San Lucas - 132 miles (212 km), 4 hours driving time - Today you will arrive in the true tourist's Baja. Take the long route to the Cape area by following Mex 1 around the east side of the Sierra de la Laguna. You'll have made reservations at one of the campgrounds near Cabo San Lucas to ensure a place to base yourself.

🚐 **Day 13 - Cabo San Lucas to Todos Santos - 45 miles (73 km), 1.25 hours driving time** - A short drive north along the west coast on Mex 19 will bring you to San Pedrito RV Park on the coast south of Todos Santos. This is an excellent place to spend several weeks along a beautiful Pacific beach or to gather yourself for the trip north.

🚐 **Day 14 through 17 - Todos Santos to Tijuana - 963 miles (1,553 km), 28 hours driving time** - You really have two choices for the return to the border. Many folks catch a ferry from La Paz to Topolobampo near Los Mochis and then drive north on four-lane Mex 15 to cross the border at Nogales near Tucson, Arizona. Others simply drive back the way they've come. By putting in decently long days of driving you could make the trip in four days with overnight stops at Ciudad Constitución (254 miles), San Ignacio (255 miles), and El Rosario (304 miles).

How This Book Is Arranged

Chapter 2 - Details, Details, Details is filled with essential background information. It tells you how to prepare your rig, how to cross the border, and how to deal with unfamiliar things while you are in Mexico.

Chapter 3 - How to Use the Destination Chapters gives a brief guide to using the information making up the bulk of the book.

Chapters 4 through 12 - These are the meat of the book. They describe the route down the Baja and also San Felipe and Puerto Peñasco. Along the way we provide a location map and description of virtually every formal campground on the Baja. You'll also find information about places to explore and things to do along the way.

Have Fun!

ESTA CARRETERA NO ES DE ALTA VELOCIDAD

THIS IS NOT A HIGH SPEED ROAD

GRACIAS POR USAR EL CINTURON DE SEGURIDAD

THANKS FOR USING YOUR SEATBELT

EN B.C.S.ES OBLIGATORIO EL CINTURON DE SEGURIDAD

IN BAJA CALIFORNIA SOUTH SEATBELTS ARE MANDATORY

PRECAUCION ZONA DE GANADO

CAUTION LIVESTOCK ZONE

PRINCIPIA TRAMO EN REPARACION A 500 m

HIGHWAY UNDER REPAIR IN 500 METERS

SI TOMA NO MANEJE

IF YOU DRINK DON'T DRIVE

DISMINUYA SU VELOCIDAD

REDUCE YOUR SPEED

TROPICO DE CANCER

TROPIC OF CANCER

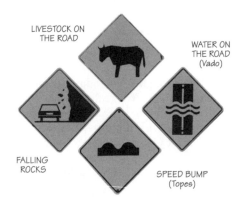

LIVESTOCK ON THE ROAD

WATER ON THE ROAD (Vado)

FALLING ROCKS

SPEED BUMP (Topes)

NO REBASE CON RAYA CONTINUA

NO PASSING WHEN CONTINUOUS LINE

CONCEDA CAMBIO DE LUCES

DIM YOUR LIGHTS FOR APPROACHING TRAFFIC

PRECAUCION CRUCE DE PEATONES

CAUTION PEDESTRIAN CROSSING

NO FRENE CON MOTOR

NO BRAKING WITH ENGINE

CURVA PELIGROSA A 400 m

DANGEROUS CURVE IN 400 METERS

PROHIBIDO TIRAR BASURA

THROWING TRASH PROHIBITED

MIRADOR DE MOLINERO

VIEWPOINT OF MILL

DESPACIO

SLOW

TOPES A 100m

SPEED BUMPS IN 100 METERS

ZONA URBANA MODERE VELOCIDAD

URBAN ZONE SLOW DOWN

km 1 0 7

KM MARKER

NO PASSING

NO TURNS

ALTO

STOP

STAY RIGHT

LEVEL OF WATER OVER ROAD

1.00
0.75
0.50
0.25

CHAPTER

· · · · · · · · · · · · · 2

DETAILS, DETAILS, DETAILS

Backroad Driving

It is hard to think of any other location in North America with such a wealth of back-road driving opportunities. While this is not a guidebook to Baja's backroad destinations we have tried to give readers some idea of what is available.

It seems that every guide to the Baja uses some system to rate the quality of the back roads. This is necessary, since they vary from wide graded roads to rocky tracks really only suitable for a burro. We've tried to skip the burro routes, but you should bear in mind that all back roads in this part of Mexico are very changeable. A winter storm can make even the best of them impassable for months and it's hard to predict when someone will run a grader along a road improving it in a major way. When you drive the back roads you must be prepared for the unexpected. Check road conditions with the locals, travel in groups of at least two rigs, and bring along equipment for getting out of trouble as well as for enduring several days in the hot dry desert. Some of the roads are very remote, you may have to save yourself if you have a problem.

We grade the roads into three types, the classifications depend upon the type of rig that is suitable:

Type 1 - An unpaved road usually suitable for motorhomes to 35 feet, and trailers that are not large or heavily loaded. Logic rules out big bus-type motorhomes, large fifth-wheels, and large trailers for travel off the pavement. These roads are occasionally graded but may have miles of washboard surfaces forcing you to creep along at very low speeds.

Type 2 - An unpaved road suitable for smaller RVs but not trailers. Our definition of smaller RVs requires good ground clearance, a maximum length of about 22 feet with no long or low rear overhangs, the ability to make steep climbs, and sturdy construction.

Type 3 - Requires four-wheel drive, lightly loaded, lots of clearance, and drivers with rugged constitutions and off-road experience.

We've rated roads based upon their normal condition but the roads do change and the ratings may become outdated. Check with someone who has recently driven the backroad route you are considering to see if conditions have changed.

Distances

As you plan your Baja trip and as you drive the highways you'll find the nearby Distance Table to be very helpful. We like to limit our driving days to no more than 200 miles on the Baja. Haste causes accidents.

Campgrounds

Mexican campgrounds vary immensely, especially on the Baja. They range from full-service campgrounds near the border comparable to anything in the U.S. to places that are boondocking sites where nothing is provided except perhaps an outhouse.

Bathroom facilities in Mexican campgrounds are often not up to the standards of Canadian and U.S. private campgrounds. Cleanliness and condition vary widely, each of our campground descriptions tries to cover this important subject. Campers in larger rigs probably won't care since they carry their own bathrooms along with them. Other campers might keep in mind that many of the campgrounds they frequent in the U.S. and Canada, especially in national, state, or provincial parks, have pit toilets and no shower facilities just like many of the places on the Baja.

In rural Mexico it is usually not acceptable to put used toilet tissue in the toilet bowl, a waste-paper basket is usually provided. Toilet tissue creates problems for marginal plumbing and septic systems, it plugs them up. Travelers who have visited other third-world countries have probably run into this custom before.

Many Baja campgrounds have hookups for electricity, water and sewer. The condition of the outlets, faucets, and sewer connections may not be of the same quality that you are accustomed to in the U.S. We find that in many campgrounds the hardware wasn't great when installed, and maintenance doesn't get done unless absolutely necessary. It is often a good idea to take a look at the connections on a parking pad before pulling in, you may want to move to another one.

Mexico uses the same 110-volt service that we use in the U.S. and Canada so your RV won't have to be modified for Mexico. Many campgrounds only have 15-amp household-type sockets so be sure that you have an adapter that lets you use these smaller sockets. Many sockets do not have a ground, either because the plug is the two-slot variety without the ground slot, or because the ground slot is not wired. It is a good idea to make yourself an adapter with a wire and alligator clip so you can provide your own ground.

It is also a good idea to test the electricity at your site before plugging in. You can buy a tester at your camping supply store before heading south that will quickly indicate the voltage and any faults of the outlet. This is cheap insurance.

Air conditioner use is something of a problem in Mexico. Heavy air conditioner use

DISTANCE TABLE

Miles

Kilometers

This page presents a triangular distance table for locations in Baja California. Distances in miles appear in the upper portion and distances in kilometers in the lower portion, read against the diagonal city labels.

City labels (along the diagonal):

- Bahía Concepción
- Bahía de los Ángeles
- Cabo San Lucas
- Catavina
- Ciudad Constitución
- El Rosario
- Ensenada
- Golfo de Santa Clara
- Guerrero Negro
- La Paz
- La Ventana
- Loreto
- Lupe Barrles
- Mexicali
- Mulegé
- Puertocitos
- Puerto Peñasco
- Rosarito
- San Carlos
- San Felipe
- San Ignacio
- San José del Cabo
- San Quintín
- San Luis Rio Colorado
- Santa Rosalía
- Tecate
- Tijuana
- Todos Santos

can cause voltage drops because most campgrounds do not have adequately sized transformers. Our understanding is that service of less than 105 volts can damage your air conditioner, so keep an eye on voltage.

Water connections are common, but you may not want to trust the quality of the water even if the campground manager assures you that it is good. See the *Drinking Water* section of this chapter for details on how to cope with this.

Sewer connections in Mexican campgrounds are often located at the rear of the site. You should make sure that you have enough hose to reach several feet past the rear of your rig before you come south. You will find it difficult to buy sewer hose south of the border.

There are two references you may see in our campground write-ups that need a little explanation. We sometimes make reference to "government campgrounds". When the Transpeninsular was built the government put in many campgrounds for travelers. These soon deteriorated, generators stopped working and most were abandoned, at least for a time. Now many are in operation again as virtual bookdocking sites run by individuals or ejidos.

You will also see references to ejidos or ejido campgrounds. Ejidos are a unique Mexican social enterprise. Space does not allow explanation of the whole idea here, but among gringos on the Baja the phrase ejido generally refers to a farming village while an ejido campground is one owned or operated by a Mexican village or family.

Caravans

An excellent way to get your introduction to Mexico is to take an escorted caravan tour. Many companies offer these tours, you'll see lots of caravans on the Baja. These range from luxury tours costing over $100 per day to months-long escort-only arrangements that are much less expensive.

A typical caravan tour on the Baja is composed of approximately 25 rigs. The price paid includes a knowledgeable caravan leader in his own RV, a tail-gunner or caboose RV with an experienced mechanic, campground fees, many meals and tours at stops along the way, and lots of camaraderie. Many people love RV tours because someone else does all the planning, there is security in numbers, and a good caravan can be a very memorable experience. Others hate caravans, and do so for just about the same reasons.

Remember that there will we a lot of costs in addition to those covered by the fee paid to the caravan company including fuel, insurance, maintenance, tolls, and groceries. We hear lots of good things about caravans, but also many complaints. Common problems include caravans that do not spend enough time at interesting places, delays due to mechanical problems with other rigs in the caravan, and poor caravan leaders who do not really know the territory or speak the language. A badly run caravan can be a disaster.

We've given the names, addresses and phone numbers below of some of the leading caravan companies. Give them a call or write a letter to get information about the tours they will be offering for the coming year. Once you have received the information do not hesitate to call back and ask questions. Ask for the names and phone numbers of people who have recently taken tours with the same caravan leader who will be in charge of the tour you are considering. Call these references and find out what they liked and what they didn't like. They are likely to have some strong feelings about these things.

Adventure Caravans, 124 Rainbow Dr., PMB 2434, Livingston, TX 77399-1024 (800 872-7897).

Baja Winters, 3760 Market St. NE, PMB #615, Salem, OR 97301 (800 383-6787).

Camping World President's Club Tours, P.O. Box 161, Osceola, IN 46561 (800 626-0042).

Eldorado Tours, P.O. Box 1145, Alma, Arkansas 72921 (800 852-2500 or 501 632-6282).

Fantasy RV Tours, P.O. Box 95605, Las Vegas, NV 89193-5601 (800 952-8496).

Good Sam Caraventures, 2575 Vista del Mar, Ventura, CA 93001 (800 664-9145).

Point South RV Tours, 11313 Edmonson Ave., Moreno Valley, CA 92555 (800 421-1394 or 909 247-1222).

Tracks to Adventure, 2811 Jackson Ave., Suite K, El Paso, TX 79930 (800 351-6053).

Cash and Credit Cards

Mexico, of course, has its own currency, called the peso. During the 1999/2000 season there were about 9.5 pesos per U.S. dollar. The currency has been relatively stable with a slow devaluation rate since a large devaluation in 1994. Some visitors, particularly on the Baja Peninsula, never seem to have any pesos and use dollars for most purchases. They pay for the privilege, prices in dollars are sometimes higher than if you pay in pesos.

Cash machines are now widespread in Mexico and represent the best way to obtain cash. If you don't already have a debit card you should take the trouble to get one before heading south, make sure it has a four-digit international number. Both Cirrus (Visa) and Plus (Master Card) networks are in place, not all machines accept both. Given a choice we would choose Cirrus, it seems to be more widely accepted. Don't be

CASH MACHINE

surprised if a machine inexplicably refuses your card, bank operations and phone lines are both subject to unexpected interruptions. If you can't get the card to work try a machine belonging to another bank or just go directly to a teller inside the bank. You should consider bringing a back-up card in case the electronic strip stops working on the one you normally use. Most cards have a maximum daily withdrawal limit, usually about $400 U.S. In Mexico the limit is sometimes lower than in the U.S.

There are cash machines in Tijuana, Rosarito, Ensenada, Tecate, Guerrero Negro,

Loreto, Ciudad Constitución, La Paz, Cabo San Lucas, San José del Cabo, Mexicali, San Felipe, and Puerto Peñasco.

Traveler's checks are a decent way to carry money for emergencies. You never know when your debit card will inexplicably stop working.

Visa and MasterCard credit cards are useful on the Baja. Restaurants and shops, particularly in tourist areas, accept them. Outside metropolitan and tourist areas their acceptance is limited. Pemex stations accept only cash but large supermarkets in Ensenada, La Paz, and Mexicali recently began accepting cards. It is also possible to get cash advances against these credit cards in Mexican banks but the fees tend to be high.

Crossing the Border
(Insurance, Tourist Cards, Fishing Licenses, Crossings)

One of the reasons campers choose the Baja over mainland Mexico is that it is easier to cross the border because less paperwork is required. Unlike the mainland, Baja does not require temporary vehicle permits.

You must have a **tourist card** if you are going to stay for over three days or travel south of Maneadero (just south of Ensenada). These are obtained at the Migración office at the border or in Ensenada. To get your card you must present identification in the form of a passport or certified copy of your birth certificate and a picture I.D. like a drivers license. The card is issued for a set length of time, you should be asked how long you plan to be in Mexico. Make sure to get a card giving you enough time even for unexpected extensions. There is a fee of 170 pesos (about $18 U.S.) per person for the card, but the money is not collected at the Migración office. Instead you take it to a bank and pay there. You have three days to do this. If you cross in Tijuana you'll probably get your card in Ensenada and find it easy to pay there. Tecate is another place with handy banks near the border station. If you cross at Mexicali we suggest you wait until you reach San Felipe to visit a bank, it's just easier.

The towns of **Puerto Peñasco** and **Golfo de Santa Clara** fall within the Sonora free zone. Neither tourist cards nor vehicle permits are required for visiting these places.

If you plan to take a ferry from Santa Rosalía or La Paz to the mainland you will have to get your **temporary vehicle permits** before you go. It may be difficult to do so in La Paz and may be impossible in Santa Rosalía so we suggest that you get your papers at the border coming south if you plan to take the ferry. Tecate would be a good place to do this because it is relatively quiet there. To get a vehicle permit you will need a driver's license for each vehicle (in other words, you need two drivers to bring two vehicles); a Visa, MasterCard, or American Express Card; and your registration and title. If the vehicle is not registered in your name you need a notarized letter from the owner stating that you can take it into Mexico. A fee of about $15 U.S. will be charged on the card for each vehicle, you will be given a packet of paperwork, and a sticker will be placed on the inside of your front window in the upper left corner. When you return to the U.S. you must stop at the Mexican border station and have them remove the sticker. They must do it, not you. If you do not have one of the credit cards mentioned above you must post a bond which is more complicated and expensive.

Your **automobile insurance** from home will not cover you in Mexico. Insurance is not required in Mexico, but you are very foolish to drive in Mexico without it. If you have an accident and have no insurance it is possible that you might be detained (in jail) for a considerable time.

Don't believe the old saw that all Mexican insurance costs the same, this is not true. Get several quotes and compare coverage. People who go into Mexico for just a short time usually buy daily coverage. This is extremely expensive, if you are planning to be in Mexico for over three weeks a six-month or one-year policy makes more sense. Some people get short-term coverage for the week or so it takes to get to their favorite campground. Once there they park the vehicle and don't use it until they buy more short term coverage for the drive home.

Longer term coverage, for six months or a year, is much cheaper. It is comparable with the cost of insurance in the U.S. Here are names and phone numbers for a few of the companies that offer Mexican insurance: Vagabundos del Mar, 800 474-BAJA; Discover Baja Travel Club, 800 727-BAJA; Sanborn's, 800 222-0158; International Gateway Insurance Brokers, Inc., 800 423-2646. Some of these are travel clubs requiring that you join, others are not. Additionally, most caravan companies (listed under *Caravans* in this chapter) also offer Mexican insurance, even to people not taking one of their caravans. We recommend that you use the phone to compare costs and coverage long before you hit the road toward the Baja.

If you are going to take a boat in to Mexico for fishing you must have a boat permit and fishing permits for each person who will be in the boat. These boat and fishing permits are available from Mexican travel clubs like Vagabundos del Mar (800 474-BAJA) and Discover Baja Travel Club (800 727-BAJA). You will need your vehicle registration form for the boat to get the boat permit. You can also directly contact the Mexican Department of Fisheries in San Diego by calling 619 233-4324. They will fax or mail you an application for boat and fishing permits so that you can do everything by mail. Their address is 2550 5th Ave., Suite 101, San Diego, CA 92103.

An important note about fishing and boat permits. You do not need a license to fish from shore, you also don't need a boat permit if you are not going to fish. However, if there is any fishing equipment in your boat at all, even a hook, you are required to have a permits for the boat and everyone on board.

There are a limited number of **border crossings** for visiting the Baja and northwest Sonora. Here are the details.

Tijuana has two crossings: San Ysidro and Otay Mesa. Of the two we prefer San Ysidro even though it is closer to the center of town. When you are heading south the route to the toll road is straightforward and not difficult. For the past several years many guidebooks have recommended the Otay Mesa crossing. There was less traffic and the eastern section of the Libramiento ring road led you fairly easily to the free road south of town. Lately, however, this crossing has become almost as busy as the main San Ysidro crossing with lines that are just as long. As Tijuana has grown the eastern Libramiento has become busier and busier. If we must cross the border near Tijuana we now prefer the San Ysidro crossing, whether heading south or returning north. Heading north there can be terrible waits at both crossings, we prefer Tecate. San Ysidro is open 24 hours a day, Otay Mesa is open from 6 a.m. to 10 p.m.

The **Tecate** crossing is small and usually not crowded. The disadvantage of the crossing is that it is a little out of the way on both sides of the border. However, the road south to Ensenada is not bad and is much less harrowing than even the short run through Tijuana from the San Ysidro crossing. Crossing northwards Tecate usually has much shorter waits than either San Ysidro or Otay Mesa. This crossing is open from 6 a.m. to midnight.

Mexicali has an in-town crossing and one about 7 miles east of town. We prefer the one east of town as it allows you to avoid driving through the center of town. Both are 24-hour crossings.

Algodones is a crossing just east of Yuma, Arizona. We do not recommend crossing here, the officials on the Mexico side have a bad reputation with RVers and connection to the road system is not as good as in nearby San Luis Río Colorado. The crossing is open 6 a.m. to 8 p.m.

The **San Luis Río Colorado** crossing is about 26 miles (42 km) south of Yuma, Arizona. It is usually not extremely busy, crosses into a small easy-to-navigate Mexican town, and is open 24-hours a day.

Finally, the **Sonoyta** crossing north of Puerto Peñasco is in a small town in the middle of nowhere. People crossing here are almost all headed for Puerto Peñasco. The crossing can be very busy on weekends, but otherwise is pretty quiet. It is open 24 hours a day.

Coming back into the U.S. you will need to be concerned about what you can bring back without duty. You are allowed $400 in purchases, 50 pounds of food, and 1 liter of alcohol per person. Some Mexican-produced food is not allowed into the U.S., we've been relieved of many fresh fruits and vegetables (especially avocados) over the years. Further information about customs allowances is available on the internet at www.customs.ustreas.gov/.

Drinking Water and Vegetables

Don't take a chance when it comes to drinking Mexican water. Even water considered potable by the locals is likely to cause problems for you. It is no fun to be sick, especially when you are far from the border in an unfamiliar environment. There are several strategies for handling the water question. Many people drink nothing but bottled water. Others filter or purify it in various ways.

We use a simple system. We purify all of the water that goes into our rig's storage tank with common bleach. Then we use a filter to remove the bleach taste, the microorganisms in the water have already been killed by the bleach. This means that we never hook up permanently to the local water supply, we always use the stored water in our rig. The advantage of this system is that you do not need to keep a separate supply of drinking water underfoot. The proof is in the results. We are almost never sick, and if we are it is usually possible to trace the problem to something we ate or drank while away from the RV. The filter we use is commonly offered as standard equipment on many RVs, it is manufactured by Everpure. Other charcoal filters probably work equally well to remove the taste of bleach.

The system we use is called superclorination. Add 1/6 ounce (1 teaspoon) of bleach (sodium hypochlorite) per each 10 gallons of water. The easiest way to do this is to measure it into the same end of your fill hose that will attach to or into your rig. That way you purify the hose too. Check the bleach bottle to make sure it has no additives, Clorox and Purex sold in Mexico are usually OK. You can tell because they have instructions for water purification right on the label.

If you don't want to bleach your water the best alternative is to drink bottled water. Everywhere in Mexico you can buy large 19 liter (approximately five-gallon) bottles of water. They are available at supermarkets, purified water shops, or from vendors who visit campgrounds. These are very inexpensive, you can either keep one of the large bottles by paying a small deposit or actually empty them into your own water tank.

Occasionally, even if you bleach your water and use a filter, you will pick up a load of water that doesn't taste too good. This is usually because it contains salt. A filter won't take this out. You can avoid the problem by asking other RVers at the camp-ground about water quality before filling up.

Another source of potential stomach problems is fruit and vegetables. It is essential that you peel all fruit and vegetables or soak them in a purification solution before eating them. Bleach can also be used for this, the directions are right on the label of most bleach sold in Mexico. You can also purchase special drops to add to water for this purpose, the drops are stocked in the fruit and vegetable department of most supermarkets in Mexico.

Drugs, Guns, and Roadblocks

Visitors to Mexico are not allowed to possess either non-prescription narcotics or guns (except those prop-erly imported for hunting). Do not take either in to Mexico, they can result in big problems and probably time spent in a Mexican jail.

Roadblocks and vehicle checks are common in Mexico. Often the roadblocks are staffed by military personnel. These stops can be a little intimidating, the soldiers carry automatic weapons and bring them right in to your rig when doing an inspection. English, other than a few words, is usually not spoken at the check-points but not much communication is really neces-sary, we have never had a problem. In general you will probably be asked where you came from (today), where are you going, do you have drugs or guns, and perhaps why you are in Mexico. It seems like every third rig or so gets inspected so don't get paranoid if

INSPECTION STATION

yours is chosen. Accompany the person inspecting the rig as they walk through to answer any questions they might have, sometimes they have trouble figuring out how to open unfamiliar cabinets and storage areas. We generally discourage offering a beverage or anything else to officials at checkpoints, this might be considered a suspi-cious bribe, or might get the inspecting soldier in trouble with his superiors.

Ferries

The company Sematur Transbordadores runs ferries between the Baja Peninsula and the mainland of Mexico. The routes are between Santa Rosalía and Guaymas, between Pichilingue (just outside La Paz) and Topolobampo (near Los Mochis) and between Pichilingue and Mazatlán. If you do not want to drive the highway both ways this is a great way to turn your Mexican trip into a loop trip and see some of the mainland. There are four-lane highways linking all of the west coast ferry ports with the U.S.

The runs take between 6 and 17 hours. Most vehicles on the routes are trucks. A lot of the provisions for the southern Baja come across on these boats. These ferries are work boats, don't expect much in the way of amenities. Cabins are available on some but not all runs.

If you plan to take your vehicle from the peninsula to the mainland you will need a vehicle permit. See the *Crossing the Border* section above for more information about this. You will need a reservation for the ferry, you can call the main reservation office in Mazatlán by dialing 01-800-696-96-00. They say you need to make reservations at least three days in advance but we recommend that you make your reservation at least a week before you want to travel. They also have a very useful web site with rates, schedules, and reservations at www.ferrysematur.com.mx. The phone number for the ticket office in La Paz is (112) 5-23-46 and the one in Santa Rosalía is (115) 2-00-14.

Fishing

Fishing is one of the most popular activities on the Baja. Today there are not as many fish as during the glory years of the 40's and 50's, but the fishing is still good. You can fish from shore, kayaks and canoes, car-top aluminum boats, trailer boats, or charter pangas or cruisers; they all can give you access to excellent fishing in the appropriate places and at the appropriate times.

Like fishing anywhere it helps to know the ins and outs of fishing on the Baja. Charter operators provide this as part of the package but if you are a do-it-yourselfer we suggest some research before you head south. See the *Internet* and *Travel Library* sections of this chapter.

Be sure to have the proper paperwork if you are going to fish or are on a boat with anyone fishing. See the *Crossing the Border* section above for details.

Fuel and Gas Stations

Choosing the brand of gas you're going to buy is easy in Mexico. All of the gas stations are Pemex stations. Pemex is the national oil company, it is responsible for everything from exploring for oil to pumping it into your car. Gas is sold for cash, no credit cards. There is usually only one kind of gas, it's called Magna Sin and is unleaded in green pumps. It has an octane rating of about 87. A new higher octane unleaded has recently become available at a few stations. Diesel is carried at many but not all stations.

All gas sells for the same thing all over the country so it will do you no good to search for the best price. The only exception to this is very small stations in very remote places. Gas in these establishments is often pumped out of drums and can cost many times the Pemex price. With proper planning you won't ever use one of these places.

Gas stations are not as common in Mexico as they are in the U.S. and Canada. On the Baja you should always be aware of how much fuel you have. One particularly bad spot is the "Baja gas gap" between El Rosario and Guerrero Negro. See Chapter 6 for more information about this.

Almost everyone you meet in Mexico has stories about how a gas station attendant cheated them. These stories are true. The attendants don't make much money and tourists are easy prey. You can avoid problems if you know what to expect.

The reason that the attendants are able to cheat people is that there are no cash registers or central cashiers in these stations. Each attendant carries a big wad of cash and collects what is displayed on the pump. Don't expect a receipt. Until the stations install a control system with a separate cashier there will continue to be lots of opportunities for attendants to make money off unwary customers.

The favorite ploy is to start pumping gas without zeroing the pump. This way you have to pay for the gas that the previous customer received in addition to your own. The attendant pockets the double payment. The practice is so widespread that at many stations attendants will point to the zeroed pump before they start pumping. Signs at most stations tell you to check this yourself.

There are several things you can do to avoid this problem. First, get a locking gas cap. That way the attendant can't start pumping until you get out of the rig and unlock the cap. Second, check the zeroed meter carefully. Do not get distracted. If several people try to talk to you they are probably trying to distract you. They'll ask questions about the rig or point out some imaginary problem. Meanwhile the pump doesn't get zeroed properly.

While the gas is being pumped stand right there and pay attention. Another trick is to "accidentally" zero the pump and then try to collect for an inflated reading. If you watch carefully you will know the true reading and won't fall for this. Sometimes the pump gets zeroed before the tank is full, so don't just assume that you can chat because you have a big tank.

The process of making change presents big opportunities to confuse you. If you are paying in dollars, which is common on the Baja, have your own calculator handy and make sure you know the exchange rate before the gas is pumped. When paying do not just give the attendant your money. He'll fold it onto his big wad of bills and then you'll never be able to prove how much you gave him. We've also seen attendants quickly turn their backs and stuff bills in a pocket. Hold out the money or lay it out on the pump, don't let him have it until you can see your change and know that it is the correct amount.

All attendants will not try to cheat you of course. You'll probably feel bad about watching like a hawk every time you fill up with gas. The problem is that when you let down your guard someone will eventually take advantage of you, probably soon and not later. It is also customary to tip attendants a peso or two, we think honest attendants deserve to be tipped more.

Green Angels

The Mexican government maintains a large fleet of green pickups that patrol all major highways searching for motorists with mechanical problems. Usually there are two men in the truck, they have radios to call for help, limited supplies, and quite a bit of mechanical aptitude. Most of them speak at least limited English. The service is free except for a charge for the cost of supplies used. The trucks patrol most highways two times each day, once in the morning and once in the afternoon. The Green Angels monitor CB channel 9.

Groceries

Don't load your rig with groceries when you head south across the border. There is no longer any point in doing so. Some Mexican border stations are checking RVs to see that they don't bring in more than a reasonable amount of food. Modern supermarkets in all of the large and medium-sized Mexican cities have almost anything you are looking for, often in familiar brand names. You can supplement your purchases in the supermarkets with shopping in markets and in small stores called *abarrotes, panaderías, tortillarías,* and *carnecerías* (canned goods stores, bakeries, tortilla shops, and butcher shops).

Internet

CCC GROCERY STORE IN LA PAZ

The internet has become a wonderful tool for research. There are a great number of web sites with information about Mexico. Rather than trying to list them all here we have set up our own web site: **www.rollinghomes.com.** On it you will find current links to other web sites with good information about Mexico.

We have another use for our web site. As a small publisher we can only afford to update our travel guides on a three to five year cycle. In order to keep the books more current we publish updated information on the web. Our site has pages for each of our books with updates referenced by page number. We gather information for these updates ourselves and also depend upon information sent in by our readers. You can contact us through our web site or by mail with update information. This information is only posted until we put out a new edition, once the new edition comes out we zero out the page and post updates only for the new book.

Pets

You can take your dog or cat into Mexico. Birds and other pets are subject to additional restrictions, taking them to Mexico is not practical. We've not heard of anyone taking a pet into Mexico who has run into problems going south, whatever requirements are in effect do not seem to be enforced, so the rules you want to watch for are the ones for bringing the animal back into the U.S. The U.S. Customs web site says that dogs coming back into the U.S. require a rabies vaccination certificate that is at least 30 days old with an expiration date that is not expired. Your vet will probably know the proper forms that are required, if not, check with customs. Your dog or cat may also be examined at the border to see if it seems to be sick, if there is a question you may be required to have it examined by a vet before it will be admitted to the U.S.

Propane

Either propane or butane is available near most larger town or cities. The LP Gas storage yards are usually outside the central area of town. Ask at your campground for the best way to get a fill-up, in many locations trucks will deliver to the campground. We've also seen people stop a truck on the street and get a fill-up.

We're accustomed to seeing only propane in much of the U.S. and Canada because butane won't work at low temperatures, it freezes. In parts of the southern U.S. and the warmer areas in Mexico butane is common and propane not available. This probably won't be a problem, most propane appliances in RVs will also run on butane. Make sure you use all the butane before you take your RV back into the cold country, however.

The fact is that you may never need to fill up with LP Gas at all. We find that if we fill up before crossing the border we have no problem getting our gas to last four months because we only use it for cooking. Some people run their refrigerators only on gas because they fear that some of the new electronic control boards can be damaged by the fluctuating electrical voltage common to Mexican campgrounds. You may want to check into this, it is virtually impossible to get an RV refrigerator fixed in Mexico.

Roads and Driving in Mexico

If there were only one thing that could be impressed upon the traveler heading south to drive in Mexico for the first time it would be "drive slowly and carefully". The last thing you want in Mexico is an accident or a breakdown, driving slowly and carefully is the best way to avoid both of these undesirable experiences.

Baja's roads are getting better. The last time we drove Mex 1 long stretches had just been resurfaced and were beautiful. On the other hand, travelers who had driven this same road just a month before reported terrible potholes. Conditions change and you can't count on great roads. Cautious driving will mean fewer flat tires and broken springs.

THE ROAD

One concern many travelers have about the Transpeninsular is that much of it is only eighteen feet wide (nine-foot lanes) with no shoulders. That is indeed narrow, wide-body RVs are eight and a half feet wide not counting the mirrors. RVer usually adjust their left-side rear-view mirror to be as close to the side of the rig as possible while still being useable. Marking the front face of the left outside mirror with high-visibility tape also helps. The best strategy to follow is to drive slowly and carefully. When you see traffic approaching; especially if it is a truck, bus, or RV; slow even more so that you have complete control of your rig, and get over as far as you safely can. The good news is that there is very little traffic on most of the Transpeninsular.

Do not drive at night. There are several reasons for this. Animals are common on roads in Mexico, even in daylight hours you'll find cows, horses, burros, goats, pigs and sheep on the road. At night there are even more of them, they're attracted by the warm road surface and they don't have reflectors. Truckers like to travel at night because they can make good time in the light traffic. Some of these guys are maniacs, in the morning you'll often see a fleet of tow trucks lined up along the edge of a highway trying to retrieve one from a gully. Truckers also often leave rocks on the road at night, this is done to keep someone from hitting them when they break down, or to block the wheels when stopped on a hill. Often these rocks aren't removed, they're very difficult to see in time at night. Finally, driving at night means that if you have a breakdown you're going to be in an unsafe position. Mexican roads are good places to avoid after dark.

No discussion of driving in Mexico is complete without a discussion of traffic cops and bribes. Traffic cops (and many other government functionaries) are underpaid, they make up for it by collecting from those who break the law. This is not condoned by the government, but it is a fact of life. Norteamericanos usually feel uncomfortable with this custom and as a result they are difficult targets for cops with a *mordida* habit. Unfortunately some cops do not yet know this.

The best way to avoid the *mordida* trap is to scrupulously follow all traffic laws. Even if everyone around you is breaking the law you should follow it. If only one person in a line of cars gets arrested for not stopping at a railroad crossing you can be sure that it will be the gringo in the fancy RV (we know this from personal experience). Obey all speed limits, especially easy to miss are those at schools and small towns along a highway. Stop at the stop sign at railroad crossings even though no one else will.

In the event that you do get stopped we recommend against offering a bribe. It is possible that you might get yourself in even worse trouble than you are already in. If you can't talk your way out of a fine the normal practice is to accompany the officer back to his headquarters (bringing your vehicle) to pay the fine. Most fines are quite reasonable by Norteamericano standards. Occasionally a police officer will suggest that such a trip can be avoided by paying a reasonable fee to him on the spot, let your conscience be your guide.

Everyone's least favorite thing is to get involved in an accident. In Mexico there are special rules. First and most important is that you had better have Mexican insurance. Your insurance carrier will give you written instructions about the procedure to follow if you get into an accident. Take a look at it before you cross the border to make sure you understand exactly how to handle an accident before it happens. See *Crossing the Border* section above for the names of some Mexican insurance companies.

Safety and Security

Mexico would be full of camping visitors from the U.S. and Canada if there was no security issue. Fear is the factor that crowds RVers into campgrounds just north of the border but leaves those a hundred miles south pleasantly uncrowded. People in those border campgrounds will warn you not to cross into Mexico because there are banditos, dishonest cops, terrible roads, and language and water problems. The one thing you can be sure of when you get one of these warnings is that that person has not tried Mexican camping him/herself.

First-time camping visitors are almost always amazed at how trouble-free Mexican camping is. Few ever meet a bandito or get sick from the water. The general feeling is that Mexico is safer than much of the U.S., especially U.S. urban areas. After you've been in Mexico a few years you will hear about the occasional problem, just as you do north of the border. Most problems could have been easily avoided if the person involved had just observed a few common-sense safety precautions. Here are the ones we follow and feel comfortable with.

Never drive at night. Night driving is dangerous because Mexican roads are completely different at night. There are unexpected and hard-to-avoid road hazards, there are aggressive truck drivers, and there is little in the way of formal security patrols. If there are really any banditos in the area they are most likely to be active after dark.

Don't boondock alone except in a place you are very sure of. Individual free campers are uniquely vulnerable. Many folks don't follow this rule and have no problems, it is up to you.

Don't open the door to a knock after dark. First crack a window to find out who is knocking. Why take chances. We've talked to a number of people who wish they'd followed this rule, even in campgrounds.

Don't leave your rig unguarded on the street if you can avoid it. Any petty crook knows your rig is full of good stuff, it is a great target. We like to leave ours in the campground while we explore. Use public transportation, it's lots of fun.

There are a couple of security precautions that you can take before leaving home, you probably have already taken them if you do much traveling in your rig. Add a deadbolt to your entrance door, some insurance policies in the states actually require this. If possible install an alarm in your vehicle, it can take a load off your mind when you must leave it on the street.

Spanish Language

You certainly don't need to be able to speak Spanish to get along just fine in Mexico. All of the people working in campgrounds, gas stations and stores are accustomed to dealing with non-Spanish speakers. Even if you can't really talk to them you'll be able to transact business.

Telephones

Telephone service is rapidly improving in Mexico but is still expensive. Almost all towns along the highway now have phones on the street that you can use to call home for a reasonable fee, if you know how. Other companies, like AT&T, have started competing with Telmex so the improvement should continue. If a town does not yet

LADATEL PHONE

have the street-side phones it usually has a phone office. You go in and the operator will dial for you and send you to a booth. When you are finished she'll get the charge and you pay her with cash.

It seems like every country has a different system of area codes and telephone numbers. Mexico is no exception. Each city on the Baja has an area code, it can have two or three digits. Here are some of them: Tijuana 66, Rosarito 661, Ensenada 617, Mexicali 65, San Felipe 657, Santa Rosalía 115, Loreto 113, La Paz 112, Cabo San Lucas 114. The individual phone numbers also have a varying number of digits, there will be 5 or 6 so that there are a total of 8 digits when the area code is included. You can find a listing of area codes in the front of Mexican telephone books.

In this book you can tell a Mexican telephone number by the way we split it up. The format is (xxx) n-nn-nn or (xx) nn-nn-nn where x's stand for an area code number and n's stand for the individual local number. This makes it easy to tell if a number is in Mexico or the states. Many Mexican businesses do maintain a number in the states to make it easy for tourists to reach them so many of the phone numbers in this book are in the U.S.

To call into Mexico from the U.S. or Canada you must first dial a 011 for international access, then the Mexico country code which is 52, then the Mexican area code and number. Often businesses will advertise in the U.S. with a number which includes some or all of these prefixes. Now that you know what they are you should have no problems dialing a Mexican number.

In recent years phones in kiosks or booths, usually labeled Ladatel or Telmex have appeared along the streets in more and more Mexican towns. To use them you buy a phone card, usually at pharmacies. These are computerized smart cards charged with 10, 20, 30, 50, or 100 pesos. When you insert them into the phone the amount of money left on the card appears on a readout on the phone. As you talk the time left counts down on the readout. This has become the cheapest way to call out of Mexico.

To dial an international call to the U.S. or Canada you dial 00 + 1 + area code + the local number. To place a collect call you dial 09 + 1 + area code + local number.

To dial a Mexican long distance number you dial 01 + area code + the local number.

To dial a local number you generally just dial the local number. However, this is changing and in some places you must also dial part of the area code. For example, in Puerto Peñasco the area code is 638 and the local number has 5 more digits. You must now dial 38 and then the remaining 5 digits. This practice varies from exchange to exchange so if you have a problem try dialing some of the area code digits to make your local call.

The latest scourge to hit the telephone-starved traveler to Mexico is credit card-accepting phones placed conveniently in many tourist areas. Many Mexican businesses have allowed these things to be installed as a convenience to their customers since a normal phone is difficult to obtain. Unfortunately they are a real problem, the rate charged is often in excess of $10 per minute for calls to numbers outside Mexico. We have talked to several unsuspecting users who found charges of several hundred dollars on their credit card statements when they returned home. You can pick up any of these phones and ask the English-speaking operator for the name of the company providing the service as well as the initial and per-minute fee. If the service is not being provided by Telmex you should be extremely cautious. Hopefully these rates will go down as people wise up and learn to ask.

Travel Library

Don't go to Mexico without a general tourist guide with information about the places you'll visit. Even if you're on the Baja for the sun and fun you'll have questions that no one seems to be able to answer. One of the best of the guides for our money is *Baja Handbook: Tijuana to Cabo San Lucas* by Joe Cummings (Moon Publications Inc., Chico, CA, 1998, ISBN 1-56691-120-6).

A cult favorite in the travel guide genre is *The People's Guide to Mexico* by Carl Franz (John Muir Publications, Santa Fe, NM, ISBN 1-56261-419-3). This book has been around since 1972, it's frequently updated, and it's filled with an encyclopedic mix of information about pretty much everything Mexican that you will wonder about during your visit. It's also so well written that it is hard to put down.

For background information about Mexican history, culture and politics you should read Alan Riding's book *Distant Neighbors*. The book was originally published in 1984. It is somewhat outdated but you will be amazed at how it predicts exactly the things that are happening in Mexico today. The book is still in print and paperback editions are not difficult to find.

Maps are very useful on the Baja, particularly if you are traveling back roads. There's a new two-volume atlas available that is invaluable. The two volumes are *Baja Almanac California Norte: Mexico's Land of Adventure* (Baja Almanac Publishers, Inc.; Las Vegas, NV; ISBN 0-9658663-0-0) and *Baja Almanac California Sur: Mexico's Land of Dreams* (Baja Almanac Publishers, Inc.; Las Vegas, NV; ISBN 0-9658663-1-9).

Baja travelers have a wealth of books available to them. Don't read Walt Peterson's *The Baja Adventure Book* (Wilderness Press, Berkeley, CA, 1999, ISBN 0-89997-231-4) if you're not sure you really want to visit the Baja because after reading it you won't be able to stay away. *The Magnificent Peninsula: The Comprehensive Guidebook to Mexico's Baja California* by Jack Williams (H.J. Williams Publications, Redding, CA, 1998, ISBN 1-891275-00-3) is just what the title says. It has lots of information about camping spots on the peninsula, and lots of other things too. A book using satellite maps of the peninsula is *The Baja Book IV: The Guide to Today's Baja California* by Ginger Potter (Baja Source, Inc., El Cajon, CA, 1996, ISBN 0-9644066-0-8). To get some good background try reading *Into a Desert Place: A 3000-Mile Walk Around the Coast of Baja California* by Graham Machintosh (W.W. Norton & Co., New York, NY, 1990, ISBN 0-393-31289-5). Fishermen will find *The Baja Catch* by Neil Kelly and Gene Kira (Apples and Oranges, Inc., Valley Center, CA, 1997, ISBN 0-929637-04-6) to be absolutely essential. For information about the landforms and plants along the highway bring along *Roadside Geology and Biology of Baja California* by John, Edwin, and Jason Minch (John Minch and Associates, Inc., Mission Viejo, CA; 1998; ISBN 0-9631090-1-4). Also lots of fun if you can find them are some old books about exploring the Baja back country by Perry Mason detective novel author Erle Stanley Gardner: *Mexico's Magic Square, Off the Beaten Track in Baja, The Hidden Heart of Baja, Hovering over Baja,* and *Hunting the Desert Whale.* Try libraries and used book stores for these classics.

A visit to Mexico is a great way to study Spanish. Make sure to bring along a good Spanish-English dictionary. If you want to study while on your trip we recommend Living Language's book *Spanish All the Way* (Crown Publishers, Inc., New York, NY, 1994, ISBN 0-517-58373-9). It is available in a package with four CDs, great for studying while on the road.

Most of these books can be purchased at Amazon.com. You can follow links from our web site: www.rollinghomes.com.

Units of Measurement

Mexico is on the metric system. Most of the world has already learned to deal with this. For the rest of us it takes just a short time of working with the metric system, and there is no way to avoid it, to start to feel at home. Conversion tables and factors are available in most guidebooks but you will probably want to memorize a few critical conversion numbers as we have.

For converting miles to kilometer, divide the number of miles by .62. For converting kilometers to miles, multiply the kilometers by .62. Since kilometers are shorter than miles the number of kilometers after the conversion will always be more than the number of miles, if they aren't you divided when you should have multiplied.

For liquid measurement it is usually enough to know that a liter is about the same as a quart. When you need more accuracy, like when you are trying to make some sense out of your miles per gallon calculations, there are 3.79 liters in a U.S. gallon.

Weight measurement is important when you're trying to decide how much cheese or hamburger you need to make a meal. Since a kilogram is about 2.2 pounds we just round to two pounds. This makes a half pound equal to about 250 grams and a pound equal to 500 grams. It's not exact, but it certainly works in the grocery store, and we get a little more than we expected for dinner.

Temperature is our biggest conversion problem. The easiest method is to just carry around a conversion chart of some kind. If you don't have it with you just remember a few key temperatures and interpolate. Freezing, of course is 32 F and 0 C. Water boils at 212 F and 100 C. A nice 70 F day is 21 C. A cooler 50 F day is 10 C. A hot 90 F day is 32 C.

Here are a few useful conversion factors:

1 km = .62 mile	1mile = 1.61 km
1 meter = 3.28 feet	1 foot = .30 meters
1 liter = .26 U.S. gallon	1 U.S. gallon = 3.79 liters

1 kilogram = 2.21 pounds   1 pound = .45 kilograms
Convert from °C to °F by multiplying by 1.8 and adding 32
Convert from °F to °C by subtracting 32 and dividing by 1.8

Vehicle Preparation and Breakdowns

One of the favorite subjects whenever a group of Mexican campers gets together over cocktails is war stories about breakdowns and miraculous repairs performed by Mexican mechanics with almost no tools. Before visiting Mexico many people fear a breakdown above all else. Our experience and that of the people we talk to is that on the main roads help is generally readily available. Lots of other RVers are traveling the same route and they will stop to help.

While it is usually possible to find someone to work on the vehicle, it is often very hard to get parts. Ford, General Motors, Chrysler, Volkswagen and Nissan all manufacture cars and trucks in Mexico and have large, good dealers throughout the country. Toyota does not. These dealers are good places to go if you need emergency or maintenance work done on your vehicle. However, many of the models sold in the north are not manufactured in Mexico and the dealers may not have parts for your particular vehicle. They can order them but often this takes several weeks.

Often the quickest way to get a part is to go get it yourself. One of our acquaintances recently broke an axle in Villahermosa. His vehicle is common in Mexico, but the type of axle he needed was not used in the Mexican models. Rather than wait an indeterminate length of time for a new axle he went and picked one up himself. He climbed on a bus, traveled to Matamoros, walked across the border, caught a cab to a dealer, picked up a new axle and threw it over his shoulder, walked back across the border, caught another bus, and was back in Villahermosa within 48 hours. This works on the Baja too, there is a steady stream of busses traveling the Transpeninsular to and from Tijuana.

Avoid problems by making sure your vehicle is in good condition before entering Mexico. Get an oil change, a lube job, and a tune-up. Make sure that hoses, belts, filters, brake pads, shocks and tires are all good. Consider replacing them before you leave. Driving conditions in Mexico tend to be extreme. Your vehicle will be operating on rough roads, in very hot weather, with lots of climbs and descents.

Bring along a reasonable amount of spares. We like to carry replacement belts, hoses, and filters. Make sure you have a good spare tire. Don't bring much oil, good multiweight oil is now available in Mexico.

RV drivers need to be prepared to make the required hookups in Mexican RV parks. RV supplies are difficult to find in Mexico so make sure that you have any RV supplies you need before crossing the border.

Electricity is often suspect at campgrounds in Mexico. It is a good idea to carry a tester that will tell you when voltages are incorrect, polarities reversed, and grounds lacking. Always carry adapters allowing you to use small 110V, two-pronged outlets. The best setup is one that lets you turn the plug over (to reverse polarity) and to connect a ground wire to a convenient pipe, conduit, or metal stake.

Sewer hookups in many Mexican campgrounds are located at the rear of the site. Make sure you have a long sewer hose, one that will reach all the way to the rear of your RV and then another couple of feet. You'll be glad you have it.

Water purity considerations (see the *Drinking Water* title in this chapter), mean that you may need a few items that you may not already have in your rig. Consider adding a charcoal water filter if you do not already have one installed. You should also have a simple filter for filtering water before it even enters your rig, this avoids sediment build-up in your fresh water tank. Of course you'll also need a hose, we have found a 20-foot length to be adequate in most cases.

It is extremely hard to find parts or knowledgeable mechanics to do systems-related work on camping vehicles. Before crossing the border make sure your propane system, all appliances, toilet, holding tanks, and water system are working well because you'll want them to last until you get home. Marginal or jury-rigged systems should be repaired. Consider bringing a spare fresh water pump, or at least a diaphragm set if yours isn't quite new. Make sure your refrigerator is working well, you'll need it and replacement parts are impossible to find.

Make sure you have all the tools necessary to change a tire on your rig, and a spare tire. Many large motorhomes no longer come with jacks, tire-changing tools, or even spares. The theory must be that it is too dangerous for an individual to change a tire on one of these huge heavy rigs. This may be true but you need to have the proper tools available so that you can find help and get the job done if you have a flat in a remote location. Mexican roads are rough and flat tires common. Even if you don't normally carry a spare you should have at least an unmounted tire that can be mounted if you destroy one on your rig, it can be difficult to find the right size tire for big rigs on the Baja.

If you do have a breakdown along the road what should you do? It is not a good idea to abandon your rig. RVs are a tempting target, one abandoned along the road invites a break-in. This is one good reason not to travel at night. Daytime drivers can usually find a way to get their broken-down rig off the road before night falls. If you are traveling with another rig you can send someone for help. If you are traveling by yourself you will probably find it easy to flag down a car or another RV. Ask the other driver to send a mechanic or *grúa* (tow truck) from the next town. Large tow trucks are common since there is heavy truck traffic on the Transpeninsular.

Weather and When To Go

The winter dry season is when most travelers visit the Baja. In a fortunate conjunction of factors the extremely pleasant warm dry season on the Baja occurs exactly when most northerners are more than ready to leave snow and cold temperatures behind. Comfortable temperatures occur beginning in November and last through May. The shoulder months of October and June may be uncomfortably warm for some people.

On the other hand, unlike the rest of Mexico the Baja is a popular summer destination too. The northern west coast of the peninsula is really a summer destination, winters can be pretty cool. Also, many people come to the Baja for the fishing, and the hot season is the best one for that.

CHAPTER

· · · · · · · · · · · · · · · · · 3

HOW TO USE THE DESTINATION CHAPTERS

The focus of this book is on campgrounds, of course. A question we often hear is "Which campground on the Baja is your favorite?" Usually the person asking the question has a personal favorite in mind. Our answer is always the same — we like them all. No one campground is the best because everyone likes different things. Also, the personality of a campground depends upon the people staying there when you visit. People traveling on their own in an environment they are not used to tend to be very friendly, this is one of the best things about Mexican camping. We can't tell you exactly who will be staying in each of the campgrounds in this book when you decide to visit, but we will try to give you a good feel for what to expect in the way of campground features and amenities.

Chapters 4 through 12 contain information about the many camping destinations you may visit on the Baja and in northwest Sonora. The chapters are arranged somewhat arbitrarily into regions that fall naturally together for a discussion of their camping possibilities.

Introductory Map

Each of the campground chapters begins with a road map. The map shows a lot of information that will allow you to use it as an index to find campgrounds as you travel. The map shows the route covered in the chapter and also the most important towns. Dotted lines on the map show areas covered in maps later in the chapter, these later maps show the actual locations of the campgrounds. An index on the map page shows the names of all route and town descriptions in the chapter and the page number where each can be found.

Introductory Text

Each chapter starts with an introduction giving important information about the region covered in the chapter. Most of this information is important to a camping traveler and much of it is not necessarily included or easy to find in normal tourist guides. On the other hand, much information that is readily available in normal tourist guides will not be found in this book. Other books do a good job of covering things like currency information, hotels, restaurants, language, and tour details. This book is designed to be a supplement to normal tourist guides, not to replace them. It provides a framework, other guides must be used to fill it the details.

For Baja travelers the roads and fuel availability are especially important so there is a section in each chapter describing the major roads and giving the location of the gas stations. When appropriate we also include sections summarizing the details of sightseeing, golf, beaches and water sports, and fishing in the area. It is handy to have some idea what to expect.

We've also included a section titled *Backroad Adventures*. Paved roads other than the Transpeninsular are scarce in remote areas of the peninsula, you'll probably find yourself on some back roads. They are the only way to reach many of the best destinations on the Baja. You must be aware, however, that these roads are not appropriate for all vehicles, especially not for all RVs. Be sure to review the section titled *Backroad Driving* in the *Details, Details, Details* chapter. Very few of the formal campgrounds on the Baja are off the paved highway system so don't be concerned if you don't have a rig that is appropriate for backroad driving.

Route and Town Descriptions

Following the introductory material in each chapter is **The Routes, Towns, and Campgrounds** section. You'll find campground overview maps showing the major roads and campground locations and text describing each route or town. There are descriptions of the driving routes and of the towns and recreational areas.

We have given population numbers for each major town. These are our estimates. Population figures are notoriously unreliable in Mexico, and the number of residents in an area can change rapidly.

We've also included many mileage figures and have used kilometer markers extensively. Almost all of the major roads on the Baja Peninsula are marked with kilometer posts. Be prepared for many missing ones, but overall they are a useful way to fix locations.

The users of this book are probably going to be both folks from the U.S. and Canada. As everyone knows the U.S. uses miles and Canada uses kilometers. We've tried to give both numbers when we mention distances. Canadians will no doubt notice our bias - the mileage figures come first. Our excuse is that most Canadians are familiar with both systems while most of us from the states aren't quite comfortable yet with kilometers.

Campground Overview Maps

Each important city or town and each region between the towns has its own campground overview maps. These maps are designed to do two things: they quickly show you the lay of the land and the campgrounds that are available, and if you examine them more carefully they will help you drive right to the campground you have decided to use.

There are two different types of campground overview maps. The first is a city map. Each city map is associated with a written description of the city and a listing of the campgrounds in that city. The second type is an area map. These usually show the road between two cities and each is associated with a description of that road and also a listing of the campgrounds on that road.

While the maps are for the most part self-explanatory here is a key.

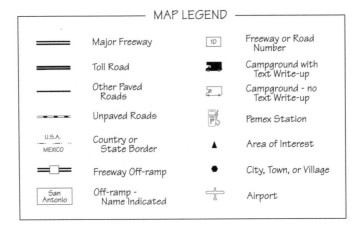

Campground Descriptions

Each campground description begins with address and telephone number, if available. While it is not generally necessary to obtain campground reservations in Mexico you may want to do so for some very popular campgrounds. If we think that reservations are necessary we say so in the campground description.

One thing you will not find in our campground descriptions is a rating with some kind of system of stars, checks, or tree icons. Hopefully we've included enough information in our campground descriptions to let you make your own analysis.

We've included limited information about campground prices. Generally you can expect that tent campers will pay the least. RV charges sometimes depend on the size of the rig but more often are based upon the number of people with a two-person minimum. If hookups are available and you are in an RV you should expect to pay for them, campground owners usually do not distinguish between those who hook up and those who don't. Some oceanside campgrounds have higher rates for spaces close to the water.

We've grouped the campground fees into the following categories in our campground descriptions:

Free	
Inexpensive	Up to $5 U.S.
Low	Over $5 and up to $10
Moderate	Over $10 and up to $15
Expensive	Over $15 and up to $20
Very Expensive	Over $20

All of these prices are winter prices for an RV with 2 people using full hookups if available. Some campgrounds, particularly near Ensenada, actually have higher rates in the summer, we've tried to indicate the summer prices in those campgrounds.

Campground icons can be useful for a quick overview of campground facilities or if you are quickly looking for a particular feature.

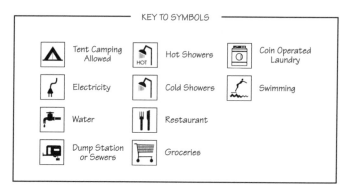

All of the campgrounds in this book accept RV's but not all accept tent campers. We've included the tent symbol for all campgrounds that do accept tents.

Hookups in Mexican campgrounds vary a great deal so we've included individual symbols for electricity, water, and sewer. For more information take a look at the written description section.

Showers in Mexican campgrounds often have no provision for hot water so we give separate shower symbols for hot and cold water. If there is provision for hot water but it was cold when we visited we list it as providing cold water only. You may be luckier when you visit.

If we've given the campground a shopping basket icon then it has some groceries. This is usually just a few items in the reception area. Check the write-up for more information.

An on-site restaurant can provide a welcome change from home-cooked meals and a good way to meet people. In Mexico almost all restaurants also serve alcohol of some kind. Often campground restaurants are only open during certain periods during the year, sometimes only during the very busy Christmas and Semana Santa (Easter) holidays. Even if there is no restaurant at the campground we have found that in Mexico there is usually one not far away.

A swimming icon means that the campground has swimming either on-site or nearby. This may be a pool or the beach at the ocean.

You'll find that this book has a much larger campground description than most guidebooks. We've tried to include detailed information about the campground itself so you know what to expect when you arrive. While most campgrounds described in this book have a map we've also included a paragraph giving even more details about finding the campground.

GPS (Global Positioning System) Coordinates

You will note that we have provided a GPS Location for each campground. GPS is a new navigation tool that uses signals from satellites. For less than $150 you can now buy a hand-held receiver that will give you your latitude, longitude, and approximate altitude anywhere in the world. You can also enter the coordinates we have given for the campgrounds in this book into the receiver and it will tell you exactly where the campground lies in relation to your position. If our maps and descriptions just don't lead you to the campground you can fall back on the GPS information.

If you don't have a GPS receiver already you certainly don't need to go out and buy one to use this book. On the other hand, if you do have one bring it along. We expect that GPS will actually be installed in many vehicles during the next few years so we thought we'd get a jump on things. If you are finding that our readings are not entirely accurate you should check to see which Map Datum your machine is set to use. The coordinates in this book are based upon the World Geodetic System 1984 (WGS 84) datum.

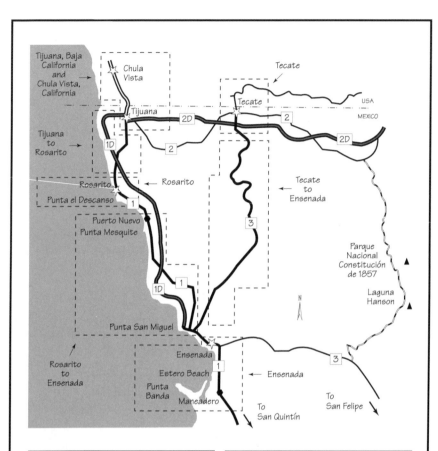

Tijuana, Baja
California
and
Chula Vista,
California

Chula
Vista

Tecate

Tijuana

2D

Tecate

USA

MEXICO

2

Tijuana
to
Rosarito

1D

2

2D

Rosarito

Rosarito

Tecate
to
Ensenada

Punta el Descanso

1

Puerto Nuevo
Punta Mesquite

3

Parque
Nacional
Constitución
de 1857

1D

1

Laguna
Hanson

N

Punta San Miguel

Rosarito
to
Ensenada

Ensenada

Estero Beach

Punta
Banda

Maneadero

1

Ensenada

3

To
San Felipe

To
San Quintín

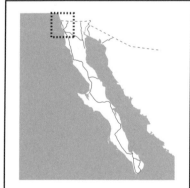

CHAPTER INDEX

Highlights .... Page 45
Roads and Fuel Availability .... Page 45
Sightseeing .... Page 46
Golf .... Page 46
Beaches and Water Sports .... Page 47
Fishing .... Page 47
Backroad Adventures .... Page 47
Tijuana, Baja California and
    Chula Vista, California .... Page 48
Tijuana to Rosarito .... Page 50
Rosarito .... Page 53
Rosarito to Ensenada .... Page 54
Ensenada .... Page 60
Tecate .... Page 67
Tecate to Ensenada
    on Highway 3 .... Page 70

SOUTH TO ENSENADA

CHAPTER

.... 4

SOUTH TO ENSENADA

INTRODUCTION

The Pacific Coast south to Ensenada is an extremely popular camping destination. So many people visit from the San Diego area across the border in southern California that it seems almost an extension of that state. In this chapter we also include the inland corridor from Tecate to Ensenada.

Highlights

Ensenada is a fun town to visit for a day or a week with lots to keep you occupied. There are many day trips to places like **La Bufadora**, **Puerto Nuevo**, the **Guadalupe Valley**, and **Laguna Hanson**. And don't forget a fishing trip on one of the many charter boats based in Ensenada.

Roads and Fuel Availability

Mex 1 begins in Tijuana. From Tijuana to Ensenada there are actually two different highways, one is the free road, Mex 1 Libre. The other is a toll road, Mex 1D. The toll road is by far the best road, it is four lanes wide and for most of its length a limited-access highway. Much of the road is extremely scenic with great views of cliffs and ocean. There are three toll booths along the 65-mile (105 km) road, an automobile or van was being charged about $ 7 U.S. for the entire distance during the late winter of 1999/2000 and double that for larger rigs. This is the only section of toll road on all of Mex 1.

The free road, Mex 1 Libre, is much less direct than the toll road. It leaves Tijuana to the south and heads directly to Rosarito. After passing through the bustling streets of Rosarito it parallels the toll road on the ocean side for 20 miles (33 kilometers) to the vicinity of La Misión. There it turns inland and climbs into the hills where after 20 miles (32 km) it rejoins Mex 1D just south of the southernmost toll booth and 5 miles (8 km) north of Ensenada. The road through the mountains is scenic and fine for carefully driven big rigs but only two lanes wide, few people drive it because it takes much longer than the toll road.

There is a good alternate to Mex 1 as far south as Ensenada. This is Mex 3 which runs from Tecate on the border to Ensenada. Actually this is a very useful highway if you are headed north since the Tecate border crossing has much shorter waiting lines to cross into the U.S. than the Tijuana crossings. Mex 3 from Tecate to El Sauzal and then on to Ensenada on the free portion of Mex 1 is 65 miles (105 km).

Mex 3 also continues eastward from Ensenada to meet with Mex 5 about 31 miles (51 km) north of San Felipe on the Gulf of California. This 123 mile (201 km) two-lane paved highway offers an alternative to Mex 5 south from Mexicali for San Felipe-bound travelers.

Fuel is readily available at Pemex stations at population centers throughout this section.

Sightseeing

This section of the Baja Peninsula offers a wealth of sightseeing opportunities. This is at least partly because there is such a large population within easy driving distance. Remember, Tijuana is Mexico's fourth largest city, and southern Californians can easily visit the entire region as day-trippers.

Tijuana gets most of the visitors, of course. The best way to visit is to walk across the border. Many sights are within walking distance of the San Ysidro crossing. To travel farther afield just use a taxi, or if you are more adventurous, catch a bus. See the Tijuana section below for specific destinations.

The town of **Rosarito** is best known for its beach. See *Rosarito* below for more details.

The small town of **Puerto Nuevo,** 9 miles (15 kilometers) south of Rosarito is well known for its restaurants. They specialize in lobster dinners. There are many of them, just pick one that looks good to you.

South of Rosarito Beach the toll highway travels along **spectacular cliffs** offering some great views. Watch for the viewpoints that have room to pull larger rigs off the highway to take a picture or two.

If you are following Mex 3 south from Tecate you will have the opportunity to visit a couple of **wineries in the Guadeloupe Valley**. This is Mexico's premier wine-growing area.

Ensenada is a popular destination for folks from north of the border. It offers shopping and restaurants and has a much more relaxed atmosphere than Tijuana. See the Ensenada section below for more information.

Golf

If you enjoy golf there are a number of possibilities in this region.

In Tijuana there is the **Club Campestre Campo de Golf Tijuana**. It is an 18-hole course near central Tijuana and is located just off the Boulevard Agua Caliente. The telephone number for reservations is (66) 81-78-55.

As you drive south along Mex 1D watch for the **Real del Mar Golf Resort** near Km 19.5. It has 18 holes and is associated with a Marriott hotel. The telephone number is (66) 33-44-01.

Farther south along the same road, near Km 78, you'll find the **Bajamar Ocean Front Golf Resort**. There are three 9-hole courses here, as well as a hotel and housing development. For reservations call (615) 5-01-51.

Just south of Ensenada is the **Baja Country Club** which has 18 holes. Call (617) 3-03-03 for reservations.

Along the border again, and just south is Tecate, there is a new course being developed. This is the **Rancho Tecate Resort and Country Club** with 9 holes.

Finally, to the east near Mexicali is the **Club Campestre de Mexicali**. It has 18 holes and is located south of town. Call (65) 61-71-30 for reservations.

Beaches and Water Sports

While there is some surfing on Rosarito Beach you'll find more surfers to the south from about Km 33 on Mex 1 Libre at Punta el Descanso south to Punta Mesquite. Off the campground at San Miguel is Punta San Miguel, one of the most popular surfing spots in Baja California.

People from Ensenada generally head for the beaches south of town at Estero Beach. Several campgrounds offer access to these beaches and are listed in the Ensenada section.

Fishing

Many people come to Ensenada for charter fishing trips. Big boats from Ensenada range far to the south along the Pacific Coast of the Baja Peninsula. They're after yellowtail and albacore tuna. Smaller boats also run out of Ensenada on day trips after bottom fish like rockfish and halibut.

Surf-casting is popular along many of the beaches along the upper northwest coast. One sandy beach where this is popular is the one in front of the Rancho Mal Paso and Baja Seasons campgrounds.

Backroad Adventures

See the *Backroad Driving* section of *Chapter 2 - Details, Details, Details* for essential information about driving off the main highway on the Baja and for a definition of road type classifications used below.

From Km 55 on Mex 3 between Ensenada and San Felipe - A national park, **Parque Nacional Constitución de 1857**, is accessible from Mex 3 east of Ensenada. A road goes north to the shallow **Laguna Hanson**, the distance to the lake is 22 miles

(36 km). There are primitive campsites at the lake and hiking trails. This is usually a Type 2 road. This lake is also accessible from Mex 2 to the north but that road is usually a Type 3. It meets the Mex 2 between Tecate and Mexicali near Km 72.

THE ROUTES, TOWNS, AND CAMPGROUNDS

TIJUANA (TEE-HWAN-AH), BAJA CALIFORNIA AND CHULA VISTA, CALIFORNIA
Population 1,350,000

Tijuana is the fourth largest city in Mexico, and perhaps the fastest growing city in North America. That means that the atmosphere can be somewhat chaotic, particularly if you are driving an RV. It's a great city to visit, but not in your own vehicle.

We think that the best base for visiting Tijuana is actually on the north side of the border in the U.S. The **Tijuana Trolley**, a light rail line, runs from San Diego to a station right at the border. Several campgrounds are located near the line. From them you can board the trolley and travel effortlessly to the border, walk across, and then either walk or use taxis to visit the city's attractions.

The border crossing between San Ysidro and Tijuana (the main Tijuana-area garita or gate) is said to be the busiest border crossing anywhere in the world. This presents a challenge for automobile travelers, but pedestrians find the crossing pretty easy.

Once in Mexico you are within walking distance of the **La Reforma District**, also known as **Avenida Revolución**. Most visitors who walk across the border never get beyond this area. They bargain for souvenirs of their trip to Mexico and perhaps visit one of the restaurants or bars in the area. Many folks come to Tijuana to watch jai alai, the game is played at The **Frontón Palacio Jai Alai de Tijuana** which is located where Calle 7 crosses Avenida Revolución. The north-south street just west of Avenida Revolución is **Avenida Constitución**, the shopping along it is less tourist-oriented but worth a look. Prices on this street are usually marked and not negotiated.

About a mile east of the La Reforma district is the **Zona Río Tijuana**. This is an area of nicer restaurants, hotels, and large shopping centers. The **Centro Cultural Tijuana** has a good cultural museum covering all of Mexico, an Omnimax theater, a performing-arts theater where a Ballet Folklórico is often performed, and crafts shops.

Another area of interest is the **Agua Caliente District** which stretches down Blvd. Agua Caliente to the southeast from the south end of the La Reforma District. Along the boulevard you'll find one of two bull rings in Tijuana as well as the **Caliente Greyhound Track**, the **Tijuana Golf and Country Club** and several large hotels.

Tijuana Campgrounds

Tijuana actually has no campgrounds, but there is excellent access from campgrounds north of the border in Chula Vista and San Diego. These campgrounds double as excellent bases for preparation for your trip south of the border.

SOUTH TO ENSENADA

🚐 CHULA VISTA RV RESORT

Address: 460 Sandpiper Way, Chula Vista, CA 91910
Telephone: (619) 422-0111 or (800) 770-2878
Fax: (619) 422-8872
Internet: www.gocampingamerica.com/chulavista
E-mail: chulavistarv@isat.com
Price: Expensive

GPS Location: N 32° 37' 40.7", W 117° 06' 16.6"

This is a first class, very popular campground in an excellent location for preparing to enter Mexico. Chula Vista is a convenient small town with all the stores and facilities you'll need, and both San Diego and Tijuana are close by. Reservations are necessary.

This campground is located adjacent to and operated in conjunction with a marina. There are 236 back-in and pull-through sites with 50-amp power and full hookups. Parking is on paved drives with patios, sites are separated by shrubbery. Large rigs and slide-outs fit fine. The bathroom facilities are excellent and there is a nice warm pool as well as a hot tub, small store, and meeting rooms. The marina next door has two restaurants and a shuttle bus provides access to central Chula Vista, stores, and the local stop of the Tijuana Trolley. Paved walkways along the water are nice for that evening stroll.

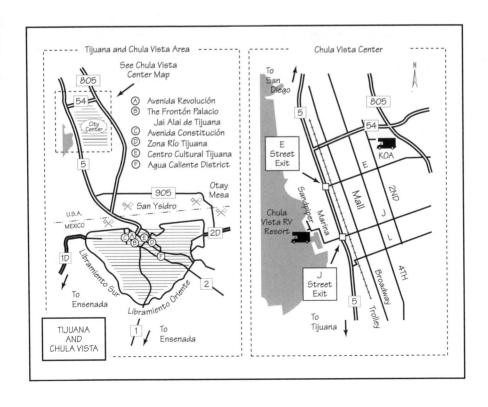

Take the J Street Exit from Highway 5 which is approximately 7 miles north of the San Ysidro border crossing and about 8 miles south of central San Diego. Drive west on J Street for 2 blocks, turn right on Marina Parkway, and drive north to the first street from the left (about 1/4 mile) which is Sandpiper, turn left here and drive one block, then follow the street as it makes a 90 degree right-angle turn, the entrance will be on your left.

SAN DIEGO METRO KOA

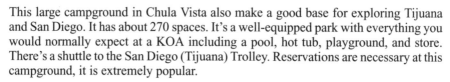

Address:	111 North 2nd Ave, Chula Vista, CA 91910
Telephone:	(619) 427-3601
Res.:	(800) KOA-9877
Internet:	www.koa.com/where/ca/05112.htm
E-mail:	reservations@sandiegokoa.com
Price:	Expensive

GPS Location: N 32° 38' 57.1", W 117° 04' 39.3"

This large campground in Chula Vista also make a good base for exploring Tijuana and San Diego. It has about 270 spaces. It's a well-equipped park with everything you would normally expect at a KOA including a pool, hot tub, playground, and store. There's a shuttle to the San Diego (Tijuana) Trolley. Reservations are necessary at this campground, it is extremely popular.

To reach the campground take the E Street Exit from I-5 in Chula Vista. Travel east on E Street until you reach 2nd Ave. Turn left here on 2nd and proceed about a mile.

TIJUANA TO ROSARITO
17 Miles (27 Km), .5 Hour (From San Ysidro crossing via Mex 1D)

There are two roads south from Tijuana to Rosarito and points south. One is the toll road, Mex 1D. The other is a free road called Mex 1. The toll road is much easier to reach from the border crossing so it is usually the preferred route, especially among those with big rigs.

Mex 1D, the toll road, is accessed by heading westward from the San Ysidro border crossing along the fence that divides Mexico and the U.S. Be alert because to reach this road along the fence you must follow a loop road that circles to the left and then crosses under the road you came in on from the U.S. Watch for signs for Mex 1D or for any of these other signs: "Toll Road", "Cuota" (this means toll road in Mexico), or "Rosarito-Ensenada Scenic Road". The signs do change from season to season so watch for any of these. You'll drive along the border fence and then make a left, descend a hill, and merge onto another highway that heads westward toward the coast. Soon you'll reach the first of three toll stations between Tijuana and Ensenada. In another 12.6 miles (20.3 km) you'll reach the northern Rosarito exit. You can join the free road here and drive through Rosarito, or you can continue south on the toll road toward Ensenada.

The free road from Tijuana to Ensenada heads south from the Libramiento or ring road that circles the southern border of Tijuana. If you were following the directions given above for reaching the toll road you would be on the Libramiento if you had gone straight instead of turning onto the toll road after leaving the border fence. While the Libramiento is better than most surface streets in Tijuana it can still be a challenge, that's why the toll road is the preferred route.

The free road branches off the Libramiento (watch for signs for Rosarito or Mex 1 or "Libre") and from that point it is only a short 7.3 mile (11.8 km) drive until you cross over the toll road and enter Rosarito. The free road is the main drag through Rosarito, watch for the many stop signs, there are dozens of them.

Some folks like to cross the border at another crossing to the east of Tijuana called Otay Mesa. See *Crossing the Border* in the *Details, Details, Details* chapter for more information.

Tijuana to Rosarito Campgrounds

ROSARITO CORA RV PARK
Res.:   Box 430513, San Ysidro, CA 92143
Telephone: (661) 3-33-05
Price: Expensive

GPS Location: N 32° 25' 33.1", W 117° 05' 32.2"

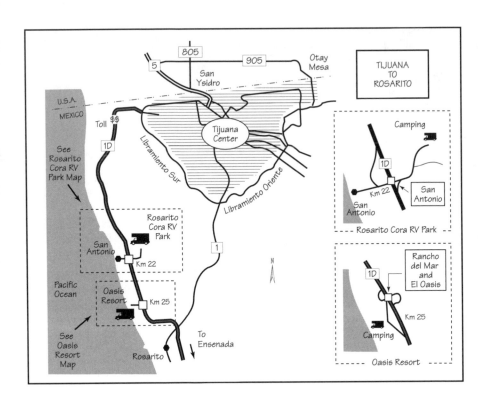

Rosarito Cora RV Park (formerly called the Rosarito KOA) is the closest campground to the border crossing in Tijuana. It could be a good overnight stop if you don't want to face the line in the evening.

The campground has about 200 grass-covered level campsites on a sloping hillside. Most are pull-throughs and have 15-amp electrical plugs and water. They also have great views of the coast far below. Unfortunately almost all of the spaces are filled with trailers that have been there for years. Travelers will have a choice of perhaps 10 spaces. While the campground is virtually full there aren't usually many people around, the facilities won't be crowded. The bathrooms are old but reasonably clean and have hot water showers. There is a laundry and a small store, a playground, and a dump station at the top of the campground. You can find groceries in Rosarito, a short drive away.

The campground is just off the toll highway Mex 1D. If you are headed south follow the signs from the border for Rosarito, Ensenada and *cuota* (toll) highway Mex 1D. Take the San Antonio exit 7.6 miles (12.2 km) south of the toll station. Use the over-pass to cross the road and then follow the cobblestone driveway up the hill for .2 miles (.3 km). If you are coming from the south or if you have taken the free road to Rosarito you should take the toll road north and exit at the San Antonio exit at the 22 Km marker. There is no toll booth between the intersection of the free road and toll road in Rosarito and the campground so free road users won't have to pay to get to the campground if they use this route.

⊠ OASIS RESORT

Address:	Km 25 Carretera Escénica No. 1
	Tijuana-Ensenada, B.C., México
Res.:	P.O. Box 158, Imperial Beach, CA 91933
Telephone:	(661) 3-32-55 (Mex), (800)-462-7472 (Reservations)
Internet:	www.oasisbaja.com
E-mail:	Oasis@telnor.net
Price:	Very Expensive

GPS Location: N 32° 23' 47.8", W 117° 05' 18.6"

This is one of the two most expensive campgrounds we've found in Mexico, reason enough to spend a night here just for the novelty. The other is the Baja Seasons farther south on this same coast. You won't spend much more than you would for a motel in the states and the facilities are great! In the winter the rates are $39 per day and summer rates about $10 higher during the week, $20 higher on weekends. Popular destinations in this part of the Baja have higher summer rates because that's when most people visit.

There are 57 back-in campsites available for visitors. Several others have big fifth-wheels permanently installed that the hotel rents as rooms. Each slot has a paved parking area, a patio, 50-amp plugs, sewer, water, TV hookup, patio, and barbecue. The whole place is beautifully landscaped, this place is posh. Before accepting a campsite check it to make sure that you can level your rig, many have an excessive slope. Make sure too that you can extend your slide-outs, some sites have trees that could interfere. There are very nice restrooms with hot showers, several swimming pools including one with a geyser-like fountain in the middle, a hot tub next to the pool, a weight room and sauna with ocean view, a tennis court, a pool room, ping-pong, a putting course, a laundry, and a very nice restaurant. There is also a convention center for groups of up to 1,200, if you need one of those. The campground is next to the beach and has beach access. Security is tight and English is spoken. Pets are not allowed. Don't be run off by this description, the place really isn't as big or threatening as it sounds.

Heading south on the toll road Mex 1D the exit for the Oasis is labeled El Oasis, it is at Km 25 and is 9.4 miles (15.1 km) south of the northernmost toll booth. Heading north there is also an exit, it is labeled Rancho del Mar.

ROSARITO (ROW-SAH-REE-TOE)
Population 60,000

The main attraction in Rosarito is a nice beach close to the U.S. and Tijuana. On school breaks and weekends, particularly during the summer, Rosarito is a busy place. At other times, particularly during the winter, the town is much more quiet. Virtually everything in town except the beach is right on Avenida Benito Juárez, the main road,

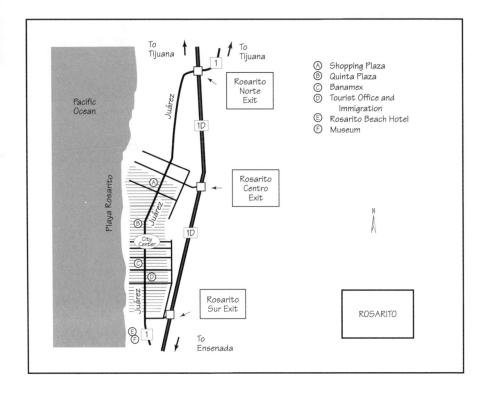

so a drive through will give you a good introduction. Watch for the stop signs! Rosarito has a large Commercial Mexicana supermarket so if you are not planning to go as far as Ensenada you may want to stop and do some shopping there. The town also has curio and Mexican crafts stores, just like Tijuana and Ensenada so you will have a chance to do some shopping if you haven't yet had a chance.

The beach here is probably the main attraction. Unfortunately it is often polluted so swimming is not recommended.

For many years the top hotel in town has been the **Rosarito Beach Hotel**. It's been around since the 20s, and has grown over the years. Today a tour of the place is on most folk's itineraries.

ROSARITO TO ENSENADA
51 Miles (82 Km), 1 Hour

Mex 1 (Libre) meets the toll highway Mex 1D at the north end of Rosarito. The free highway runs through town while the toll road bypasses it, then they meet and run side by side for about 25 miles (41 km) south. There are lots of developments of various types along this double road, one of the most interesting is **Puerto Nuevo**, about 13 miles (21 km) south of Rosarito. This has become the place to go to get a lobster dinner, there are about 30 restaurants in the small town, they cover the spectrum in price and quality.

For access to campgrounds immediately south of Rosarito we recommend that you stay on the free road. Otherwise stay on the toll road. Near La Misión the free road passes under the toll road and heads inland. From that point south all campgrounds are accessible from the toll road only. You'll have to get on the toll road at a point somewhat north of the point it passes under the freeway, the southernmost on-ramp is at Km 59 of the free road (and Km 66 of the toll road) and is called Los Alisitos.

Rosarito to Ensenada Campgrounds

PLAYA ENCANTADA
    Address: Km 30 Carr. Tijuana-Ensenada Libre, B.C., México
    Price: Low

GPS Location: N 32° 18' 47.3", W 117° 02' 51.0"

This is little more than a place to park in a large flat dirt lot next to and overlooking the ocean. The entrance is at a row of shacks along the highway, it is marked with a sign that promises bathrooms and showers. The fee is collected at the entrance. Bathrooms are marginal, think of this as a boondocking site with a fee. Much of the bluff area above the ocean is occupied by older rigs and semi-permanent buildings. There is a nice little cove with a beach below the low bluff.

The campground is located just south of Rosarito on the free road. The entrance is near Km 30.

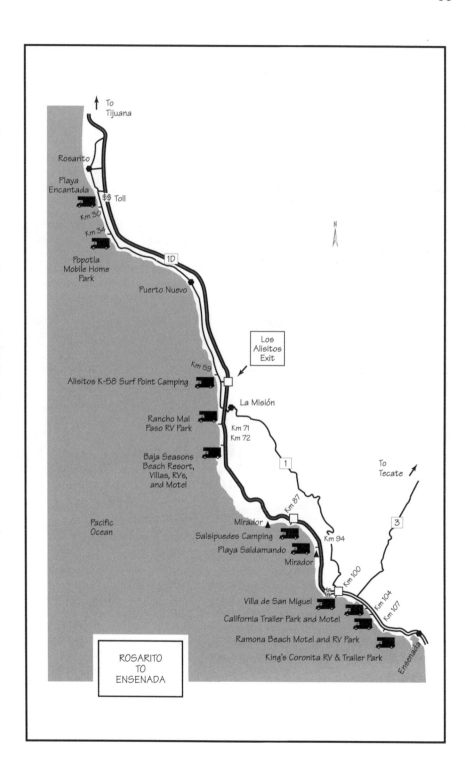

To Tijuana

Rosarito

Playa Encantada

$$ Toll

Km 30

Km 34

Popotla Mobile Home Park

1D

Puerto Nuevo

N

Los Alisitos Exit

Km 59

Alisitos K-58 Surf Point Camping

La Misión

Rancho Mal Paso RV Park

Km 71
Km 72

Baja Seasons Beach Resort, Villas, RVs, and Motel

1

To Tecate

3

Pacific Ocean

Mirador

Km 87

Salsipuedes Camping

Km 94

Playa Saldamando

Mirador

Km 100

Villa de San Miguel

Km 104

California Trailer Park and Motel

Km 107

Ramona Beach Motel and RV Park

King's Coronita RV & Trailer Park

Ensenada

ROSARITO TO ENSENADA

POPOTLA MOBILE HOME PARK

Address:	Km 34 Carr. Tijuana-Ensenada Libre; Rosarito, B.C. México
Res.:	P.O. Box 431135, San Ysidro, CA 92143
Telephone:	(661) 2-15-01
Price:	Expensive

GPS Location: N 32° 16' 48.5", W 117° 01' 48.0"

This is a large gated RV park mostly filled with permanent residents, but is has a very nice area set aside for short-term campers. We usually find these sites mostly empty, perhaps surprising considering the location next to the ocean, but probably reflecting the fact that we visit mostly during the winter.

There are 40 spaces here for overnighters, all with ocean views. They are large back-in spaces suitable for large rigs with full hookups. Electrical outlets are 30 amp and all sites have parking pads. Some sites are set near the water near a small cove, others are above along the bluff. There are bathrooms with hot showers and a swimming pool. The campground is fenced and secure and there is a bar and restaurant on the grounds. No dogs are allowed.

The campground is located near Km 34 on the free road about 7 km (4 miles) south of Rosarito.

ALISITOS K-58 SURF POINT CAMPING

Address:	Km 59 Carr. Tijuana-Ensenada Libre, B.C., México
Telephone:	(663) 6-11-69
Price:	Moderate

GPS Location: N 32° 07' 24.1", W 116° 53' 08.4"

This is another basic no-frills place to park on a bluff above the ocean. There is a large open field with no hookups, plenty of room and easy access make it suitable for any size rig. There are new flush toilets and cold showers available and the owners seem to make an effort to keep the place clean. Beer and ice are available. A paved access trail leads down to a long sandy beach.

The entrance is located near the Km 59 point of the free road south of Rosarito.

RANCHO MAL PASO RV PARK

Address:	Km 71 Carr. Tijuana-Ensenada; B.C., México
Price:	Low

GPS Location: N32° 04' 31.0", W 116° 52' 46.2"

This primitive campground offers excellent access to the same beach as Baja Seasons. Access is easy and this campground is suitable for even the largest rigs.

Camping is on a huge area of solid fill right next to the beach. Sites are not delineated, rigs can park along at least a quarter-mile of beach. Facilities are limited to flush and pit toilets and cold water showers.

Access to the campground is directly from the south-bound lanes of the toll road at the 71 Km marker. There's no access from the north-bound lanes, you'll have to drive north to the Alisitos exit and return to reach the campground. There is a walking overpass right beyond the exit so watch for it so you don't miss the turn. You'll drive into a small compound where you'll pay the fee and then drive on through to the beach.

🚌 **BAJA SEASONS BEACH RESORT, VILLAS, RVS, AND MOTEL**
    Res.:   1177 Broadway Ave., Suite 2, Chula Vista, CA 91911
    Telephone: (800) 754-4190 or (619) 422-2777 (U.S. Res.)
               or (615) 5-40-15 (Mex)
    Fax: (615) 5-40-19 (Mex)
    Price: Very Expensive

GPS Location: N 32° 03' 55.0", W 116° 52' 42.3"

The Baja Seasons is a large and very nice beachside RV park within reasonable driving distance of Ensenada. The drive into town is about 30 miles (50 km) on good four-lane highway, complicated only by a fascinating area where there seems to be an unending construction project to stabilize the road and keep it from sliding into the ocean. The only problem is that you'll pay more to stay here than you would north of the border, about $40 in the winter and $50 in the summer.

The campground has about 140 very nice camping spaces with electricity (some 50 amp, the rest 30 amp), sewer, water, TV, paved parking pad, patios and landscaping. The streets are paved, they even have curbs. There's a huge central complex with a restaurant and bar, swimming pool, hot tub, small store, tennis courts, sauna and steam baths, mini golf, game room, library and coin-op laundry. There are also restrooms with hot showers. The entire set-up is on a wide, beautiful beach. English is spoken and reservations are accepted.

The campground is right next to Mex 1D just south of the Km 72 marker. Going south watch the kilometer markers and turn directly off the highway. Going north you will see the campground on your left but cannot turn because of the central divider. Continue north 4.1 miles (6.6 km) to the Alisitos exit to return.

🚌 **SALSIPUEDES CAMPING**
    Address: Km 87 Carr. Escénica No. 1 Tijuana-Ensenada;
                B.C., México
    Price: Low

GPS Location: N 31° 58' 51.0", W 116° 46' 57.6"

This campground offers primitive camping in an olive tree grove. It is popular with surfers who clamber down a steep trail to the beach. The name of the campground suggests the problem for big rigs, Salsipuedes means "leave if you can" in Spanish. A very steep access road winds down about a half-mile from the highway far above. It is not suitable for rigs larger than vans.

After the initial descent you'll enter a compound where the managers live. They'll collect a fee for camping, then you drive down another steep section of road to a bluff above the beach. Back from the bluff there is an olive orchard. Campers set up on the bluff where they can watch the surfing or back in the orchard where there is some shade. There's lots of room. Facilities include flush toilets, cold showers, and sometimes a small taco stand.

To find the campground watch for the Salsipuedes exit sign near Km 87 of the toll road. The entrance gate has a gatehouse next to it, we've always found it abandoned. The access road is very steep, we think anything larger than a van would have problems with this road.

PLAYA SALDAMANDO

Address:	Km 94 Carr. Escénica No. 1 Tijuana-Ensenada; B.C., Mex.
Telephone:	(619) 582-8333 (U.S., for reservations)
E-mail:	saldamando@k-online.com
Internet:	www.mexonline.com/playasal.htm
Price:	Low

GPS Location: N 31° 55' 58.7", W116° 45' 16.5"

This campground, like Salsipuedes, has a steep access road. This one's not as bad, we think it is good for rigs to about 24 feet. No trailers though! The drop from the toll road to this campground is not nearly as great as the descent to Salsipuedes.

There are some 30 or 40 camping sites spread along at least a half-mile of rocky coastline. Roads and campsites are lined with white-painted rocks. Someone has put in a lot of time with a paint brush. Most sites are pretty well separated from each other and sport picnic tables. Almost all have excellent view locations, you can watch the waves and surfers below. There are no hookups, pit toilets and flush toilets with cold water showers are available.

The access road to this campground is just north of the Mirador de Ballenas which is just south of the Km 94 marker. It is easiest to pull off at the mirador (overlook) and then drive back to the entrance road along a small side road. About .5 mile (1 km) down the hill is an entrance gate where the fee is collected.

VILLA DE SAN MIGUEL

Address:	Km 99 Carr. Tijuana-Ensenada; Apdo. 55; Ensenada; C.P. 22760 B.C., México
Telephone:	(617) 4-62-25
Price:	Moderate

GPS Location: N 31° 54' 07.6", W 116° 43' 42.6"

This campground is very popular with surfers. The point just to the west is Punta San Miguel, this is one of the most popular surfing locations along the northern Baja coastline.

The campground itself is little more than a large gravel parking lot next to the beach. There are hookups. They form a line of about 30 pull-alongside or back-in sites at the back of the parking lot with 15-amp power plugs, water and sewer. There is a cement-block building with flush toilets and cold showers, it was dirty and in poor repair when we visited. Above the beach area are a large number of permanently-situated rigs, there's also a popular restaurant.

The campground is located off the four-lane coastal highway just south of the southernmost toll station. The exit is marked San Miguel and is near the Km 99 marker. There is an entrance gate near the exit where the fee is collected, then the road descends to the beach. The entrance road and campsite are suitable for the largest rigs.

🚐 **CALIFORNIA TRAILER PARK AND MOTEL**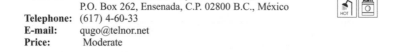

Address:	Km 103-700 Carretera Tijuana-Ensenada,
	P.O. Box 262, Ensenada, C.P. 02800 B.C., México
Telephone:	(617) 4-60-33
E-mail:	qugo@telnor.net
Price:	Moderate

GPS Location: N 31° 53' 04.5", W 116° 41' 10.4"

This is a small hotel with just a few campsites for rigs to about 26 feet. The sites are back-in, most with paved pads, there are about 8 of them. There are 15-amp power plugs, water and sewer hookups. The restrooms are small but offer flush toilets and hot showers.

The motel is located on the ocean side of the 4-lane highway north of Ensenada near the Km 104 marker. Reservations are accepted.

🚐 **RAMONA BEACH MOTEL AND RV PARK**

Address:	Carr. Transp. Km 104, Apdo. 513,
	Ensenada, B.C., México
Telephone:	(617) 4-60-45
Price:	Low

GPS Location: N 31° 52' 57.7", W 116° 41' 08.1"

The facilities at this campground are older and in poor repair. It is located just south of the Motel California. Driving by you might think it abandoned, often there seems to be no one around. However, usually the campground is open, the office is in the Ramona Beach Motel just to the south.

Access is good and the 30 or so sites are suitable for large rigs. The campground is located next to the ocean with just a low bluff down to the water. If you decide to stay check for a site with working hookups. Most have 15-amp plugs, water, and sewer but many do not work. There are flush toilets and hot showers but they're hard to find. They're located just above the beach directly behind the motel office in a small white building.

🚐 **KING'S CORONITA RV & TRAILER PARK**

Address:	Hwy. Tijuana-Ensenada Km 107,
	Ensenada, C.P. 22860, B.C., México
Res.:	P.O. Box 5515, Chula Vista, CA 91912
Telephone:	(617) 4-45-40 or (617) 4-43-91
Price:	Moderate

GPS Location: N 31° 51' 58.3", W 116° 39' 50.2"

This is an older well-kept campground that is almost full of permanently located rigs. There are generally a few sites available for overnighters but you would do well to call ahead if you wish to stay here.

Campsites have full hookups with 15-amp plugs. Most are small although some would allow large rigs, access to the campground is not a problem for larger rigs. Restrooms are clean with flush toilets and hot showers. The campground is located on a bluff above a marina, but sites for overnight rigs would be back from the bluff and would not offer much in the way of views.

The campground is located off the four-lane coastal highway near Km 107.

ENSENADA (EHN-SEH-NAH-DAH)
Population 400,000

Ensenada is the Baja's third most populous town and one of the most pleasant to visit. It is an important port and is more than ready for the tourist hordes that make the short-and-easy 68 mile (109 km) drive south from the border crossing at Tijuana or disembark from the cruise ships that anchor in Todos Santos Bay. There are many, many restaurants and handicrafts stores in the central area of town, English is often spoken so this is not a bad place to get your feet wet if you have not visited a Mexican city before. Try walking along **Calle Primera**, also called Avenida López Mateos, it is lined with restaurants and shops and is located just one block inland from the coastal Blvd. Costero (also known as Blvd. Gral. Lázaro Cárdenas). There are also many supermarkets and Pemex stations so Ensenada is the place to stock up on supplies before heading down the peninsula. Many banks have ATM machines so you can easily acquire some pesos.

When you tire of shopping and eating Ensenada has a few other attractions. The best beach is at **Estero Beach** which also has several campgrounds, they are discussed below. The **fishing** in Ensenada is good, charters for yellowtail, albacore, sea bass, halibut and bonito can be arranged at the fishing piers. Ensenada has the largest fish market on the Baja, it is called the **Mercado Negro** (black market) and is located near the sport fishing piers. Nearby is a nice **Malecón** or waterfront walkway where you can take a good look at the fishing fleet. The waterspout at **La Bufadora**, located south near Punta Banda (see below) is a popular day trip. **Whale watching trips** are a possibility from December to March.

Important fiestas and busy times here are **Carnival** in February, spring break for colleges in the U.S. during late March, the Rosarito to Ensenada Bicycle Race and Newport to Ensenada Yacht Race in April, a wine festival in August, another Rosarito to Ensenada bicycle race in October, and the Baja 1000 off-road race in November.

If you did not get a tourist card when you crossed the border in Tijuana you can obtain one and get it validated at the immigration office in Ensenada. It is located on the north side of the road soon after you cross the speed bumps next to the port when entering town from the north on Mex 1.

The **Estero Beach** area is really a suburb of Ensenada. The road to Estero beach leads

SWIMMING POOL AT THE ESTERO BEACH HOTEL/RESORT

west from near the Km 15 marker of Mex 1 about 7 miles (11 km) south of Ensenada. There's not much here other than beaches, the resorts, and vacation homes.

Punta Banda is another small area that is virtually a suburb of Ensenada. To get there follow the road west from near the center of Maneadero near the Km 21 marker, about 11 miles (18 km) south of Ensenada on Mex 1. It is then another 8 miles (13 km) out to Punta Banda. Punta Banda has grown up around the large RV parks here. The beach is known for its hot springs, you can dig a hole and make your own bath tub. A few miles beyond Punta Banda is the La Bufadora blow hole. There are several small campgrounds without hookups or much in the way of services near La Bufadora.

Ensenada Campgrounds

This section includes campgrounds in Ensenada itself and south to Maneadero. This includes Estero Beach and Punta Banda.

CAMPO PLAYA RV PARK

Address:	Blvd. Las Dunas & Calle Agustin Sanginés, Apdo. 789; Ensenada; B.C., México
Telephone:	(617) 6-29-18
Price:	Moderate

GPS Location: N 31° 51' 01.4", W 116° 36' 50.1"

SOUTH TO ENSENADA

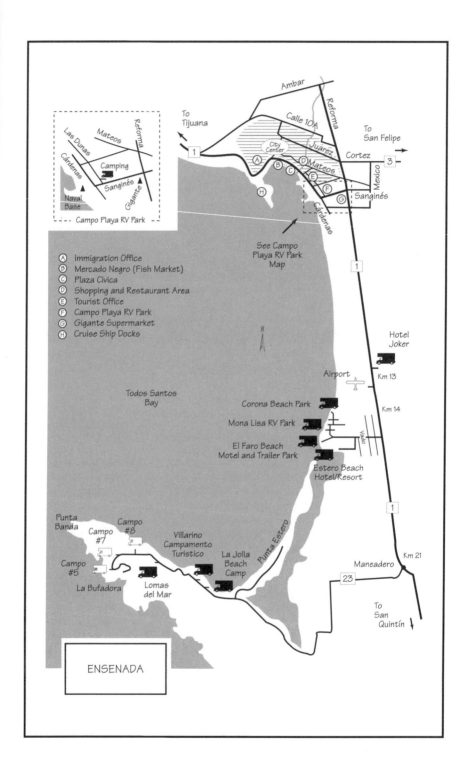

To Tijuana

To San Felipe

Ambar
Calle 10A
Reforma
City Center
Juarez
Mateos
Cortez
Mexico
1
3

Las Dunas
Mateos
Reforma
Cárdenas
Camping
Sanginés
Gigante
Naval Base

Campo Playa RV Park

Cárdenas
Sanginés

(A) Immigration Office
(B) Mercado Negro (Fish Market)
(C) Plaza Civica
(D) Shopping and Restaurant Area
(E) Tourist Office
(F) Campo Playa RV Park
(G) Gigante Supermarket
(H) Cruise Ship Docks

See Campo Playa RV Park Map

1

Hotel Joker

Airport   Km 13

Todos Santos Bay

Corona Beach Park

Km 14

Mona Lisa RV Park

Vado

El Faro Beach Motel and Trailer Park

Estero Beach Hotel/Resort

1

Punta Banda
Campo #8
Campo #7
Villarino Campamento Turistico
La Jolla Beach Camp
Punta Estero
Km 21
Maneadero

Campo #5

23

La Bufadora
Lomas del Mar

To San Quintín

ENSENADA

The Campo Playa is the only RV park actually in urban Ensenada and is the best place to stay if you want to explore the town. The downtown area is about 2 miles distant, the campground is right on the preferred route that you will probably be following through town, and there is a large Gigante supermarket just up the street.

There are about 50 spaces in the park set under palm trees. Most are pull-throughs that will accept a big rigs with slide-outs. The spaces have 15-amp plugs, sewer, water and patios. There are also some smaller spaces, some with only partial utility availability. The restrooms are showing their age but are clean and have hot showers. The campground is fenced but the urban location suggests that belongings not be left unattended.

The campground lies right on the most popular route through Ensenada. Entering town from the north on Mex 1 zero your odometer as you cross the obnoxious topes (speed bumps) next to the harbor. You'll pass a shipyard on your right with huge fishing boats almost overhanging the highway. Take the first major right in .5 miles (.8 km) following signs for La Bufadora, this is Blvd. Lázaro Cárdenas. You'll pass a Sanborn's coffee shop on the right and also a plaza with statues of three heads. At 1.8 miles (2.9 km) turn left onto Calle Agustin Sanginés, drive one block and turn left. The trailer park will be on your right after the turn.

🚐 HOTEL JOKER

Address:	Carretera Transpeninsular Km 12.5; Ensenada; B.C., México
Telephone:	(617) 7-44-60
Fax:	(617) 7-44-60
Price:	Expensive

GPS Location: N 31° 48' 12.3", W 116° 35' 42.6"

Just south of Ensenada, right on Mex 1, is a quirky little motel with a few RV slots. Once you enter the gates you'll probably find you like the place. The hotel specializes in special-event parties, there are play areas with castle-like crenellations, a piñata party plaza, a barbecue area and a general atmosphere of good clean family fun.

The Joker has about 6 spaces, although most are pull-throughs they are small, rigs larger than 24 feet or so will have difficulty maneuvering and parking. The slots have 15-amp plugs, sewer, water, and patios with shade, flowers, and barbecues. There's also a large grass area that is perfect for tents. The restrooms are older but clean and in good repair and have hot water. The hotel also has a restaurant and a tiny swimming pool.

The Joker is on the east side of Mex 1 just north of the Km 13 marker. Heading north watch for it after you pass the airport, about 1.4 miles (2.2 km) north of the Estero Beach road. Heading south there are really no good markers, just watch for the hotel on your left.

SOUTH TO ENSENADA

ESTERO BEACH HOTEL/RESORT

Address:	Apdo. 86; Ensenada; B.C., México
U.S. Res.:	PMB. 1186, 482 W. San Ysidro Blvd.,
	San Ysidro, CA 92173
Telephone:	(617) 6-62-25
Fax:	(617) 6-69-25
E-mail:	estero@telnor.net
Internet:	www.hotelesterobeach.com
Price:	Expensive (Winter), Very Expensive (Summer)

GPS Location: N 31° 46' 40.8", W 116° 36' 15.0"

The Estero Beach Hotel has one of Mexico's finest RV parks, comparable in many ways with the very expensive places on the road between Tijuana and Ensenada. For some reason, perhaps because it is slightly off the main road, it doesn't cost as much as those places. This is really a huge complex with a hotel as the centerpiece and many permanent RVs in a separate area from the RV park. Reservations are recommended because caravans often fill this place unexpectedly. English is spoken.

The modern RV park has 38 big back-in spaces with 30-amp plugs, sewer, and water. There is also a very large area for parking if you don't want utilities. There is grass under trees for tenters. The parked RVs look across an estuary (excellent birding) toward the hotel about a quarter-mile away. There's a paved walkway along the border of the estuary to the hotel. The restrooms were showing some age last time we visited and there was no hot water, but we're assured that normally there is. The hotel also has another area with full hookups for about 20 smaller units, they call it their trailer park. Check to see if there is room there for you if the RV park happens to be full.

The resort also has a restaurant, bar, museum, several upscale shops, boat launching ramp, tennis courts, and playground. There's also a brand-new beautiful swimming pool with hot tubs.

To reach the Estero Beach Hotel take the Estero Beach road west from Mex 1 some 5.2 miles (8.4 km) south of the Gigante supermarket on the corner of Ave. Reforma (Mex 1) and Calle General Agustin Sanginés. Drive 1 mile (1.6 km) west and turn left at the sign for the Estero Beach Hotel. You'll soon come to a gate. There is a very long entrance drive and then a reception office where they'll sign you up and direct you to a campsite.

EL FARO BEACH MOTEL AND TRAILER PARK

Address:	Apdo. 1008, Ensenada, C.P. 22800 B.C., México
Telephone:	(617) 7-46-20
Price:	Low

GPS Location: N 31° 46' 48.1", W 116° 37' 04.0"

The El Faro is a popular destination for beach-goers from Ensenada. Busses bring loads of them to the small beach that is located between the El Faro and the Estero Beach Hotel. That means that on sunny days there are probably too many people wandering through the camping area for a really enjoyable experience. The mascot here is Leonardo, a huge male lion kept in a cage near the entrance. At one time it was a cute little cub, but, they say, "it just kept getting bigger!"

This is a simple place, parking is right next to the beach on a sandy lot surrounded by a low concrete curb. There is room for about 3 rigs to back in for spaces with low-amp electricity. Much more space, enough for some 20 more rigs is available without hook-ups. Showers are old, in poor repair, and cold. You'll be happier if you bring your own bathroom facilities along with you. However, hot showers are available for a fee at a place about a quarter-mile up the road.

To reach the El Faro take the Estero Beach road west from Mex 1 about 5.2 miles (8.4 km) south of the Gigante supermarket on the corner of Ave. Reforma (Mex 1) and Calle Agustin Sanginés. Drive 1.9 mile (3.1 km) west, taking the left fork of the Y at 1.6 miles (2.6 km). The El Faro is at the end of the road.

🚐 MONA LISA RV PARK

Address:	Apdo. 200, Chapultepec, B.C., México
Telephone:	(617) 7-49-20
Price:	Expensive

GPS Location: N 31° 47' 07.5", W 116° 36' 55.2"

This is a interesting family-run campground, a fun place to visit. The name apparently comes from the murals painted on every available wall. They depict scenes from Mexico's history and are themselves worth a special trip to the Mona Lisa.

The campground has 13 fairly large back-in spaces. All are paved and some have palapa-shaded tables. All also have 50-amp plugs, sewer, and water. The restrooms are old and last time we visited they were so dirty that they were unusable although this may not always be the case. There is also a restaurant, bar, and motel on the property. The Mona Lisa is near beaches but rock rip-rap fronts the actual RV park property, the current RV sites don't overlook the water. There's also a playground. English is spoken and reservations are accepted.

To reach the Mona Lisa take the Estero Beach road west from Mex 1 5.2 miles (8.4 km) south of the Gigante on the corner of Ave. Reforma (Mex 1) and Calle General Agustin Sanginés. Drive west and then north, taking the right fork of the Y at 1.6 miles (2.6 km). At 1.8 miles (2.9 km) turn left and you'll see the Mona Lisa ahead.

🚐 CORONA BEACH PARK

Address:	P.O. Box 1149, Ensenada, México
Price:	Moderate

GPS Location: N 31° 47' 21.9", W 116° 36' 53.3"

This is a simple campground with parking in a large flat area with no view of the beautiful sandy beach to the north of the campground. There is parking for 28 rigs with 15-amp plugs and water. There is also a dump station. The restrooms are clean and have cold water showers. A small grocery store sits next to the camping area. English is spoken.

To reach the Corona Beach take the Estero Beach road west from Mex 1 some 5.2 miles (8.4 km) south of the Gigante on the corner of Ave. Reforma (Mex 1) and Calle

General Agustin Sanginés. Drive west and then north, taking the right fork of the Y at 1.6 miles (2.6 km). At 1.9 miles (3.1 km) the road makes a quick right and then left to continue straight. You'll reach the campground at 2.1 miles (3.4 km).

VILLARINO CAMPAMENTO TURISTICO

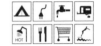

Address: Km 13 Carr. a la Bufadora, Apdo. 842,
                 Ensenada, B.C., México
Telephone: (615) 4-20-45
Fax: (615) 4-20-44
Price: Moderate

GPS Location: N 31° 43' 03.5", W 116° 40' 00.9"

This campground with lots of permanents also has a good-size transient area. It's close to Ensenada, on the beach, and a little off the beaten path.

Behind a glass-fronted terrace overlooking the beach is a large packed dirt area with some trees and about 20 larger sites. Some sites have 15-amp plugs, sewer, and water and some have only electricity and water. Most sites have picnic tables, some have fire rings. The restrooms are very clean and well maintained, they have hot showers. In front of the campground is a restaurant, a small store, a post office, and a public phone.

Take the road toward La Bufadora from Mex 1 about 9.1 miles (14.7 km) south from the Gigante on the corner of Ave. Reforma (Mex 1) and Calle General Agustin Sanginés in Ensenada. You will see the Villarino on the right 7.9 miles (12.6 km) from the cutoff.

LA JOLLA BEACH CAMP

Address: Apdo. 102, Punta Banda, Ensenada,
                 C.P. 22791 B.C., México
Telephone: (615) 4-20-05
Fax: (615) 4-20-04
Price: Low

GPS Location: N 31° 43' 00.1", W 116° 39' 52.2"

The La Jolla Beach Camp is a huge place. There are a lot of permanently-located trailers here but most of the transient trade is summer and holiday visitors using tents or RVs. Several big empty dirt lots, both on the waterfront and on the south side of the highway, have room for about 400 groups. During the winter these areas are practically empty. You can park on the waterfront and run a long cord for electricity from a few plugs near the restroom buildings. Water is available and there's a dump station. Restrooms are very basic, like what you'd expect next to a public beach, there are a few hot showers available. There is a small grocery store and basic English is spoken.

Take the road toward La Bufadora from Mex 1 about 9.1 miles (14.7 km) south from the Gigante on the corner of Ave. Reforma (Mex 1) and Calle General Agustin Sanginés in Ensenada. You will see the La Jolla on the right 7.8 miles (12.6 km) from the cutoff.

LOMAS DEL MAR

Address: Km 16, Carr. La Bufadora, Apdo. 190, Pob.
                 Punta Banda, C.P. 22791 B.C., Mex.
Telephone: (615) 4-23-74
Price: Low

GPS Location: N 31° 43' 28.5", W 116° 41' 07.1"

This new campground is on the grounds of a housing development on the road out to La Bufadora. There are 20 pull-through sites with full hookups (15-amp plugs) situated on the side of a hill with excellent views north toward Ensenada. All of the sites seem to have a downhill slope and the sandy soil is beginning to erode making the place seem almost abandoned. There are no restrooms.

Take the road toward La Bufadora form Mex 1 about 9.1 miles (14.7 km) south from the Gigante on the corner of Ave. Reforma (Mex 1) and Calle General Agustin Sanginés in Ensenada. 9.2 miles (14.9 km) from the junction you'll see the campground on the left.

Other Camping Possibilities

Out near La Bufadora there are at least three small camping operations. These are very basic no-frills camping sites. They offer no facilities except pit toilets, but some have great views. These places tend to have difficult access, they are not recommended for big rigs.

TECATE (TEH-KAW-TAY)
Population 80,000, Elevation 1,850 ft. (560 m)

Tecate is probably the most relaxed and pleasant border town in Mexico. Besides being a great place to cross into Baja (there are decent roads south to Ensenada and east to Mexicali) the town is well worth a short visit.

Tecate is an agricultural center that is gradually turning industrial as the maquiladora industries arrive. The center of town is dominated by the park-like square which is just a couple of blocks from the laid-back border crossing. Probably the most famous tourist attraction here is the Tecate brewery.

Tecate Campgrounds

POTRERO REGIONAL PARK

Res.:   5201 Ruffin Road, Suite P,
            San Diego, CA 92123-1699
Telephone: (Reservations) (858) 565-3600, (Info) (858) 694-3049
Internet: www.co.san-diego.ca.us/parks
Price: Moderate

GPS Location: N 32° 36' 45.6", W 116° 35' 41.2"

This is a good campground on the U.S. side of the border near Tecate. If you are headed south and want to get a good start in the morning consider spending the night here. It is only 5 miles (8 km) from Tecate, the small nearby town of Potrero offers a café. Another nearby town, Campo, has an interesting railroad museum.

There are 32 back-in sites with electrical and water hookups set under oak trees for shade. Large rigs will find plenty of room in most sites. Picnic tables and fire pits are provided. Areas are also set aside for tents and there are hot water showers. There is a dump station. Reservations are accepted but probably not necessary during the winter season.

Follow Hwy. 94 from San Diego toward Tecate. Zero your odometer where Hwy. 188 to Tecate cuts off to the right but continue straight. Drive 2.3 miles (3.7 km) to the outskirts of Potrero and turn left. Then after another .3 miles (.5 km) turn right on the entrance road to the campground.

▦ TECATE KOA, RANCHO OJAI

Address:	P.O. Box 280, Tecate, CA 91980 (U.S.)
Telephone:	(665) 5-30-14
Fax:	(665) 5-30-15
E-mail:	rojai@telnor.net
Internet:	www.tecatekoa.com
Price:	Expensive

GPS Location: N 32° 33' 32.6", W 116° 26' 09.5"

Rancho Ojai is something a little different in Baja campgrounds. This is a former working ranch located in the rolling hills just east of Tecate off Mex 2. The facilities are brand-new and nicely done. It is now a KOA. This is normally a summer destination, the area is known for its mild summer weather, but winters have an occasional frost.

There are 75 campsites, 41 have full hookups with 30-amp plugs, sewer, and water. The tiled restrooms are brand new and clean with hot water showers. The ranch offers a ranch-style clubhouse, a barbecue area, swimming pool, grocery shop, sports areas for volley ball and horseshoes, bicycle rentals and a children's playground. The campground is fenced and there is 24-hour security. There's a good restaurant just outside the grounds, just a pleasant stroll through the pasture will take you there.

The Rancho is located about 13 miles (21 km) east of Tecate on the north side of the free highway near the Km 112 marker. It is not accessible from the toll highway. There is a stone arch entrance near the highway and you can see the camping area across the valley.

▦ HACIENDA SANTA VERÓNICA

Address:	Blvd. Agua Caliente No. 4558, Piso No. 1,
	Ofic. 105 Torres de Agua Caliente,
	Tijuana, C.P. 22420 B.C., Mex.
Telephone:	(668) 1-74-28 (Tijuana), (664) 8-52-34 (On site)
Price:	Moderate

GPS Location: N 32° 27' 34.3", W 116° 21' 46.6"

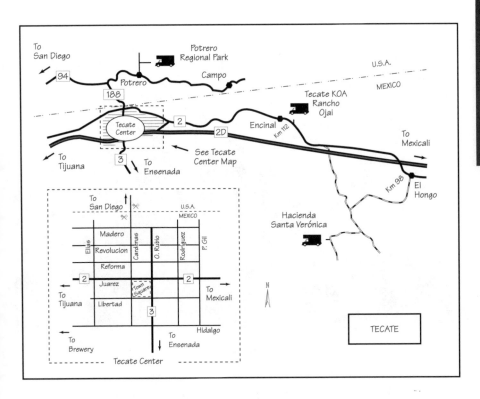

Slightly farther east of Tecate than the Tecate KOA is Hacienda Santa Verónica. To get there you must negotiate a partially paved back road but once you've reached the campground you're likely to want to spend some time. This is a 5,000 acre rancho. It is described in its own brochures as rustic, but other than the no-hookup campground it is really surprisingly polished. The rancho is very popular with off-road motorcycle riders and also offers quite a few amenities: rental rooms, a huge swimming pool with a bar in the middle, good tennis courts, a nice restaurant and bar, horseback riding, and occasionally even a bullfight. This is a popular summer destination, in the winter things are pretty quiet except on weekends.

The camping area is a grassy meadow with big oak trees for shade. Spaces are un-marked, you camp where you want to. The restrooms are near the pool, not far from the camping area. In the summer when the pool is in use they have hot water showers. The Santa Veronica also has a nice full-hookup campground that has been closed down because it wasn't getting enough use. Perhaps they'll open it again if enough of us visit!

To find the hacienda head east on Mex 2 from the Tecate KOA to the small town of El Hongo, a distance of 8.7 miles (14 km) from the Tecate KOA. Near the center of town there is a small road heading south through the village, it is marked with an easy-to-miss Hacienda Verónica sign. After 1.1 miles (1.8 km) the road curves right and leaves

THE DOMECQ WINERY SOUTH OF TECATE

town. You'll reach a Y after 4.7 miles (7.6 km) take the right fork and you'll reach the gate in another 1.5 miles (2.4 km).

TECATE TO ENSENADA ON HIGHWAY 3
67 Miles (108 Km), 2 Hours

Highway 3 is a good two-lane paved road that runs 63 miles (102 km) south from Tecate to meet with the four-lane coastal road just before it enters Ensenada. The route is suitable for larger rigs if they take it easy, it does cross some higher elevations. Some 45 miles (73 km) south of Tecate the road passes through the Guadalupe Valley, Mexico's premier wine-growing region. Several wineries are located there. The Pedro Domecq winery, hard to miss on the west side of the highway, offers tastings and tours as does the nearby L.A. Cetto winery.

Tecate to Ensenada on Highway 3 Campground

RANCHO SORDO MUDO (DEAF RANCH)

Address:	P.O. Box 1376, Chula Vista, CA 91912 or	
	Apdo. 1468, Ensenada, B.C.., Mex.	
Price:	Donation	

GPS Location: N 32° 06' 41.3", W 116° 32' 47.7"

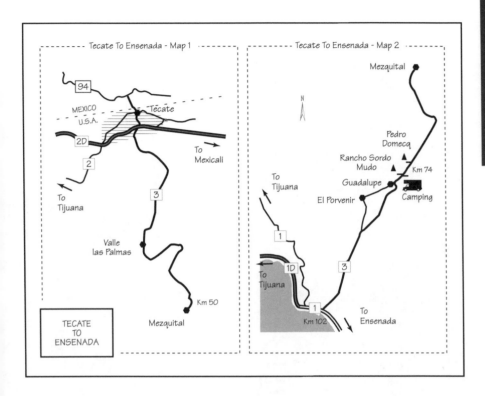

If you decide to follow the inland route on Mex 3 south from Tecate to Ensenada you might decide to spend the night at Rancho Sordo Mudo, about 24 miles (39 km) north of Ensenada. The ranch is actually a school for deaf children, the campground was originally constructed for the use of visitors helping at the school. The income from the RV park goes to a good cause and the surroundings are very pleasant.

There are 9 back-in spaces in a grassy field with full hookups including 50-amp plugs. Eighteen more pull-through spaces offer electricity and water only. The bathrooms are modern and clean and have hot water. The campground is likely to be deserted when you stop, just pull in and park and someone will eventually come across from the school to welcome you. The campground is located in a beautiful valley, the Domecq winery is just a mile up the road and offers tours.

The campground is well-signed on Mex 3. Driving south start watching as you pass the Domecq winery, it will be on your left right next to the highway just after the Km 74 marker. Heading north it is even easier to spot just north of the village of Guadalupe.

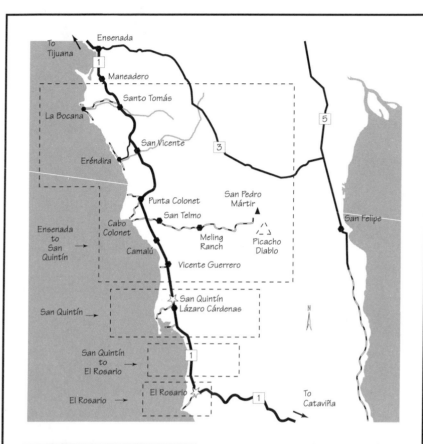

To Tijuana
Ensenada
1
Maneadero
Santo Tomás
La Bocana
San Vicente
3
Eréndira
5
Punta Colonet
San Pedro Mártir
Cabo Colonet
San Telmo
San Felipe
Ensenada to San Quintín →
Meling Ranch
Picacho Diablo
Camalú
Vicente Guerrero
San Quintín →
San Quintín Lázaro Cárdenas
N
San Quintín to El Rosario →
1
El Rosario →
El Rosario
1
To Cataviña

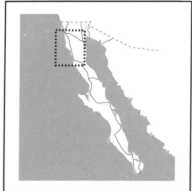

CHAPTER INDEX

Highlights .... Page 73
Roads and Fuel Availability .... Page 74
Sightseeing .... Page 75
Beaches and Water Sports .... Page 76
Fishing .... Page 76
Backroad Adventures .... Page 76
From Ensenada to San Quintín .... Page 78
San Quintín .... Page 81
San Quintín to El Rosario .... Page 85
El Rosario .... Page 85

SOUTHERN NORTHWEST COAST

CHAPTER

· · · · · · · · · · · · · · 5

SOUTHERN NORTHWEST COAST

INTRODUCTION

South of Maneadero the character of the Baja changes considerably. There are far fewer people and less traffic. In the beginning the road climbs into coastal hill country, much of it is covered with greenery. One of the valleys you will cross is the Santo Tomás Valley, known for its vineyards. After some time the road flattens out and runs along a coastal plain. There is much irrigated farming in this fast-growing region with occasional roads toward the ocean which is out of sight to the west. Near San Quintín roads lead west to Bahía San Quintín, a sheltered estuary offering a place to launch boats and also some history. Finally the road climbs to cross a barren mesa and then descends steeply into the town of El Rosario.

Enjoy the hustle and bustle of the small farming towns that often line the road, at the south end of this section you will be turning inland and driving through some of the Baja's most remote countryside.

Highlights

The **Santo Tomás Valley**, about 22 miles (35 km) south of Ensenada, is another of Mexico's wine regions. Many of the grapes from this area go to the Santo Tomás Winery, Mexico's largest, which is located in Ensenada. The ruins of the old **Mission Santo Tomás de Aquino** are located near the Balneario El Palomar.

Bahía San Quintín, about 110 miles (177 km) south of Ensenada, is a popular fishing destination. The bay provides a protected place to launch boats and the fishing outside the bay is excellent. Wide sandy beaches are easy to reach from the highway just to the south of Bahía San Quintín. In the 1890s an English company failed in an attempt to develop an agricultural town in the area, remains of a grain mill, pier, and cemetery can still be seen.

Inland from this stretch of road is the **Parque Nacional San Pedro Mártir** (San Pedro Mártir National Park). Access to this high pine country is via a long rough dirt road. See this chapter's *Backroad Adventures* for information about visiting this park.

One hundred and forty-six miles (235 km) south of Ensenada the road turns sharply left and heads inland. The small town here, **El Rosario**, is traditionally the spot to get gasoline and prepare for the isolated road to the south.

Roads and Fuel Availability

Much of the road in this section of the book is built to the narrow Baja Peninsula standard of about 18 feet wide. Additionally, there are seldom any shoulders. That means that all drivers much be cautious, particularly those driving large rigs. See the *Roads and Driving in Mexico* section in the *Details, Details, Details* chapter.

This section of Mex 1 is marked by kilometer markers that begin in Ensenada and end at Lázaro Cárdenas near Bahía San Quintín with Km 196.

Gasoline is not hard to find in this part of the Baja. There are several stations in Maneadero and also stations in most small towns along the route. The stations, the

MODERN PEMEX STATIONS HAVE BECOME QUITE COMMON

distances between them, and the type of fuel sold are as follows: **Santo Tomás**, gas and diesel; **San Vicente**, 24 miles (39 km), gas and diesel; **Punta Colonet**, 23 miles (37 km), gas and diesel; **Camalú**, 19 miles (31 km), only gas; **Vicente Guerrero**, 9 miles (15 km), gas and diesel; **San Quintín**, 8 miles (13 km), gas and diesel; **Lázaro Cárdenas**, 3 miles (5 km), gas and diesel; and **El Rosario**, 37 miles (60 km), gas and diesel.

A word of warning is in order about fuel. It is very important to fill up with gas or diesel in either San Quintín or El Rosario at the south end of this section. There will probably be no fuel available from filling stations until you reach Villa Jesús María, some 22 miles (35 km) north of Guerrero Negro. This is a gas gap of 195 miles (315 km). When we visited during the winter of 1999/2000 the old filling stations at Cataviña and at the Bahía L.A. Junction had been closed down and the pumps removed. Individuals with drums of gasoline in the back of their pickups were selling fuel at these stations, but we wouldn't want to count on this being the case if we were in dire need. They didn't have any diesel at all.

Sightseeing

The **Parque Nacional Sierra San Pedro Mártir** is located high in the sierra east of the highway. It is an area of pine forest that is so free from human interference that there is actually an astronomical observatory at 9,300 feet in the park. On Saturdays you can drive to the observatory, tours are given from 11 a.m. to 1 p.m. **Picacho Diablo**, the highest mountain in Baja California at 10,150 feet, is accessible to climbers from the park. See *Backroad Adventures* in this chapter for more information about this road.

The ruins of several **Dominican missions** can be viewed as you travel down the peninsula in this section. Since all were constructed of adobe they have suffered from the occasional rain over more than 100 years and give the appearance of having melted. At Santo Tomás the ruins of **Misíon Santo Tomás de Aquino** are actually located on the grounds of a campground, the Balneario El Palomar. Ask for directions for finding them at the office. The ruins of **Misíon San Vicente Ferrer** are located in the town of San Vicente, about 43 miles (69 km) south of the La Bufadora cutoff in Maneadero. To find them take the dirt road west from about Km 88. Near Vicente Guerrero is the **Misión Santo Domingo**. It is accessible by taking a road east at about Km 169 to the village of Santo Domingo. Finally, near El Rosario there are the ruins of **Misión el Rosario**. The directions for finding the mission can be found in the *Backroad Adventures* section below.

One of the few **tourist information centers** on the Baja is located near Km 178 just south of the town of Vicente Guerrero. It might be worth a stop although we find the information offerings pretty slim.

The late 19th century wheat-farming scheme at San Quintín left a few remnants that you might want to track down. Near the Old Mill Trailer Park is the restored **grist mill** and near the Old Pier Motel and RV Park is the **old pier**. Just south of the latter is the **Old English Cemetery**.

Beaches and Water Sports

There are miles of long sandy beaches along this section of coast. The primary activities are surfing and surf fishing. Road access is actually not bad, see *Backroad Adventures* below for some ideas. Since many of the back roads lead to beaches in this area we've discussed the attractions in that section. Water temperatures along the coast are cool but that just makes the fishing better.

South of the mouth of the San Quintín estuary is a long beach called **Playa Santa María** at the north end and **Playa Pabellón** farther south. Both surfing and fishing are popular, access is from the Cielito Lindo and El Pabellón RV parks, see the campground descriptions below for directions.

Fishing

From Punta Banda at the north end of the area covered by this chapter and south for about 200 miles upwelling water from the ocean depths brings nutrients that make fishing near the shore extremely good. The problem with this area is that it is unprotected and not really very safe for small boats. Launching sites for larger boats are scarce.

One way around this problem is to beach cast. Surf fishing is good along much of the coast for surf perch and rockfish.Another solution is to hire a panga and guide to take you out. You can do this at Puerto San Isidro, La Bocana near Puerto Santo Tomás, or at San Quintín at the Old Mill Trailer Park or the Cielito Lindo, also an RV park.

If you do decide to use your own boat the best launch site is San Quintín. However, from there you must find your way out through the weeds of the estuary, not easy to do for someone without local knowledge. There are also poor launch ramps at Puerto San Isidro and La Bocana that might be usable for small boats if the tide and weather are just right.

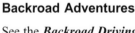
Backroad Adventures

See the *Backroad Driving* section of *Chapter 2 - Details, Details, Details* for essential information about driving off the main highway on the Baja and for a definition of road type classifications used below.

In the area covered by this chapter there are many small roads branching off the highway to the west and east. Most of those to the west are headed for the coast, one to the east is headed up into the Sierra San Pedro Mártir and the national park there. There are quite a number of people living between the highway and the coast, that means that there are a great number of roads of varying quality. Many of them are farm roads but they often reach the coast in places that offer good surf fishing and surfing. Most are not suitable for any RVs. High clearance vehicles, especially with four-wheel drive are your best bet. The condition of these roads changes, we advise getting local information about road conditions before heading out.

Some places to try roads like this are as follows. In Santo Tomás near Km 51 a road leads to the coast at Punta San José and southwards all the way to Eréndira. The area is popular for surf fishing and surfing. There is also a web of roads west of Punta

Colonet. They reach the long beach at San Antonio del Mar which is good for surf fishing and also Bahía Colonet, Punta Colonet, and Punta San Telmo. Surfing is popular south of the points, particularly south of Punta San Telmo which is widely known as "Quatro Casas". In Colonia Vicente Guerrero the same road that leads out to the Posada Don Diego Trailer Park continues out to Playa San Ramón, good for surfing and fishing. Consider these roads to be Type 3 roads unless you have local knowledge. More possibilites follow.

From Km 47 Near Santo Tomás - One and nine tenths miles (3.1 km) north of the El Palomar campground a gravel road goes along the Santo Tomás valley to **La Bocana** and then north along the coast to **Puerto Santo Tomás**. La Bocana is at the mouth of the Santo Tomás River and is 17.6 miles (28.7 km) from Mex 1. Puerto Santo Tomás is about three miles (5 km) to the north. This is usually a Type 2 road.

From Km 78 between Santo Tomás and San Vicente - A paved but sometimes rough road leads about 11 miles (18 km) to the coast at the ejido town of **Eréndira**. The road continues up the coast to **Puerto San Isidro**. You can also cross the river near the coast and drive south on dirt roads to Malibu Beach Sur RV Park, see the description below for this campground and instructions for reaching it. The paved road to Eréndira is usually a Type 1 road, beyond Eréndira the road is usually Type 2.

From Km 141 North of San Quintín - About 34 miles (55.5 km) north of San Quintín a road goes east to San Telmo, the **Meling Ranch**, and the **Parque Nacional Sierra San Pedro Mártir**. The road as far as the Meling ranch at about 32 miles (52 km) is usually a Type 2 road. The ranch is about a half-mile off the main road, it has an airstrip and offers overnight accommodations. Beyond the ranch to the park entrance gate at about 51 miles (83 km) the road may not be as good and is sometimes a Type 3 road. The road continues to an astronomical observatory at 65 miles (106 km). There are undeveloped campsites in the park and lots of hiking opportunities. You should be aware that the road may be closed due to snow in the winter.

From the northern border of the town of Lázaro Cárdenas - A road runs to **Bahía Falsa** on the coast where there is an oyster farm. The distance is 9 miles (14 km) along a graded gravel and sand road that is normally a Type 2 road. Bahía Falsa is the outer bay of the San Quintín estuary, the road takes you around the north end of Bahía San Quintín and past the volcanic cones that protect the bay. There are other less developed sand and dirt roads along the outer peninsula. The outer coast is a popular surfing destination.

From the 90-degree turn in the town of El Rosario - Heading south the highway takes a sharp left. If you go right here, then almost immediately left you will cross the river and within a mile reach the village of El Rosario de Abajo (Lower El Rosario). The ruins of **Misión el Rosario** are in this town on the right side of the road. Roads lead about 10 miles (16 km) out to the coast from here to Punta Baja and points south along the Bahía Rosario. The sandy beach along the bay is a popular surf-fishing location. This is usually a Type 3 road. The road is suitable for high-clearance vehicles only, the river crossing right at El Rosario is sometimes a problem, there is a makeshift bridge made from a large culvert that sometimes washes out. Fortunately you will reach this less than a mile from the highway so you won't waste much time if the crossing is not possible.

THE ROUTES, TOWNS, AND CAMPGROUNDS

ENSENADA TO SAN QUINTÍN
116 Miles (187 Km), 4 Hours

Mex 1 as it leaves Ensenada runs through some 7 miles (11 km) of suburbs until it reaches the town of Maneadero. At the north end of Maneadero is the road west out to La Bufadora, and you'll find several campgrounds there, they are described in the preceding chapter.

Leaving the south edge of Maneadero the road climbs into brush-covered hills. This is a scenic section of road but exercise caution because the road is narrow. Fifteen miles (24 km) after leaving Maneadero the road descends into the Santo Tomás Valley.

For a few miles the road runs along the valley floor which is used to grow grapes and olives. Then it once again climbs into the rolling hills. You'll pass through the small farming towns of San Vicente and Punta Colonet.

After Punta Colonet the road runs along a broad coastal plain which is covered with irrigated farmland. Along this section are the villages of Camalú, Vicente Guerrero, San Quintín, and Lázaro Cárdenas. These last two towns almost seem to be one as

CACTUS FARM SOUTH OF ENSENADA

they merge into one another along the highway, they and the bay that almost adjoins them to the west form the area that for the sake of convenience is often called San Quintín.

Ensenada to San Quintín Campgrounds

BALNEARIO EL PALOMAR

Res.:	Avenida Ruíz #339 Interior,
	Ensenada, B.C., México
Telephone:	(615) 3-80-02 (Campground),
	(617) 8-80-02 (Reservations in Ensenada)
Price:	Moderate

GPS Location: N 31° 33' 24.1", W 116° 24' 42.7"

Balnearios (swimming resorts) are very popular in Mexico, they often make a good place to camp. This is the best example of such a balneario on the Baja. In 1997 it celebrated its fiftieth anniversary.

The El Palomar has six pull-throughs large enough for big rigs to about 30 feet and about 20 very small back-in spaces. All have 15-amp plugs, sewer, water, patios and barbecues. Many also have picnic tables. Two restroom buildings are clean and in

SOUTHERN NORTHWEST COAST

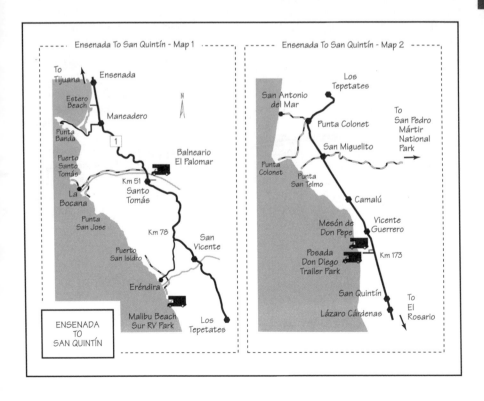

good repair, they have hot water for showers. There are two swimming pools near the camping area and a small lake and water slide about a half-mile away. There's also a small zoo and large areas for picnicking. Across the street in the main building there is a store, a restaurant, and a small gas station. The store has a good collection of Baja books and Mexican handicrafts. Two words of warning are in order. Take a look at the steep entrance before entering and be aware that this is a very popular place with people from Ensenada on weekends during the summer and on holidays. It might be better to avoid the campground during those times since many of the sites are pretty much right in the center of things.

The El Palomar is at the north entrance to the town of Santo Tomás about 30 miles (49 km) south of Ensenada on Mex 1. The office is on the west side of the road and the campground on the east.

▄ MALIBU BEACH SUR RV PARK　　　　　
　　Price:　　Low

　　　　　GPS Location: N 31° 14' 15.1", W 116° 21' 26.3"

This is an isolated campground with decent facilities on a very nice beach. If you have a smaller rig that allows you to drive to it without problems you'll find it hard to beat.

There are 14 pull-through sites with full hookups. Plugs are 15 amps. Sites have cement patios and the 7 in front overlook the ocean. There is a 15-foot bluff here with stairs leading down to the beach. Sixteen more sites with no hookups or patios are located behind the serviced sites. The bathroom building has hot showers and there is also a washing machine and dryer. Fishing from the beach is excellent here.

A portion of the access road to this campground is ungraded dirt road. We recommend that motorhomes over about 24 feet and trailers do not attempt to use this campground without local knowledge. The road condition undoubtedly changes from year to year and you may also have to do a little route-finding. To reach the campground leave Mex 1 just south of the Km 78 marker on the road toward Eréndira. Follow this paved road 10.2 miles (16.5 km), then take a left turn at a somewhat faded sign for Malibu Beach Sur RV Park. This is an unpaved track that will take you across the (hopefully) dry riverbed and up the bank on the other side through a group of houses. Continue following signs for the campground through a region of fields along the ocean. You'll reach the campground 3.2 miles (5.2 km) after leaving the pavement. If you reach a branch in the road that is not marked (there are several branches), just follow the one that seems to lead south along the coast. The countryside is open and you'll have a good view of the area.

▄ MESÓN DE DON PEPE　　　　　
　　Address:　　Callejon del Turista No. 102, Apdo. No. 7,
　　　　　　　　Col. Vicente Guerrero, C.P. 22920 B.C, México
　　Telephone:　(616) 6-22-16
　　Fax:　　　　(616) 6-22-68
　　Price:　　Low

　　　　　GPS Location: N 30° 42' 44.7", W 115° 59' 50.1"

This campground and the one following are in the town of Vicente Guerrero, about 8 miles (13 km) north of San Quintín. Both of these parks have been popular for a long time with travelers heading south or north, they are a comfortable day's drive from the border. Both are located on the same entrance road, they're within a half-mile of each other. The Don Pepe is the one on the highway and the first one the visitor reaches, it is also the smaller of the two.

There are really two transient camping areas at this park. Just below the restaurant is a grassy area with electrical outlets and water that is set aside for about 10 tent and van campers. Farther from the restaurant on the far side of a few permanents is the RV camping with about 20 pull-through spaces with electricity, sewer, and water. Both camping areas have restrooms, they are older but clean and have hot water showers. The restaurant at the Don Pepe is well known and considered to be very good.

The entrance to the trailer park is on the west side of Mex 1 just south of Col. Vicente Guerrero where the road starts to climb a small hill at the Km 173 marker. There are actually two entrances, the farthest north is well signed and will lead you into the RV camping area. The second is near the top of the hill, just north of the gas plant, this will take you to the restaurant/office. After checking in you'll see a road curving around the back of the trailer park to lead you back down the camping areas.

⛺ POSADA DON DIEGO TRAILER PARK

Address: Apdo. 126, Col. Vicente Guerrero,
              C.P. 22920, B.C., México
Telephone: (616) 6-21-81
Price: Moderate

GPS Location: N 30° 42' 58.9, W 115° 59' 21.7"

This second Col. Vicente Guerrero trailer park is very popular with caravans, it is roomy and has lots of spaces, in fact it is the only large campground with full hookups in this area.

The campground has 100 spaces, almost 50 of these are usually occupied by permanents. Most of the available slots are large enough for big rigs with slide-outs, they have 15-amp plugs, water, and patios. About half have sewer, there is also a dump station available. The restrooms are in good repair and clean, they have hot water showers. The campground also has a restaurant/bar, a store, a meeting room and a playground.

To reach the Posada Don Diego follow the road going west from just north of the gas plant at Km 173. This is just south of Col. Vicente Guerrero. The same road runs right past the restaurant at the Don Pepe, described above. The campground is about .5 miles (.8 km) down this sometimes rough but passable gravel road.

SAN QUINTÍN (SAHN KEEN-TEEN)
Population 25,000 in the area

San Quintín is an interesting place, both geological and historically. The area is a large salt water lagoon system which fronts a fertile plain. Long sandy beaches stretch north and south. The lagoon and plain probably would have eroded away long ago except that there are eight small volcanoes (seven onshore and one an island offshore) that shelter the area from the sea. For the last few decades the plain has been heavily farmed, unfortunately there is not enough fresh water in the aquifer and salt water has started to displace the fresh water. Farming has gradually retreated to the east side of Mex 1.

Farming is also responsible for the interesting history of the area. During the late 19th century the region was the focus of a settlement scheme by an American company and then later an English company under a grant from Mexican President Porfirio Díaz. The plan was to grow wheat but it turned out that there wasn't enough rainfall. Today there are several ruined structures to remind visitors of the colony, they include the Molino Viejo (old mill), the Muelle Viejo (old pier), and the English cemetery.

Outdoorsmen love the area. Goose and duck hunting is good in the winter, fishing offshore is excellent. The protected waters are a good place to launch a trailer boat if you've pulled one south, but the shallow waters of the bay are difficult to navigate and the offshore waters can be dangerous.

San Quintín Campgrounds

🚐 CIELITO LINDO MOTEL AND RV PARK

Address:	Apdo. 7, San Quintín, B.C., México
Telephone:	(619) 222-8955 (U.S. Res.),
	(619) 593-2252 (Voice mail in the U.S.)
Price:	Low

GPS Location: N 30° 24' 30.9", W 115° 55' 21.1"

The Cielito Lindo Motel has been around for a long time. It is well-known for its restaurant and fishing charters. At one time it had a large camping area near the beach, that location has been abandoned and is not recommended. There is a second camping area near the hotel which we enjoy. The long and sandy Playa Santa María is a short walk from the campground.

The hotel camping area has 8 back-in slots, they have generator produced electricity with 15-amp plugs, water and sewer. There is a row of pine trees to provide shade and some shelter from the frequent wind in this area. Electricity is produced by an on-site generator so it is available from 7 a.m. to 11 a.m. and from 3 p.m. until the bar closes. The bar also serves as a restaurant, some people come here just because of the food. There is also a small area set aside for tent campers not needing hookups. Restrooms with hot showers are located in a building on the north side of the central courtyard area.

The Cielito Lindo is located near the San Quintín La Pinta Motel. The paved road with lots of potholes leads west from Mex 1 near the Km 11 marker. It is signed for both the La Pinta and the Cielito Lindo. Follow the road west for 2.8 miles (4.5 km) past the La Pinta entrance to the Cielito Lindo entrance.

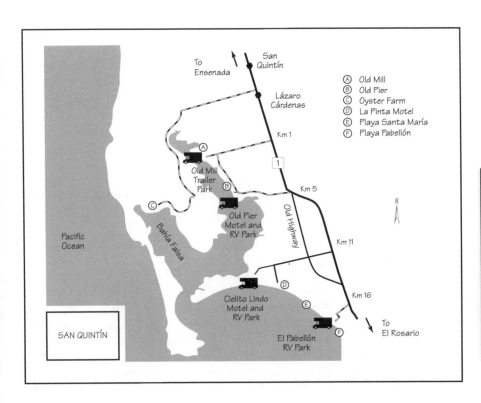

🚐 OLD MILL TRAILER PARK

Address: Apdo Postal 90, Valle de San Quintín, B.C., México
Telephone: (800) 479-7962 (U.S. Reservations) or
(619) 428-2779 (U.S. Reservations)
Price: Expensive

GPS Location: N 30° 29' 09.8", W 115° 58' 32.5"

The Old Mill Trailer Park is becoming more and more popular both as an overnight stop and a fishing destination. It is located some 3 miles (5 km) off Mex 1 on a washboard but otherwise fine dirt road. Big rigs don't hesitate to come here.

The campground has 20 spaces. They all have paved parking pads, patios, electricity with 15-amp plugs, sewer, and water. Fifteen are in the front row with a good view of the estuary and its birds. There is also an area set aside for dry or tent campers. The bathrooms are only a few years old, they have hot water showers. Check in at the bait shop across the driveway from the restaurant or, if it is closed, at the bar. Fishing is good in the area. There's a boat launch if you've brought your own or you can hire a boat and guide.

The access road to the Old Mill leads west from Mex 1 south of Col. Lázaro Cárdenas.

It is well- signed at the 1 Km marker. The wide dirt road leads west for 3.3 miles (5.3 km), then you'll see a sign pointing left to the restaurant and RV park. Don't follow signs for Old Pier, that is a different place.

⛟ OLD PIER (MUELLE VIEJO) MOTEL AND RV PARK

Address:	Fracc. Juan Maria Salvatierra,
	Bahía de San Quintín, San Quintín, B.C., México
Telephone:	(616) 3-42-06
Price:	Inexpensive

GPS Location: N 30° 28' 10.6", W 115° 57' 04.5"

This older motel overlooks the bay from the east side. It is located directly south of the old pier or Muelle Viejo which dates from the days of the Mexican Land and Colonization Company.

The motel has about 7 RV spaces overlooking the bay at the north end of the property next to the motel buildings. There are no hookups but there are flush toilets in a dedicated building nearby. RVers use a motel room for showers. The restaurant is reported to be pretty good however electricity for the motel and restaurant are only available in the evening as they are provided by an on-site generator.

To reach the motel take the road west from Mex 1 that is used to access the Old Mill RV Park. It is located south of Col. Lázaro Cárdenas near the 1 Km marker. Follow it west for 2.3 miles (3.8 km). Turn south here, there should be a sign pointing the way. The motel is 1.4 miles (2.3 km) down this sandy side road on the right. Road conditions vary, when we last visited there was a great deal of soft sand so exercise caution.

⛟ EL PABELLÓN RV PARK

Price:	Inexpensive

GPS Location: N 30° 22' 27.3", W 115° 52' 08.7"

Miles of sand dunes and ocean. That's El Pabellón RV Park. There really isn't much else. This is a large graded area set in sand dunes close to the ocean. It is being gradually improved. There have been flush toilets and hot showers for some time. There are also six pull through spaces with sewer drains and water. Recently a long line of interesting table-like structures with sinks and barbecues have been built, these will apparently someday be pull-through campsites. Everyone just ignores the campsites anyway and parks where they want. Caravans often stop here and circle wagon-train style. Tenters pitch in the dunes in front of the campground or behind rows of trees that provide some shelter if the wind is blowing. There is usually an attendant at the entrance gate.

The turn for El Pabellón is between Km 16 and 17 south of San Quintín. Turn south at the sign and follow the 1.2 mile gravel road to the campground.

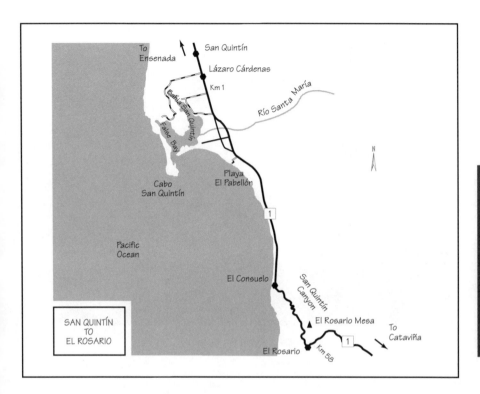

SOUTHERN NORTHWEST COAST

SAN QUINTÍN TO EL ROSARIO
37 Miles (60 Km), 1.25 Hours

After leaving San Quintín the road continues southward along the coastal plain. It soon crosses a long bridge over the Río Santa María, which is usually dry. After a few more miles the ocean is within sight to the west, occasionally a small track leads to the bluff above the ocean. About 40 miles (65 kilometers) south of Lázaro Cárdenas the road turns inland into the San Quintín Canyon and begins to climb to the top of El Rosario Mesa. Soon after reaching the top of the mesa the road descends steeply into the town of El Rosario.

EL ROSARIO (EL ROE-SAHR-EEYOH)
Population 4,000

For many years El Rosario was as far south as you could drive unless you were an off-roader. Today's road turns inland here and heads for the center of the peninsula, it won't return to the west coast until it cuts back to Guerrero Negro, and even there it won't stay for long. **Espinosa's Place**, a local restaurant, has been famous for years

SOUTHERN NORTHWEST COAST

RUINS OF THE MISIÓN EL ROSARIO

for its seafood burritos (lobster and crab meat). The town of El Rosario is actually in two places, El Rosario de Arriba is on the main highway, El Rosario de Abajo is a 1.5 miles (2.4 km) away down and across the arroyo (river bed). Each has the ruins of an old mission, the first is in El Rosario de Arriba, it was abandoned when the mission moved to El Rosario de Abajo. Little remains of the first except the foundations, there are still standing walls at the second, which was abandoned in 1832. See *Backroad Adventures* in this chapter for directions to the mission.

El Rosario Campground

🚐 MOTEL SINAI RV PARK

Address:	Carret. Transp. Km 56 #1056,
	El Rosario, B.C., México
Telephone:	(616) 5-88-18
Price:	Moderate

GPS Location: N 30° 04' 00.6", W 115° 42' 55.0"

In the last few years this little hotel has installed RV spaces on the hillside behind. This is a welcome addition to the peninsula campgrounds because it reduces the longest gap between campgrounds with utilities by about 30 miles (49 km). It is 219 miles (358 km) between El Rosario and the next ones to the south in Guerrero Negro (unless you make a side trip to Bahía de los Angeles).

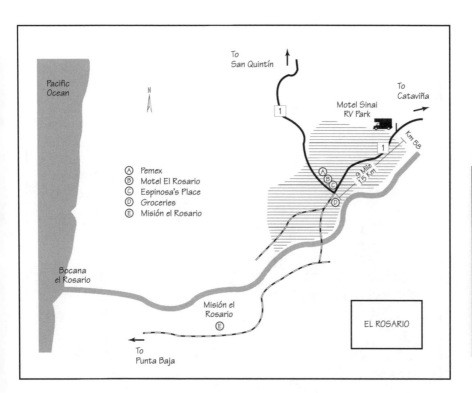

There are 12 paved pads for RVs, but they are so close together that there will probably be room for fewer campers most of the time. All sites have electricity, water and sewer drains are available to most of them. There is a very nice toilet cubicle and two nice little shower rooms with hot water. The campground is up a small slope behind the motel. There is plenty of room for big rigs to maneuver and sites are flat. The motel also has a little restaurant. Limited English is spoken.

The Motel Sinai is near the eastern outskirts of El Rosario on the north side of the highway. It is exactly .9 miles (1.5 km) east of the 90-degree turn in the middle of town.

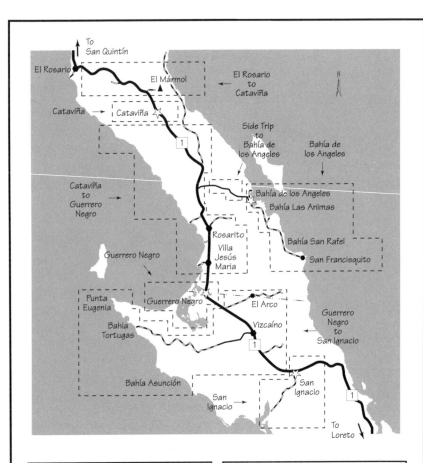

To
San Quintín

El Rosario

El Mármol ▲

El Rosario
to
Cataviña →

N

Cataviña → Cataviña

1

Side Trip
to
Bahía de
los Angeles

Bahía de
los Angeles
↓

Cataviña
to
Guerrero →
Negro

Bahía de los Angeles

Bahía Las Animas

Bahía San Rafel

San Francisquito

Rosarito

Villa
Jesús
Maria

Guerrero Negro
↓

Guerrero
Negro
to
San Ignacio ←

Punta
Eugenia

Guerrero Negro

El Arco

Vizcaíno

1

Bahía
Tortugas

Bahía Asunción

San
Ignacio →

San
Ignacio

1

To
Loreto ↓

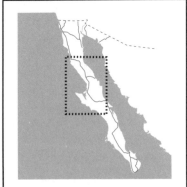

CHAPTER INDEX	
Highlights	Page 89
Roads and Fuel Availability	Page 90
Sightseeing	Page 90
Beaches and Water Sports	Page 91
Fishing	Page 91
Backroad Adventures	Page 92
El Rosario to Cataviña	Page 95
Cataviña	Page 96
Cataviña to Guerrero Negro	Page 98
Guerrero Negro	Page 100
Side Trip to Bahía de los Angeles	Page 103
Bahía de los Angeles	Page 104
Guerrero Negro to San Ignacio	Page 108
San Ignacio	Page 110

CENTRAL BAJA

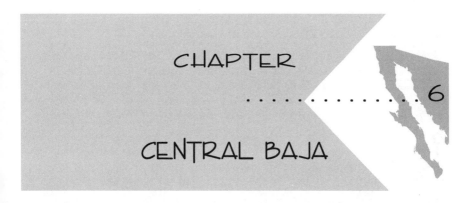

CHAPTER
· · · · · · · · · · · · 6

CENTRAL BAJA

INTRODUCTION

This central section of the Baja Peninsula is much different than that to the north. The area has far fewer people, and the landscape is definitely desert. In fact, the area from El Rosario to the cutoff to Bahía de los Angeles has some of the most scenic and interesting desert country in the world.

Highlights

The desert country around **Cataviña** is filled with huge granite boulders. Between them grow a variety of desert cactus, this is great country for short hikes and photography. In this area you'll see a unique type of cactus, the **cirio** or boojum tree. These large cactus look like upside-down green carrots. The Baja is the only place in the world that you are likely to see them.

The **Ojo de Liebre** lagoon near Guerrero Negro is one of only three places on the Baja where you can get right up close to **California gray whales**. They give birth to their young in the lagoon, you can see them from January to March each year. A second location for this is **Laguna San Ignacio**, accessible from San Ignacio and also described in this chapter.

Bahía de los Angeles is beautiful, you'll want to see it. The bright blue bay and string of islands offshore are a real spectacle as you approach on the highway. The town itself can be a bit of a letdown, but there are some very popular primitive but accessible camping sites near town and excellent summer fishing locations some distance to the south.

Roads and Fuel Availability

The main road, Mex 1, from El Rosario to Guerrero Negro and on to San Ignacio is in good condition. The countryside is made up of rolling hills so the road rises and falls and snakes around looking for the best route. This may be the area where you really begin to notice the 9-foot-wide lanes. Just keep your speed down and watch for traffic. When you meet someone, slow to a safe speed and get as near the right edge of the pavement as you safely can.

Kilometer markers in this section are in three segments. The first two count up as you go south: El Rosario to a point near the Bahía de los Angeles Junction (60 to 280) and Bahía L.A. Junction to the Baja/Baja Sur Border (0 to 128). From the border to San Ignacio (and for the rest of the trip south) the kilometer markers run from south to north. They begin at the border with Km 221 and reach Km 74 at San Ignacio.

The road out to Bahía de los Angeles is paved but lately has been in very poor condition. It is rough and has lots of potholes. The last time we traveled it we managed an average of 25 miles per hour for the distance of 42 miles (68 km). It took us an hour and forty minutes to reach Bahía de los Angeles, but was worth it!

This section of the road is the famous " Baja Gas Gap". It is the one place on the Baja highway where even cautious travelers might run in to trouble. From the gas station at El Rosario to the gas station at Villa Jesús María just north of Guerrero Negro is a distance of 195 miles (315 km). If you make the round trip to Bahía de los Angeles you add at least 85 miles (137 km) to this trip. If either the gas station at El Rosario or the one at Villa Jesús Maria was temporarily out of fuel the gap would be even larger. Even so, few vehicles are permanently lost in the "gas gap", just be sure to fuel up before entering it.

Fuel locations, types available, and distances between stations is as follows: **El Rosario**, gas and diesel; **Villa Jesús María**, gas and diesel, 195 miles (315 km); **Guerrero Negro**, gas and diesel, 27 miles (44 km); **Vizcaíno**, gas and diesel, 44 miles (71 km); and **San Ignacio**, gas and diesel, 43 miles (69 km).

Sightseeing

El Mármol is an abandoned onyx mine located in the desert about nine miles north of the highway. From the early 1900's to about 1950 this was the world's major source of onyx, if you have some this is probably where it came from. Today the place is abandoned but there is a well-known onyx-walled schoolhouse and blocks of onyx scattered around. See the *Backroad Adventures* section below for driving instructions.

Near **Cataviña** there is an area of extremely photogenic cactus set among rounded granite boulders. The highway goes right through the middle of this area so you can't miss it.

From late December to about the middle of April the **California gray whales** come to the Baja. They congregate in shallow bays along the west coast where their young are born. It is possible to take a ride in a panga out to see them up close. There are three places where this is done: Guerrero Negro, Laguna San Ignacio, and Bahía Magdalena.

This is discussed in much more detail in the sections about Guerrero Negro and San Ignacio later in this chapter.

Misión San Fernando Velicatá, Misión Santa Maria, and **Misión San Borja** are located in the area covered by this chapter. See the *Backroad Adventures* section below for detailed information about visiting the sites.

The **28th Parallel** forms the border between the states of Baja California and Baja California Sur. The spot is marked by a huge metal statue of an eagle, also by a huge Mexican flag at the military base located at the base of the statue. The road runs right by both so you'll have a good look.

San Ignacio appears to be a classic desert oasis, and it really is. The town has thousands of date palms, as well as an attractive square bordered by the Misión San Ignacio. There is also a museum describing the cave paintings found in the surrounding Sierra de San Francisco, they're known as **rupestrian art**. Guides are available in Guerrero Negro, San Ignacio, Mulegé, Loreto and also near some of the sites and are required. You must also register to visit many of the sites at the museum in San Ignacio.

Beaches and Water Sports

Surfing in this area, of course, is limited to the Pacific Coast. Since the main highway runs far from the coast, road access to surfing generally requires long drives on pretty poor roads. Exceptions are the places accessible from El Rosario in the north and also where the road nears the coast north of Rosarito.

One of the popular surfing spots near Rosarito is Punta Santa Rosalillita, also known as "The Wall". See *Backroad Adventures* below for more about this location. This is also a popular sailboarding location, it is sometimes called "Sandy Point".

A few miles south is Punta Rosarito, also a surfing destination. To the south of the point is the long Altamara beach. See *Backroad Adventures* below for driving instructions.

Still farther south, near Villa Jesús María a roads lead out to Laguna Manuela. This is a popular fishing destination, but there is a long beach called Playa Pacheco to the north of the lagoon. Between the beach and the lagoon is Morro Santo Domingo, a high headland ringed with small coves. There's also a small beach near the fish camp at the end of the road at the lagoon, it is often used by the folks from Guerrero Negro for picnics. Watch for soft sand, access to the long Playa Pacheco is very sandy and requires 4WD or a walk. See *Backroad Adventures* below for more about this road.

Kayaking is popular on the Gulf of California coast. Winds tend to be from the north so long-distance kayakers tend to travel from north to south. Bahía de los Angeles makes a good place to explore with beaches for camping that don't require long passages.

Fishing

Since much of this route is inland fishing possibilities are limited to Bahía de los Angeles and areas that you can reach using back roads.

The **Bahía de los Angeles** area is probably the most popular destination on the Baja for fishermen with large and small trailer boats. There are good boat launches, a reasonable number of fish, and the weather is much warmer than on the west side of the peninsula at this latitude.

Unfortunately, boating conditions can be dangerous here. A combination of often very strong winds (generally either from the north or the west) and very active tidal currents can make boating a challenge.

The best fishing is in the summer and fall and the most popular fishing is for yellowtail. Expect daytime temperatures to 100 degrees Fahrenheit in the middle of the summer.

Unfortunately the fishing is not as good as it once was due to commercial overfishing. Your best fishing opportunities are north and south of the bay. Access to the north by vehicle is nonexisting much past Playa La Gringa, but to the south there are several fishing destinations for those with the rigs to travel rough roads. Destinations include Bahía las Animas (30 miles south), Playa San Rafael (45 miles south of L.A. Bay with good shore fishing), and Bahía San Francisquito (85 miles south of L.A. Bay). See the *Backroad Adventures* of this section for more information about access to these locations.

At the southern end of the section covered by this chapter is Laguna Manuela. You reach it on a marked road heading westward from Villa Jesús Maria. You can launch small boats across the beach here and fish the lagoon for bass, halibut, sierra, and corvina. See *Backroad Adventures* for road information.

Backroad Adventures

See the *Backroad Driving* section of *Chapter 2 - Details, Details, Details* for essential information about driving off the main highway on the Baja and for a definition of road type classifications used below.

From Km 114 Between El Rosario and Cataviña - The ruin of **Misión San Fernando Velicatá** is a short distance off the highway on this road east of El Rosario. This is usually a Type 2 road, the distance is about 3 miles (5 km).

From Km 143 Between El Rosario and Cataviña - The virtually abandoned onyx mining area called **El Mármol** makes an interesting day trip. The access road is about 19 miles (31 km) west of Cataviña. This is a graded road that is about 10 miles long, it is usually a Type 1 road. Take a look at the old school house built entirely of onyx. The mine was very active in the early part of the century, the quarried onyx slabs were shipped by water from Puerto Santa Catarina about 50 miles west on the Pacific coast. You might also want to make the 3-mile hike (6 miles round trip) from the mine to El Volcán where you can see a small seep forming new onyx.

From Km 229 Between Cataviña and L.A. Bay Junction - This road runs to the coast and then north all the way to Puertecitos (81 miles (131 km)) and then San Felipe. It is a long rough Type 2 road that is planned for an eventual upgrade so that there will be paved access from the north along the east side of the Baja Peninsula.

From Km 38 Between L.A. Bay Junction and Guerrero Negro - A good road leads west to the small community of Santa Rosalillita, Bahía Santa Rosalillita, and Punta Santa Rosalillita. It leaves Mex 1 near Km 38, some 8 miles (13 km) north of Rosarito. The road leads 9.5 miles (15 km) to the village. At about 8 miles (13 km) a side track leads north toward the community of San José de las Palomas giving access to many more beaches. The road to Santa Rosalillita is usually Type 1, the others in the area vary, some are Type 2 or even 3, watch for soft sand.

From Km 52 Between L.A. Bay Junction and Guerrero Negro - Another mission, **Misión San Borja** is also accessible if you have four-wheel drive or a lightly loaded pickup with good ground clearance. From Rosarito, located about 97 miles (158 km) south of Cataviña on Mex 1 drive east, roads leave the highway both north and south of the bridge over the arroyo. At about 15 miles (24 km) the road reaches Rancho San Ignacio, the mission is beyond at about 22 miles (36 km). Misión San Francisco de Borja was built in 1759 and has been restored by the government. This is usually a Type 3 road.

From Km 68 Between L.A. Bay Junction and Guerrero Negro - A short 2.8 mile (4.5 km) road leads to **El Tomatal** which is popular for surfing, board sailing, and surf fishing. There is also room for boondocking. This road is usually Type 1, but watch for soft sand.

From Km 96 Between L.A. Bay Junction and Guerrero Negro - From the town of Villa Jesús María a road heads 7 miles westward to the Laguna Manuela. This area is popular for fishing, primitive camping, and the beach. Drive about a mile west on a paved road, then turn south on a graded dirt road, you'll reach the lagoon in another 6 miles (10 km). This is usually a Type 1 road.

From Bahía de los Angeles - A road leads south from Bahía de los Angeles for many miles. Along the way it passes beaches on the southern curve of Bahía de los Angeles, an abandoned silver-smelting operation at Los Flores, a side road to Bahía las Animas, Bahía San Rafael, and eventually reaches Punta and Bahía San Francisquito. The road is a badly washboarded Type 1 for about 10 miles (16 km), then becomes a bad Type 2 road.

From Km 189 Between Guerrero Negro and San Ignacio - From 16 miles east of Guerrero Negro a road that was paved at one time goes north to the almost-abandoned mining town of **El Arco**. The road is very poor, many drivers actually find the sand alongside to be faster and smoother. The distance is 26 miles (42 kilometers). The road continues beyond El Arco for 23 miles (37 km) to **Misión Santa Gertrudis**, which is being restored. The road to El Arco is usually a marginal Type 1, the one to the mission usually a Type 3 road.

From Km 144 Between Guerrero Negro and San Ignacio - There's a junction here at Ejido Vizcaíno for a road that runs southwest to the coast at **Bahía Tortugas**, only the first twenty miles or so are paved, the remainder is a Type 1 road often with soft sand in places. The distance to the coast is about 107 miles (173 km), this is a long, rough, lonely road across Baja's dryest desert, but fuel trucks do travel to Bahía Tortugas, which is a popular refueling station for power boats traveling between California and Cabo. Type 2 and 3 side roads allow you to travel on to Punta Eugenia or off to the southwest to Bahía Asunción and other coastal locations.

CENTRAL BAJA

From Km 118 Between Guerrero Negro and San Ignacio - This is a 22-mile (35 km) drive into the Sierra San Francisco to the village of **San Francisco**. This is a cave-art location, **Cueva Ratón** is located near the village. Guides can take you to other caves too, some trips require several days. Before visiting you must register in San Ignacio. This is usually a Type 2 road.

From San Ignacio - This 40-mile (65 km) road leads southeast from the village to **Laguna San Ignacio**. This is one of the best California gray whale observation sites on the peninsula. Most people opt to leave their rigs in San Ignacio and ride down with a van tour. You can drive it yourself although route-finding can be difficult due to there being many alternate tracks in some areas. Panga operators at the lagoon give whale-watching tours. This is usually a Type 2 road, watch out for soft sand.

A VADO IN THE CATAVIÑA DESERT

THE ROUTES, TOWNS, AND CAMPGROUNDS

EL ROSARIO TO CATAVIÑA
73 Miles (118 Km), 2.25 Hours

From El Rosario the highway heads northeast for about four miles (6 km) along the north side of the El Rosario River. It then crosses and follows a climbing canyon into rolling hills that can be surprisingly green during the winter. This is the beginning of the longest mountainous section of Mex 1 as the highway passes along the western edge of the Peninsular Range for some 180 miles (290 km) but never crosses to the Gulf of California side.

From this point until well past Cataviña the scenery is fascinating, you are in what is known as the Sonoran Desert Vegetation Region. You'll soon see your first cirios (boojum trees) and as you drive along there will be more and more of them. Other cactus include huge cardóns, barrel cactus, chollas, and agaves. Many of these cactus are found only in this area.

Near Km 114 a short road runs south to the ruins of **Misión San Fernando Velicatá**. See *Backroad Adventures* for more information about this road.

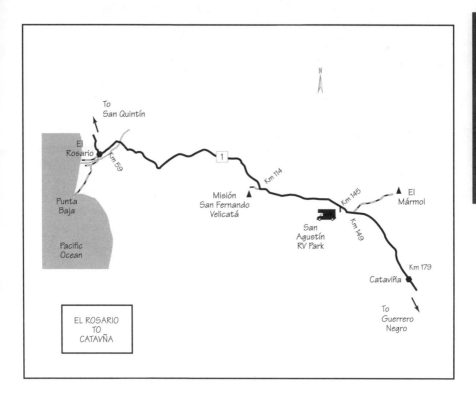

EL ROSARIO
TO
CATAVÑA

Near Km 149 is the cutoff to the north to **El Mármol**. See the *Backroad Adventures* section above for a description of this road and destination.

As you near Cataviña, near Km 160, you enter a region of large granite boulders. These are known as the Cataviña boulder fields. Around and among them grow all types of cactus, and together they are extremely photogenic. You'll be tempted to pull off and camp on one of the short roads leading into the boulders, but you'll be much safer at one of the inexpensive campgrounds just a few miles ahead.

El Rosario to Cataviña Campground

🚐 SAN AGUSTÍN RV PARK
    Price: Inexpensive
                GPS Location: N 29° 55' 17.3", W 114° 58' 42.3"

This fenced group of campsites appears to be one of the old government campgrounds although an aficionado would see some differences. For one thing, there are no concrete tombstones between the sites. There is little here other than a fenced place to park for the night, the restrooms and hookups (other than sewer) are no longer usable. This place is only open intermittently but was open last time we checked with a family living in the old building.

The campground is located right off Mex 1 near Km 145 marker. This is 55 miles (89 km) east of El Rosario.

CATAVIÑA (CAT-AH-VEE-NYA)

You can't really call Cataviña a town. There is little more here than a Hotel La Pinta, an abandoned Pemex, an old government-built campground, and a few shacks and restaurants. The area, however, is one of the most interesting on the Baja. The Cataviña boulder fields (formal name is Las Vírgines - the Virgins) are striking. The road threads its way for several miles through a jumble of huge granite boulders sprinkled liberally with attractive cacti and desert plants. It is a photographer's paradise. Gas is sometimes still available at the La Pinta Motel, they have a Pemex gas pump with limited and irregular supplies.

Cataviña Campgrounds

🚐 PARQUE NATURAL DESIERTO CENTRAL TRAILER PARK
    Price: Inexpensive
                GPS Location: N 29° 43' 51.6", W 114° 43' 19.6"

This is one of the fenced compounds that were built by the government soon after the road south was finished. None of the hookups other than sewer work any more, but this is still an attractive campground. The landscaping has boulders and cactus, just

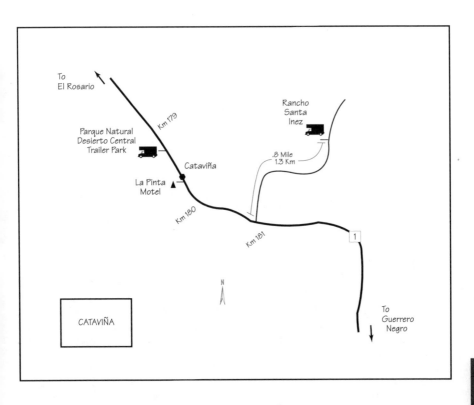

like the surrounding area. There are bathrooms with toilets that are flushed with a bucket of water but no showers. Many people use this campground, there aren't a lot of other choices on this stretch of road.

The campground is located in Cataviña off Mex 1 just west of the La Pinta Motel and the abandoned Pemex on the south side of the road.

RANCHO SANTA INEZ

Price: Inexpensive

GPS Location: N 29° 43' 47.9", W 114° 41' 53.0"

Many folks drive right by the entrance road to this camping spot, and that's a mistake. We think it is the best place to stay in this area.

The camping area is a large flat dirt lot with only one tree for shade. There's room for lots of rigs, that's why many of the caravans stay here. Other facilities include a water faucet and a small building with a flush toilet. Best of all is the small restaurant.

To reach the campground turn north on the well-marked road near Km 181, less than a mile east of the La Pinta Motel. Follow the paved side road for about .8 miles (1.3 km), the camping area is on the left.

CATAVIÑA TO GUERRERO NEGRO
145 Miles (234 Km), 4.25 Hours

The two-lane highway continues snaking its way southeastwards from Cataviña. It passes signs for a few small ranchos, along the road is the occasional small restaurant, often with a truck or two parked out front. Eighteen miles (29 km) from Cataviña on the right side of the road you'll see a very large pile of rocks. The small mountain is called **Cerro Pedregoso** (rocky hill). It has long been a landmark for travelers along the highway.

About 15 miles (24 km) beyond Cerro Pedregoso the highway descends and runs along **Laguna Chapala**. This is a large dry lake bed, before the current highway was completed a very rough road followed pretty much the same route in this region. Here it ran over the dry lake bed, it was very dusty and often heavily rutted.

Just north of the lake bed, near Km 229 you may see a road headed northeast. It is signed for San Felipe and Calamajué, they're both on the Gulf of California. See *Backroad Adventures* for more information about this road.

Thirty miles beyond the dirt road to San Felipe is the cutoff to Bahía de los Angeles, often called the **L.A. Bay Junction**. The road to Bahía de los Angeles and the attractions there are discussed in a separate section later in this chapter. In the past there was a gas station at this junction, the buildings remain but the pumps are gone. Sometimes you will find an entrepreneur here in a pickup with gas drums in the back, a welcome sight if you are low on gas.

South of the L.A. Bay Junction the road begins to gradually approach the west coast. There are roads out to the coast at Km 38 to **Santa Rosalillita**, Km 68 for **El Tomatal**, and Km 96 for **Laguna Manuela**. See *Backroad Adventures* above for more about all of these roads.

In Rosarito, 33 miles (53 km) south of the L.A. Bay Junction there is a back road northeastwards to the **Misión San Borja**. See *Backroad Adventures* for more about this trip.

Fifty-six miles (90 km) from L.A. Bay Junction you will reach the small town of Villa Jesús Maria which has a Pemex gas station with both gas and diesel. This is also the cutoff for the road out to Laguna Manuela.

Twenty-two miles (35 km) beyond Villa Jesús Maria is the border between Baja California and Baja California Sur. The **border** is marked by a huge metal **statue of an eagle**, as you approach the border you can see it for miles, it looks like a huge tuning fork from this direction. At the border there is a military base with a huge flag, a motel, a restaurant with RV parking behind, and an RV park. A checkpoint at the border will check to make sure you have tourist cards and fumigate the wheels of your rig. They charge a small fee for doing this. Just a short distance beyond the checkpoint is the side road in to the town of Guerrero Negro.

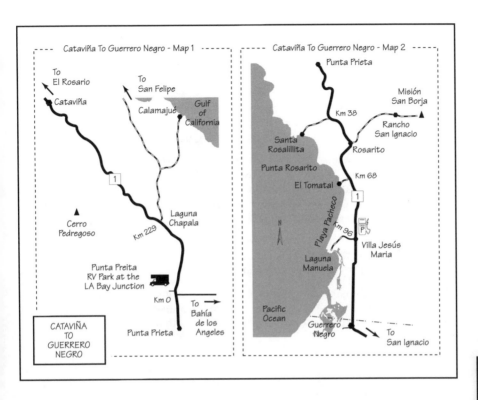

Baja California Sur observes Mountain time while Baja California observes Pacific time so you will have to change your clocks at the border.

Cataviña to Guerrero Negro Campground

🚐 PUNTA PRIETA RV PARK AT THE L.A. BAY JUNCTION
   Price: Inexpensive
   GPS Location: N 29° 02' 51.0", W 114° 09' 13.1"

This is another of the old government campgrounds. It is often closed, but occasionally the gates are open and someone is operating the place. It has the standard nice desert plant landscaping, as well as the standard non-functional hookups. Toilets are flushed using a bucket of water and there are no showers.

The campground is very near the cutoff to Bahía de los Angeles, just to the north on Mex 1. While we wouldn't depend on it being open on the way south we might stop here going north if we had noticed that it was open on our southward journey.

GUERRERO NEGRO (GEH-RER-row NEH-GROW)
Population 8,000

The 28th parallel is the dividing line between the states of Baja North and Baja South. You'll know when you pass over the line because it is marked by a very large statue of a stylized eagle, most people think it looks like a tuning fork and it is visible for miles. Two miles (3 km) south of the eagle the road to Guerrero Negro goes west.

Guerrero Negro is one of the newest towns on the Baja, and it's a company town. Founded in 1955 the town owes its existence to the Exportadora de Sal (ESSA) salt works. Large flats near the town are flooded with seawater which quickly evaporates leaving salt. This is gathered up using heavy equipment and shipped on barges to Isla Cedros offshore where there is enough water to allow cargo ships to dock.

More recently the town has gained fame for the California gray whales that congregate each winter in the nearby Ojo de Liebre or Scammon's Lagoon. There is now a lively tourist industry catering to the many people who come here to visit the whales.

The town itself is small and the places of interest, restaurants and stores, are almost all arranged along the main street. Guerrero Negro has a small supermarket and also two Pemexes. A third one is under construction to the north near the border crossing.

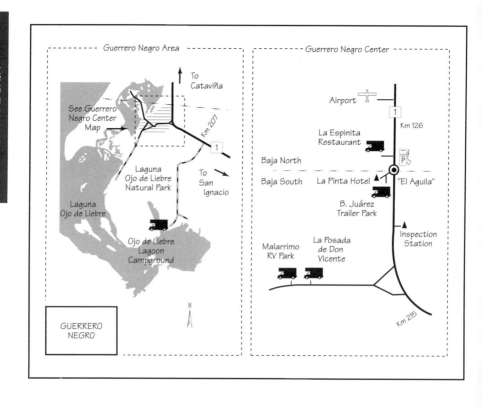

Guerrero Negro Campgrounds

🚐 LA ESPINITA RESTAURANT

    Price: Free with dinner

        GPS Location: N 28° 00' 23.3", W 114° 00' 40.7"

This is a restaurant along the road just north of the border between Baja Norte and Baja Sur. The restaurant has a large fenced parking lot to the side and behind and you can stay for free if you eat in the restaurant. There are restrooms with flush toilets at the rear of the restaurant building, otherwise there are no amenities.

La Espinita is located .2 mile (.3 km) north of the giant eagle that marks the border.

🚐 BENITO JUÁREZ TRAILER PARK

    Address: Asunción Morian Canales, Apdo. 188,
                   Guerrero Negro, B.C.S., México
    Price: Low

        GPS Location: N 27° 59' 55.6", W 114° 00' 51.6"

The Benito Juárez is another of the government-built trailer parks. This one is run by the Ejido Benito Juárez. It is the only one left on the Baja that offers electrical hook-ups, however, watch the voltage, it sometimes varies dramatically and can cause damage to your equipment.

This is a large campground. The spaces are pull-throughs with electricity, sewer, and water. Cactus are planted throughout for landscaping, there's a pretty complete collection of the different types you've been seeing along the road on the way south, including boojums. The restrooms are old but work, there are hot showers. The campground is fully fenced and has a manager who speaks some English.

This is an easy campground to find. Just watch for the eagle monument at the border between North and South Baja. The campground is just to the west.

🚐 MALARRIMO RV PARK

    Address: Blvd. Emiliano Zapata S/N,
                   Guerrero Negro, C.P. 23940 B.C.S., México
    Res.:   P.O. Box 284, Chula Vista, CA 91912
    Telephone: (115) 7-01-00
    Fax: (115) 7-01-00
    E-mail: malarimo@telnor.net
    Internet: www.malarrimo.com
    Price: Moderate

        GPS Location: N 27° 58' 03.7", W 114° 01' 04.3"

The Malarrimo is generally considered the best place to stay in Guerrero Negro. Not only are the campground facilities pretty good, the restaurant is the best in this section of Baja.

There are 36 RV spaces with 15-amp electrical plugs, sewer, and water located behind

CENTRAL BAJA

the restaurant. Guerrero Negro electricity is marginal, watch voltage while hooked up to avoid damage to your rig. Restrooms are modern and clean and have hot water showers. This is a well-run place and English is spoken. They run tours to see the gray whales and cave art, and even have a gift shop. Many people make a special point to overnight in Guerrero Negro so they can eat at the restaurant.

Recently they completed work on a second camping area across the street from the motel so that caravans can be accommodated without displacing independent travelers. There are 16 sites with full hookups in this new section.

To find the campground drive in to Guerrero Negro from the east. Almost immediately after entering town you will see the Malarrimo on the right.

LA POSADA DE DON VICENTE,
LAS CAZUELAS RESTAURANT-BAR
     Address: Blvd. Emiliano Zapata S/N,
                   Guerrero Negro, C.P. 23940 B.C.S., México
     Telephone: (115) 7-02-88
     Price: Low

GPS Location: N 27° 58' 05.1", W 114° 01' 31.1"

WHALE WATCHING AT OJO DE LIEBRE LAGOON

This place is a motel with an enclosed courtyard and a restaurant out front. It has 8 back-in RV slots with 15-amp electrical plugs and water hookups but no sewer facilities. Guerrero Negro electricity is marginal, watch voltage while hooked up to avoid damage to your rig. There are bathrooms with flush toilets and hot showers. There is limited maneuvering room so rigs over about 30 feet may find things a little tight. This is a fairly new place and it seemed to us that they needed to sort things out a bit, no one was staying here while Malarrimo's just down the street was practically full. Also, the owner was talking about opening another place nearby. Time will tell.

To find the campground just drive in to Guerrero Negro from the east. This facility is well signed, it is on the right about a block before you reach Malarrimo's.

Ojo de Liebre Lagoon Campground
Price: Inexpensive

GPS Location: N 27° 44' 55.9", W 114° 00' 42.2"

One of the top attractions of the Baja Peninsula is a whale-watching trip. One way to do this is to drive across the salt flats to the edge of Laguna Ojo de Liebre (Scammon's Lagoon). It costs a little less to take a tour here than from in town, and camping along the edge of the lagoon is excellent. This place is only accessible during the whale-watching season, approximately the middle of December to the middle of April.

When you arrive at the lagoon there is an entrance kiosk where a $3 fee is collected. There is a large parking lot where visitors on whale-watching trips can park. A large new building is under construction which will house the tour ticket sales as well as a museum and restaurant. Until then kiosks handle ticket sales and there is also a simple restaurant. Camping is beyond the parking lot along a long loop road with pullouts along the beach of the lagoon for camping. Pit toilets are provided.

To reach the lagoon turn westward from Mex 1 at about Km 207. This is 5 miles south of the turnoff for the town of Guerrero Negro. The turn is marked with a large sign for Laguna Ojo de Liebre. The road is graded dirt, it is fine for even the largest rigs. At 4 miles (6 km) you will reach an entrance gate where your name will be recorded as you enter the salt flats working area. You'll probably see heavy equipment collecting the salt from the flats. At 13.8 miles (22.3 km) there is a Y, go right as indicated by the sign. Finally, at 14.9 miles (24 km) you will reach the entrance gate at the lagoon.

CENTRAL BAJA

Side Trip to Bahía de los Angeles
42 Miles (68 Km), 1.75 Hours

From a junction on Mex 1 a paved road runs 42 miles (68 km) down to the coast at Bahía de los Angeles. In recent years the road has been in very bad shape, it really needs to be re-paved. Despite the condition of the road this is a worthwhile trip. Even if you only average 25 mph the trip only takes an hour and forty minutes.

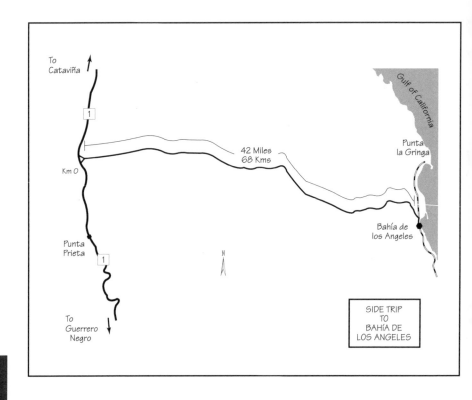

BAHÍA DE LOS ANGELES (BAH-HEE-AH DAY LOES AHN-HAIL-ACE)
Population 500

The Bahía de los Angeles (Bay of the Angels) is one of the most scenic spots in Baja California with blue waters and barren desert shoreline backed by rocky mountains. The huge bay is protected by a chain of small islands, and also by Isla Angel de la Guarda, which is 45 miles (75 km) long. Even with this protection boating is often dangerous because of strong winds from the north and evening "gravity" winds that whistle downhill from the west. Fishing, boating, diving, and kayaking are good in the bay, among the islands, and offshore and there are several launch ramps in town. Exercise caution, these are considered dangerous waters due to the frequent strong winds.

There is a turtle hatchery in Bahía de los Angeles near the Brisa Marina RV Park where you can see some of these endangered animals. The village itself doesn't offer much except a couple of motels, several RV parks and a few small stores. Electricity in town is produced by a generator that only runs part time.

CENTRAL BAJA

Bahía de los Angeles Campgrounds

This area offers many places to camp. You may find, as we do, that the campgrounds in town with hookups are much less attractive than the much more informal places outside town to the north and south.

GUILLERMO'S HOTEL AND RV PARK

Address: Expendio #11, Boulevard Bahía de Los Angeles, C.P. 22950 B.C. Norte, México

Telephone: (665) 0-32-09, (617) 6-49-46 (Ensenada)

Price: Low

GPS Location: N 28° 56' 52.3", W 113° 33' 32.5"

This campground has about 40 camping spaces, some have working full hookups with 15-amp plugs, others are in poor repair. Sites have patios and some palapas. This is a dirt and gravel lot next to the road with a few small trees to provide a little shade, permanents here block any view of the water. The restrooms around front have hot showers. There is a restaurant, bar, store and also a launch ramp. Bear in mind that electricity in Bahía de los Angeles gets turned off during the middle of the day and at night.

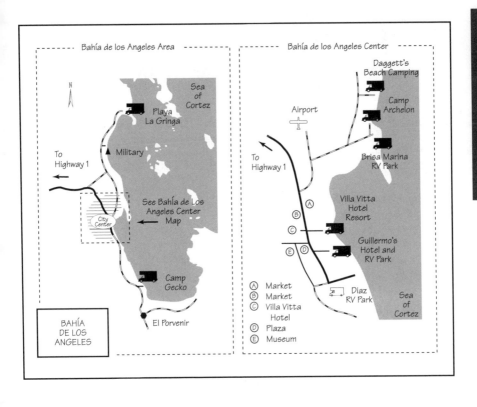

To find Guillermo's drive into town, pass the Villa Vitta, and you'll soon see the campground on the left.

🚐 VILLA VITTA HOTEL RESORT

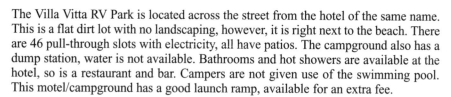

Res.:   509 Ross Drive, Escondido, CA 92029 (Res. in U.S.)
Telephone: 760 741-9583 (Res. in U.S.A.)
Price: Low

GPS Location: N 28° 57' 03.9", W 113° 33' 29.7"

The Villa Vitta RV Park is located across the street from the hotel of the same name. This is a flat dirt lot with no landscaping, however, it is right next to the beach. There are 46 pull-through slots with electricity, all have patios. The campground also has a dump station, water is not available. Bathrooms and hot showers are available at the hotel, so is a restaurant and bar. Campers are not given use of the swimming pool. This motel/campground has a good launch ramp, available for an extra fee.

You'll find that the Villa Vitta is hard to miss, you'll see the hotel on the right and the RV park on the left soon after entering town.

🚐 CAMP GECKO

Price: Inexpensive

GPS Location: N 28° 54' 50.2", W 113° 32' 24.8"

This waterside campground has an idyllic location on a long sandy beach with a few rocks. Unfortunately you must drive almost four miles of washboard gravel road to reach it.

Camp Gecko has about 10 camping spaces with palapas, a few are suitable for RVs. There are no hookups but the camping area does have flush toilets and cold water showers. There are also cabins for rent and a small boat ramp.

As you head south through Bahía de los Angeles village you will come to a rock wall and the entrance to Diaz RV park. Go the right around it and follow a washboard gravel road south. At 4.0 miles (6.5 km) take the sandy road left toward the beach and Camp Gecko.

🚐 BRISA MARINA RV PARK

Price: Inexpensive

GPS Location: N 28° 58' 06.0", W 113° 32' 50.5"

This is one of the old government RV parks. It is located next to the bay, and along the front of the campground is a sea turtle research project. Sea turtles are kept in tanks, visitors are allowed.

The campground is little more than a place to park and boondock. Only the sewer hookups are useable and there are no bathroom facilities. Still, there are generally a few people staying here since it is a quiet place in a decent location with a low price.

The road to the campgrounds north of Bahía de los Angeles leaves the highway near the point where the highway enters town and is usually marked for the airport. It is a fairly rough gravel road and runs a quarter-mile or so back from the beach. After .8 miles (1.3 km) follow the road as it curves right (the airport is straight) and follow it straight to the beach in .5 mile (.8 km). The Brisa Marina is straight ahead.

CAMP ARCHELON
Price: Low

GPS Location: N 28° 58' 17.2", W 113° 32' 49.1"

This camping area is more appropriate to tent-campers than RVers. There are four palapas near the beach. Pit toilets are provided as are charcoal-fired hot water showers. Parking space for RVs is limited.

To reach Camp Archelon follow the directions above to Brisa Marina. Turn left when you reach Brisa Marina and drive north parallel to the beach for just a tenth of a mile to Camp Archelon.

DAGGETT'S BEACH CAMPING
Price: Low

GPS Location: N 28° 58' 30.8", W 113° 32' 48.2"

This is one or our favorite places to stay in Bahía de los Angeles. There are 18 beachside palapas with room to park an RV alongside. There are no hookups but there is a dump station, flush toilets, and hot showers. There's a restaurant next door, kayak rentals, and fishing and snorkeling charters.

To drive to the campground follow the north beaches road from Bahía L.A. After .8 mile (1.3 km) the road jogs right, than in .5 miles (.8 km) it jogs left to continue north. .3 mile (.5 km) after this last turn you'll see the sign for Daggett's Beach to the right. Follow the road to the beach and campground.

PLAYA LA GRINGA
Price: Inexpensive

GPS Location: N 29° 02' 26.3", W 113° 32' 40.6"

This beach seems to be known by beach campers throughout the Baja, it is a real favorite. There is absolutely nothing in the way of facilities, just a long sandy beach backed by mostly solid side roads branching from the main gravel road and providing access to camping sites above the beach.

To reach the campground just drive north from town along the north beaches road as described in the descriptions above. Playa La Gringa is 7 miles (11.3 km) north of town. The road is passable in any rig, but sections of bad washboard often make it slow going.

GUERRERO NEGRO TO SAN IGNACIO
89 Miles (144 Km), 2.25 Hours

Now that you have crossed the border you will note that the kilometer markers are counting down instead of up as they have been doing in the state of Baja California. All sections of kilometer markers on Mex 1 in Baja California Sur go from south to north. The markers for this section of road begin in Santa Rosalía, the town where the highway reaches the coast of the Gulf of California.

About 5 miles from the Guerrero Negro junction you will see a sign and a road headed toward the coast. This is the access road for whale watching at Laguna Ojo de Liebre, or Scammon's Lagoon. The distance is about 17 miles to the lagoon on a road that is usually passable for any rig but often washboarded. The road to the lagoon is only open during the whale-watching season from December through some time in April.

The highway from Guerrero Negro to the mountains runs across the Vizcaíno Desert. Much of the way you are crossing stabilized sand dunes that have blown eastward from the Laguna Ojo de Liebre area. The most noticeable vegetation is datilillo, a member of the yucca family, and small mesquite trees.

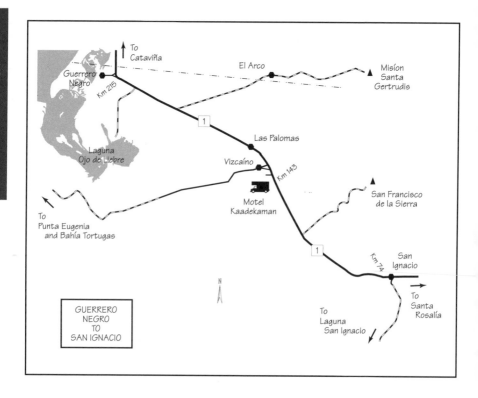

Sixteen miles (26 km) south of the Guerrero Negro junction is the road northeast to an old mining town, El Arco. See *Backroad Adventures* in this chapter for more information about this trip.

Forty-four miles (71) km) from the Guerrero Negro cutoff you will reach the small community of **Vizcaíno**. There's a junction there for a road that runs southwest to the coast at Punta Eugenia and Bahía Tortugas. See the *Backroad Adventures* section above for more information.

The road begins a gradual climb into Sierra San Francisco that form the spine of the peninsula at about 70 miles (113 km) from the Guerrero Negro junction. The pass through the mountains used by the highway is fairly mild with no major grades on the western slopes. As you near the mountains you will begin to see the large cardón cactus.

Fifty-nine miles from the Guerrero Negro cutoff there is a road to the left that leads to the most accessible of the pinturas rupestres or cave painting locations in this section of the Baja. Cueva Ratón is near the small village of **San Francisco de la Sierra**. See the *Backroad Adventures* section above for more information about this road. You must register and obtain information at the cave painting museum in San Ignacio before visiting the cave.

Finally, 86 miles (139 km) from the Guerrero Negro junction you will enter the outskirts of San Ignacio. The road to the right to San Lino is first, then you'll see the side road leading to the village of San Ignacio.

Guerrero Negro to San Ignacio Campground

🚐 MOTEL KAADEKAMÁN

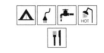

Address:	Carretera Transpeninsular Km 143,
	Vizcaíno, B.C.S., México
Telephone:	(115) 4-08-12
Price:	Low

GPS Location: N 27° 38' 46.1", W 113° 23' 05.8"

If you find yourself on the road east of Guerrero Negro when night falls you have no problem, the Motel Kaadekamán makes a convenient place to pull off the road and spend the night with electricity and water hookups.

This is a very small motel with five RV sites next door. Fifteen-amp plugs and water are available to the sites. The motel has no restroom facilities set aside for RVers but will put a room with hot shower at your disposal if you need them. Home-cooked meals are available.

The campground is located near the Km 143 marker on Mex 1 in the town of Vizcaíno. It is .4 miles (.6 km) east of the Pemex station.

CENTRAL BAJA

SAN IGNACIO (SAHN EEG-NAH-SEE-OH)
Population 4,000, Elevation 510 ft (155 m)

San Ignacio is a date-palm oasis built around lagoons formed by damming a river which emerges from the earth nearby. The town is located just south of Mex 1. The road into town is paved and big rigs should have no problems since they can drive around the main square to turn around. The main square is also the location of the **mission church of San Ignacio**, one of the easiest to find and most impressive mission churches on the Baja. This one is built of lava rock and has four foot thick walls.

From San Ignacio it is possible to take a guided tour to see rock paintings in the surrounding hills. You should visit the rock art museum located just south of the church, next door is where you register to visit rock-art sites. It is also possible to follow the thirty mile long unpaved road to **Laguna San Ignacio** to see gray whales from January through March. Tours to do this are available in San Ignacio.

San Ignacio Campgrounds

RICE AND BEANS OASIS
 Telephone: (115) 4-02-83
 Price: Moderate

GPS Location: N 27° 17' 54.7", W 112° 54' 20.1"

San Ignacio has a brand new RV park, something to celebrate. The campground also boasts a new restaurant, arguably the best place to eat in San Ignacio. Both the RV park and associated restaurant are owned and operated by the same family that has the popular Rice and Beans Restaurant in San Felipe.

There are 29 spaces all with full hookups with 15-amp plugs. They are located on two terraces overlooking San Ignacio's date palm forest. Since this is a brand new place there is not any shade, hopefully that will come. Restrooms are separate rooms with flush toilets and hot showers. The restaurant is at the entrance, we found the food to be excellent.

The campground is not located on the main road into San Ignacio like the other two mentioned here. Instead it is in the village of San Lino. The paved road to the campground leaves Mex 1 some .3 miles (.5 km) west of the main road in to San Ignacio. The campground is .4 miles (.6 km) from the highway on the right.

RV PARK EL PADRINO
 Telephone: (115) 4-00-89
 Price: Low

GPS Location: N 27° 17' 06.2", W 112° 54' 01.2"

The El Padrino is the closest RV park to town, you can easily stroll in to the zócalo or over to the nearby La Pinta Motel for dinner.

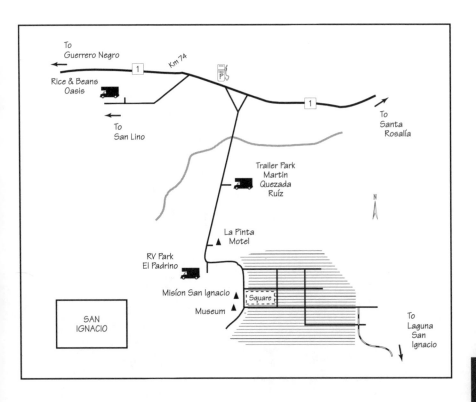

There are about 9 back-in spaces with electricity and water and the campground has a dump station. There are also large areas for camping without hookups. The restrooms have flush toilets but are in poor condition, they do have hot water showers. A centrally located restaurant also serves as an office. The campground offers gray whale watching tours to San Ignacio Lagoon which is about two hours away.

Take the San Ignacio cutoff near the Pemex. The campground is just past the La Pinta, 1.3 miles (2.1 km) from the cutoff.

⛺ TRAILER PARK MARTIN QUEZADA RUÍZ

    Price: Inexpensive

               GPS Location: N 27° 17' 22.6", W 112° 54' 20.1"

This is a grass-covered clearing in the trees with a pit toilet and dribbling cold water shower. There is room for a rig of any size, tent camping is pleasant. You'll probably find dates drying on platforms near the front of the property.

To find Martin's zero your odometer at the exit from Mex 1 and head toward town. The campground entrance is on the left at 1.1 miles (1.8 km). If no one is around don't worry, someone will be around to collect

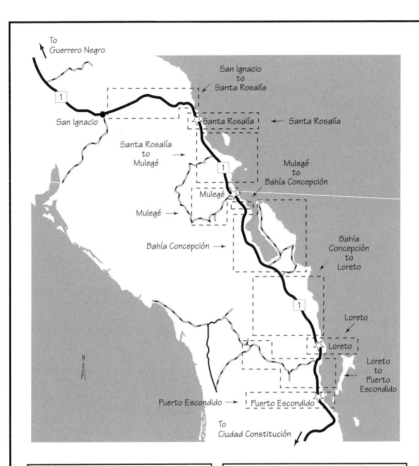

To
Guerrero Negro

1

San Ignacio

San Ignacio
to
Santa Rosalía

Santa Rosalía ← Santa Rosalía

Santa Rosalía
to
Mulegé →

1

Mulegé
to
Bahía Concepción

Mulegé →

Mulegé

Bahía Concepción →

Bahía
Concepción
to
Loreto

1

Loreto

Loreto → Loreto

Loreto
to
Puerto
Escondido

Puerto Escondido → Puerto Escondido

To
Ciudad Constitución

N

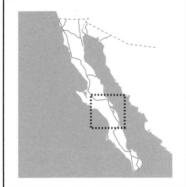

CHAPTER INDEX

Highlights . . . . Page 113
Roads and Fuel Availability . . . . . . Page 113
Sightseeing . . . . Page 114
Golf . . . . Page 114
Beaches and Water Sports . . . . . . Page 114
Fishing . . . . Page 115
Backroad Adventures . . . . Page 115
San Ignacio to Santa Rosalía . . . . . Page 117
Santa Rosalía . . . . Page 118
Santa Rosalía to Mulegé . . . . Page 120
Mulegé . . . . Page 122
Mulegé to Bahía Concepción . . . . . . Page 125
Bahía Concepción . . . . Page 125
Bahía Concepción to Loreto . . . . . . Page 131
Loreto . . . . Page 131
Loreto to Puerto Escondido . . . . . . Page 135
Puerto Escondido . . . . Page 136

CENTRAL GULF COAST

INTRODUCTION:

The section covered in this chapter is one of the most popular areas of the whole Baja Peninsula. Here the Transpeninsular reaches the warm Gulf of California for the first time. There are tourist resorts, quiet tropical towns, and sandy beaches suitable for RV parking. What more could you want?

Highlights

The many sandy beaches lining **Bahía Concepción** are the primary destination for many RVers headed down the Baja. Here you can camp right next to the water, there are enough nearby services so that you can stay for an extended period, and there is plenty to keep you busy with sightseeing trips to the north and south and water sports right at your doorstep.

Loreto, a town toward the southern end of this section, is just about the only fly-in destination with scheduled air service north of La Paz and Cabo. It has hotels, restaurants, a golf course, and resort-type services like guided fishing, diving, and sightseeing trips.

Roads and Fuel Availability

The Transpeninsular is all two lanes in this section, just as it is along most of the peninsula. It is narrow but relatively uncrowded, so continue to exercise caution and keep the speed down.

Kilometer markers along here decrease as you drive south. The segment from San Ignacio to Santa Rosalía counts down from 74 to zero. In Santa Rosalía a new segment of mileposts begins with 197, it counts down to zero at Loreto. At the Loreto cutoff the kilometer posts start again at 120, these reach zero at the 90 degree corner in Ciudad Insurgentes on the west side of the Sierra Gigante where the road turns south toward La Paz and the Cape.

Fuel is readily available in this section. Here are the locations, with types, and distances between stations: **San Ignacio**, gas and diesel; **Santa Rosalía**, gas and diesel, 45 miles (83 km)(watch these guys!), **Mulegé**, gas and diesel but poor access for RVs, 38 miles (61 km); **just south of Mulegé**, gas and diesel and good for RVs, 3 miles (5 km); and **Loreto**, gas and diesel, 80 miles (129 km). From Loreto to the next station at **Ley Federal de Aguas Número Uno** is a distance of 62 miles (100 km).

Sightseeing

At the northern end of this section is the coastal town of **Santa Rosalía**. It has an unusual history for a Baja town and some unusual sights, including a church designed by the same man who designed the Eiffel tower, an excellent French-style bakery, and wood buildings dating from the 19th century. See the Santa Rosalía section for more information.

Mulegé is a date-palm oasis located on an estuary along the Gulf of California. It's a friendly little town that is well-accustomed to visitors from north of the border. It also has some interesting sights including an old mission and a jail that only locked the doors at night when it was in operation.

You can visit some missions in this section. One is the **Misión Santa Rosalía de Mulegé** mentioned above. The other is the well-preserved Jesuit **Misión San Javier** in the hills behind Loreto, the road is described in *Backroad Adventures* below. Easiest of all to visit is the **Misión Nuestra Señora de Loreto** right in central Loreto, it also has a museum with exhibits about the Jesuit missions in the region.

There are several **rock-art sites** in the mountains behind the coast. Most popular is probably the one near Rancho La Trinidad. You can find a guide in Mulegé and you don't have to register in San Ignacio for this one. The drive is described below in the *Backroad Adventures* section.

Golf

Just a few miles south of Loreto is a resort - Nopoló. This is a FONATUR complex. FONATUR is the Mexican governmental agency that has planned and constructed places you are probably more familiar with: Cancun, Cabo San Lucas, Ixtapa, and Bahías de Huatulco. The resort has a golf course, the only one between Ensenada and Cabo San Lucas. It is an 18-hole course and tee-time reservations are easy to get, call (113) 5-07-88. There is also a driving range and a tennis center.

Beaches and Water Sports

Punta Chivato is a campground offering excellent water sports opportunities. The beach is fine for swimming with nice sand, snorkeling is good along rocky reefs just offshore, winds are good for board-sailing, and the fishing is good too. There is a nearby boat ramp and a sheltered area for small boats right at the campground.

The white sand beaches on the west side of **Bahía Concepción** are one of the area's biggest attractions. The waters of the bay are protected and excellent for swimming and water sports. Kayakers especially love the area. Most beaches near the highway are available for camping, they are listed under *Bahía Concepción Campgrounds* below.

Kayakers also like to make 1 to 2 week trips from Mulegé to Loreto or even from Puerto Escondido south to La Paz.

Fishing

It is not too hard to find launching ramps in this section. There are ramps in Santa Rosalía, San Lucas Cove, Punta Chivato, Mulegé, Bahía Concepción, Loreto, and Puerto Escondido. Some are better than others, in fact some are just beaches with hard sand, but you should be able to find a place to launch most any trailer boat along here somewhere.

In this section the two most popular fisheries are probably for yellowtail during December through January and for Dorado in July and August. The winter yellowtail season coincides with great weather for camping.

Pangas can be chartered in many places along this coast so don't think that you can't fish if you don't have a boat.

San Lucas Cove, located between Santa Rosalía and Mulegé, has two campgrounds and is very popular with fishermen. It offers protected waters for your boat at the campgrounds and easy access to 10-fathom water in Craig Channel behind Isla San Marcos.

Backroad Adventures

See the *Backroad Driving* section of *Chapter 2 - Details, Details, Details* for essential information about driving off the main highway on the Baja and for a definition of road types used below.

🚙 **From Km 169 Between Santa Rosalía and Mulegé** - This is a usually Type 2 road that leads 9 miles (14 km) to the village of **San José de Magdalena**. This town is known as the garlic capital of the Baja. You can buy long braids of garlic here from March to December. The road continues beyond town but deteriorates to a Type 3.

🚙 **From Km 136 at Mulegé** - This road leading westward from near the Mulegé cutoff leads quite a distance into the mountains, but the most popular destination is **Rancho La Trinidad** and nearby cave art in La Trinidad canyon. You can find a guide in Mulegé. The road to the rancho is usually a Type 2 but beyond it deteriorates to Type 3 requiring 4WD. Eventually the road circles around to San José de Magdalena, reaching it 50 miles (81 km) after passing Rancho La Trinidad. From **San José de Magdalena**, of course, you can return to Mex 1 at Km 169 as described above.

🚙 **From Km 77 Between Bahía Concepción and Loreto** - This road takes you around the south end of Bahía Concepción, up the east side of the bay, and then across the tip of the peninsula on the far side to an old mine site on the coast. The distance is about 35 miles (56 km) out to the mine. This is usually a Type 3 road. There's a Y at about 5 miles (8 km) that takes you across the peninsula to **San Sebastian** on the coast, the distance from the Y is 9 miles (15 km), this is usually a Type 3 road. San Sebastian can more easily be reached as described below.

From Km 62 Between Bahía Concepción and Loreto - From this point a graded road leads 10 miles (16 km) to the village of **San Nicolas**, then 6 miles (10 km) along the coast northward to **San Sebastian**. This is usually a Type 2 road.

From Km 118 Between Loreto and Puerto Escondido - The **Misión San Javier** is a popular excursion for tourists in Loreto. You can probably make the drive your-

EL REQUESÓN BEACH ON BAHÍA CONCEPCIÓN

self. The distance from the junction to the church is 22 miles (35 km) on a graded Type 2 road with some steep sections. At about 18 miles (29 km) you will pass a cutoff for the long road to San Miguel de Comondú and San Jose de Comondú. That is usually a Type 3 road, you can reach these two towns more easily from the far side of the mountains on better roads.

THE ROUTES, TOWNS, AND CAMPGROUNDS

SAN IGNACIO TO SANTA ROSALÍA
45 Miles (73 Km), 1.25 Hours

The road in this section is passing through the Sierra San Francisco. Grades are not difficult, other than the descent to the coast, but the road is sinuous in places so you'll want to keep the speed down.

About 20 miles eastward from San Ignacio you may notice that the road is crossing lava flows. They are from **Las Tres Vírgines** (The Three Virgins), a volcanic mountain with three separate cones on the north side of the highway. In a short distance you'll pass the road left to an experimental geothermal electrical plant. The volcano is

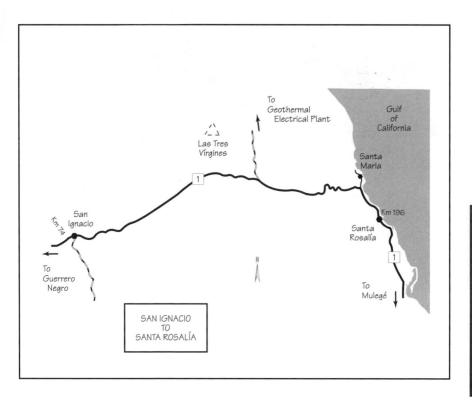

thought to have last shown significant activity about 1847 in the form of quite a bit of vapor. At about this point the road begins a long descent toward the Gulf of California.

Thirty-five miles from San Ignacio the descent becomes much steeper. This grade is called the **Cuesta del Infierno** (loosely translated as Grade to Hell), it is about 2.5 miles (3.1 km) long and the steepest grade on Mex 1. Be sure to gear down and keep the speed low as you descend, there are several curves. Soon the grade becomes less steep and after another 4 miles (6.5 km) or so you'll reach the coast and turn south to enter Santa Rosalía.

SANTA ROSALÍA (SAHN-TAH ROH-SAH-LEE-AH)
Population 15,000

Don't pass through Santa Rosalía without stopping. This old mining town is unlike any other town on the Baja. Located at the point where Mex 1 finally reaches the Gulf of California, Santa Rosalía was founded in the 1880's by a French company to extract the large amounts of copper ore located here. The mining operation lasted until the 1950's. Now the town is a fishing and ferry port, it serves as a hub for the surrounding area. The ferries run from here to Guaymas on Mexico's west coast.

EIFFEL'S CHURCH IN SANTA ROSALÍA

Much of the town is constructed of wood imported from the Pacific Northwest, the building designs are French colonial. **Santa Rosalía's church** is unique, it was designed by A.G. Eiffel who is better known for his tower in Paris. It was prefabricated in France and shipped by boat around Cape Horn. The town also has a well-known **French-style bakery**.

It is best not to drive a large rig in to town, although the town is built on a grid plan the roads are fairly constricted. It is better to park along the road north of town and then walk in.

Santa Rosalía Campground

🚐 LAS PALMAS RV PARK

Address:	Apdo. 123, Santa Rosalía, B.C.S., México
Telephone:	(115) 2-20-70
Price:	Moderate

GPS Location: N 27° 18' 52.9", W 112° 14' 35.0"

The Las Palmas is the most convenient place to stay if you want to be close to Santa Rosalía. It's a well-done full-hookup facility, but suffers from being away from the water.

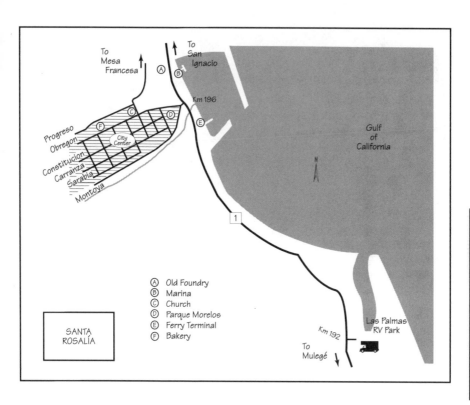

A   Old Foundry
B   Marina
C   Church
D   Parque Morelos
E   Ferry Terminal
F   Bakery

There are 30 large grassy spaces separated by concrete curbs arranged around the edge of the campground. All have electricity with 15-amp plugs, sewer, and water. The restrooms are decently maintained, they have hot water showers. There is a coin-operated laundry. When we visited the owner did not stay on site, he stopped by in the evening to collect.

The Las Palmas is just off Mex 1 about 2 miles (3.2 km) south of Santa Rosalía on the east side of the highway.

SANTA ROSALÍA TO MULEGÉ
37 Miles (60 Km), 1 Hour

As you make the short climb out of Santa Rosalía watch for the Las Palmas RV park to the left. It's a good place to base yourself if you find Santa Rosalía to be an interesting town.

Nine miles (15 km) south of Santa Rosalía, is San Lucas. Caleta San Lucas, a large cove just a half mile east of town, is the location of two RV parks popular with fishermen. They are RV Park San Lucas Cove and much smaller RV Camacho, both discussed below. The island offshore is Isla San Marcos, there is a large gypsum mine on the island.

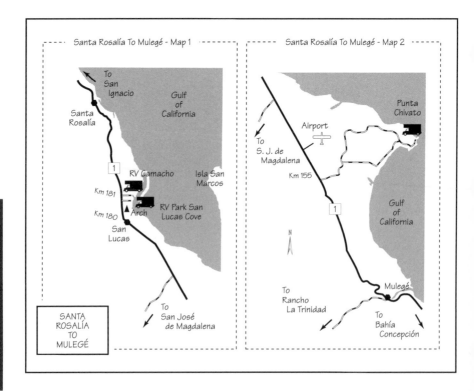

Twenty-five miles (41 km) south of Santa Rosalía, near Km 155, is a road leading to the coast and a campground known as Punta Chivato. The road is 11 miles (18 km) long, unpaved and dusty, but usually suitable for any rig. The waterfront camping area is very popular with folks who know about it, it is covered below.

You'll arrive at Mulegé 37 miles (60 km) from Santa Rosalía, near Km 136. Do not take the left in to town, the roads are narrow and not at all suitable for RVs. Instead stay on the main highway, go on across the bridge and watch for the turns to any of three RV parks located there. They all make good bases for exploring Mulegé.

Santa Rosalía to Mulegé Campgrounds

⊒ RV CAMACHO
Price: Inexpensive

GPS Location: N 27° 13' 16.3", W 112° 12' 50.3"

This is a small campground just north of the much larger RV Park San Lucas Cove. There are 10 waterfront sites with palapas. A large area behind the waterfront sites provides lots of room for additional parking. There are hot water showers and flush toilets as well as a dump station. The campground is fenced and there is a small office at the entrance gate which is usually manned.

To reach the campground watch for the sign at Km 181 south of Santa Rosalía. The .6 mile (1 km) dirt road east to the campground is fine for any size rig.

⊒ RV PARK SAN LUCAS COVE
Address: Apdo. 50, Santa Rosalía, B.C.S., México
Price: Low

GPS Location: N 27° 13' 07.4", W 112° 12' 49.4"

This is a waterfront campground that may remind you of those farther south on Bahía Concepción. It is not quite as scenic as those but has a similar ambiance. The fishing in this area is excellent and most of the campers in this park are here for the fishing.

There are about 20 parking sites along the beach and at least 40 more on a large hard-packed sandy area behind. The campground now has flush toilets and a hot water shower as well as a dump station, so it is possible to make an extended visit. Folks either pull their boats up on the beach or anchor them out front.

The campground entrance is .2 miles (.3 km) south of the Km 181 mark south of Santa Rosalía. This is about 8 miles (13.1 km) south of Santa Rosalía. The road in to the campground is packed sand and is about .5 miles (.8 km) long. Big rigs will have no problems negotiating it.

⊒ PUNTA CHIVATO
Price: Low

GPS Location: N 27° 04' 27.4", W 111° 56' 52.4"

CENTRAL GULF COAST

Punta Chivato has long been a popular beachside camping spot with few amenities, a good trade-off for having the ocean just outside your front door. This area is associated with a nearby hotel which has been a fly-in fishing destination for years. Many homes have been built along the coast, mostly to the east of the hotel between it and the camping area. The hotel has been purchased by a new owner and is being refurbished. The future of the camping area is uncertain at this time. It appears that the new owner may intend to upgrade the facility and continue to offer it as a camping destination.

Camping is in a large parking area behind a sandy beach. A small spit provides enough protection for small fishing skiffs. Restrooms were being built at the time we visited, workers said they would have flush toilets and showers. Water is available at the camping area and there is a dump station back near the hotel and airport.

Access to the resort and camping area is via a long dirt road. It too has been upgraded recently and now takes a more direct route to the resort than in former years. The access road leaves Mex 1 just south of Km 155 between Santa Rosalía and Mulegé. The distance from Mex 1 to the camping area is 11.2 miles (18.1 km). We found the road solid and fine for any vehicle, however, conditions undoubtedly vary and you should check with someone who has driven the road lately before attempting it in your rig. After 2.1 miles (3.4 km) there is a fork in the road, take the right fork for the new road. The road nears the shoreline at 5.4 miles (8.7 km) and turns left to parallel the shoreline some quarter-mile back from the beach. At about 8.5 miles (13.7 km) from the highway the road turns inland and rounds the end of a runway, then returns toward the beach reaching the resort at 10.5 miles (16.9 km). Turn left here following signs for Playa Camping and proceed another .7 mile (1.1 km) eastward to the camping area. En route you will pass through a row of houses which overlooks the beach and campground.

MULEGÉ (MOO-LAH-HAY)
Population 6,000

Situated near the mouth of the palm and mangrove-lined Río Santa Rosalía, Mulegé is a welcome tropical paradise after the long drive across desert country to the north. In many ways Mulegé may remind you of San Ignacio, both have a definite desert oasis ambiance. Mulegé is a popular RVer destination, many permanents make their seasonal home here, there are three decent RV parks, and the beaches and coves of the Bahía Concepción begin only 12 miles (19.6 km) to the south.

Fishing, diving, and kayaking are all popular here. Yellowtail are often thick during the winter and summer anglers go offshore for deep water fish. The nearby Santa Inés Islands are popular diving destinations, dive shops in Mulegé offer trips to the islands and other sites. Kayakers love Bahía Concepción and the coastline north and south.

Sights in Mulegé itself are limited. The **Misión Santa Rosalía** is located about 2 miles (3.3 km) upstream from the bridge on the right bank (facing downstream). It is usually locked except during services but the excursion offers excellent views of the town and river. Mulegé is also known for its **prison**. Now closed the prison building houses a museum and you can take a look at the cells. You can drive out to the mouth of the river (if you have a smaller rig) on the north shore, there you'll find a rock formation known as El Sombrerito, you can't miss it.

Mulegé is accustomed to visitors and takes them in stride, there's a large Norteamericano population. There are quite a few good restaurants and some small grocery shops. Street-side phones are available. A few miles south of town is a self-service Pemex, it has lots of room for big rigs and is an excellent place to fill up.

Mulegé Campgrounds

⊞ THE ORCHARD RV PARK

Address: Apdo. 24, Mulegé, C.P. 23900 B.C.S., México
Telephone: (115) 3-05-68
Price: Expensive

GPS Location: N 26° 53' 44.3", W 111° 58' 25.8"

The Orchard is an attractive park set under date palms near the Mulegé River.

There are now about 30 spaces with 30-amp plugs, sewer, and water with parking on gravel or packed dirt. Some have palapas. The campground seems to be gradually filling with attractive permanent-type units. Restrooms are modern and have hot wa-

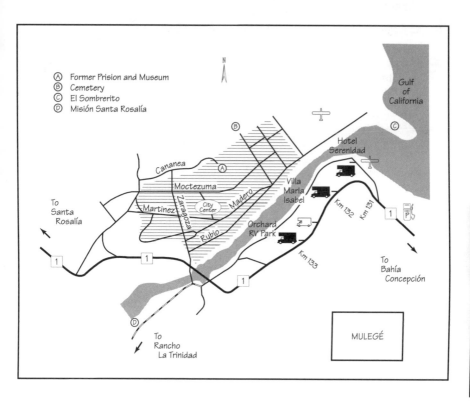

ter showers. Rental canoes are available for boating on the estuary at the back of the property. Caravans often use this campground so it is sometimes full.

The Orchard is located .5 miles (.8 km) south of the Mulegé bridge off Mex 1.

⏚ VILLA MARIA ISABEL RECREATIONAL PARK

Address:	Apdo. 5, Mulegé, C.P. 23900 B.C.S., México
Telephone and Fax:	(115) 3-02-46
Price:	Moderate

GPS Location: N 26° 53' 49.0", W 111° 57' 50.8"

This is an excellent place to stay if you are looking for an RV park with full hookups in Mulegé. Like the other Mulegé campgrounds it sits near the south shore of the Mulegé River. Although there are a lot of permanents here there also is a special grass-covered area set aside for travelers. There is a very popular little bakery, a great swimming pool, and a laundromat.

The campground has 18 pull-through spaces with 30-amp plugs, sewer, and water. Parking is on grass and the slots will accommodate larger rigs. There is also an area for tent campers with a shared palapa. The restrooms have hot water showers. The swimming pool is a big attraction, especially during hot summer weather and the bakery draws people from well outside the campground. There is a boat ramp and a dry long-term storage area.

The campground is 1.3 miles (2.1 km) south of the Mulegé bridge off Mex 1.

⏚ HOTEL SERENIDAD

Address:	Apdo. 9, Mulegé, C.P. 23900 B.C.S., México
Telephone:	(115) 3-05-30
Fax:	(115) 3-03-11
Internet:	www.serenidad.com
Price:	Moderate

GPS Location: N 26° 53' 49.6", W 111° 57' 32.0"

The Serenidad is a hotel located on the south bank of the Mulegé River near the mouth. It has its own airstrip and was a popular fly-in fishing destination even before the Transpeninsular Highway was built.

The hotel has 8 RV spaces along a wall at the back of the property. The location is hot and unappealing considering the nearby alternatives, but there are full hookups with 15-amp plugs. Restrooms are available with hot showers. The hotel has nice facilities, there is a swimming pool and restaurant, a pig roast draws people from around the area on Saturday night.

The entrance to the Serenidad is the farthest south along Mex 1 of all the Mulegé campgrounds. If you zero your odometer at the bridge you'll see the entrance road at 2.2 miles (3.5 km). There's a half-mile gravel entrance road leading along the side of the airstrip to the hotel.

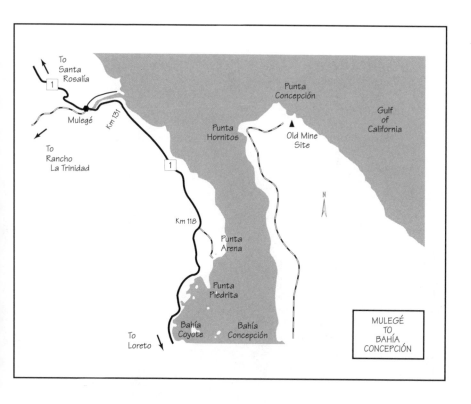

MULEGÉ TO BAHÍA CONCEPCIÓN
12 Miles (19 Km), .25 Hour

This is only a short drive to the northernmost of the beaches, of course it's a lot farther to the southernmost beaches on the bay. An important stop along the road is the Pemex station 3 miles (5 km) south of the Mulegé bridge. It has excellent access for big rigs.

BAHÍA CONCEPCIÓN (BAH-HEE-AH KOHN-SEP-SEE-OHN)

For many people, especially RVers, Bahía Concepción is the ultimate Baja destination. This huge shallow bay offers many beaches where you can park your camping vehicle just feet from the water and spend the winter months soaking in the sunshine. Mex 1 parallels the western shore of the bay for about 20 miles (33 km), you'll see many very attractive spots and undoubtedly decide to stop. The many beaches offer different levels of services. Full hookups are seldom available, but many have toilets, showers, water, and restaurants. Information about the most popular beaches is of-

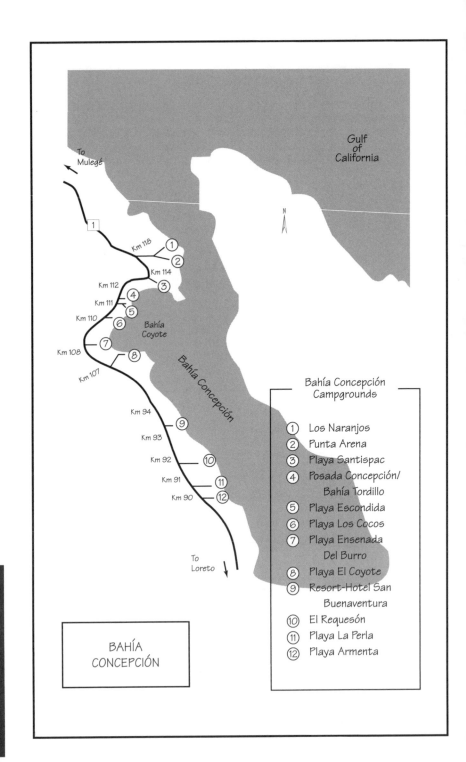

BAHÍA CONCEPCIÓN

Bahía Concepción
Campgrounds

1. Los Naranjos
2. Punta Arena
3. Playa Santispac
4. Posada Concepción/
   Bahía Tordillo
5. Playa Escondida
6. Playa Los Cocos
7. Playa Ensenada
   Del Burro
8. Playa El Coyote
9. Resort-Hotel San
   Buenaventura
10. El Requesón
11. Playa La Perla
12. Playa Armenta

CENTRAL GULF COAST

fered below. While many of these places seem to have no formal organization do not be surprised if someone comes by in the evening to collect a small fee. This usually covers keeping the area picked up, trash removal and pit toilets. Ask one of your fellow campers about arrangements if you have questions. The closest place to get supplies is Mulegé.

Bahía Concepción Campgrounds

LOS NARANJOS

Price: Inexpensive

GPS Location: N 26° 47' 02.1", W 111° 51' 48.8"

Two camping areas occupy Punta Arena. The one to the north is Los Naranjos.

This campground occupies the actual point. To the north along open beach there is a large open parking area. Along the more protected beach to the south are permanent structures, however there is some space to camp behind them. There is a small restaurant, as well as primitive restrooms with flush toilets and hot showers. There's also a dump station.

The entrance to Playa Los Naranjos is .2 miles (.3 km) south of the Km 118 marker. It is marked with a sign to Punta Arena. The road in to the beach is rough but should be negotiable by any RV at very slow speeds. It is 2.1 miles (3.4 km) long, at .4 miles (.7 km) there is a Y where you go left for Playa los Naranjos and right for Playa Punta Arena.

PUNTA ARENA

Price: Inexpensive

GPS Location: N 26° 46' 44.1", W 111° 52' 23.2"

There are actually two different camping area on this large beach: Playa los Naranjos to the north and Playa Punta Arena to the south. The entry road branches not far from the highway and you make your decision there. Punta Arena is the fork to the right.

The beach at Punta Arena is long and not nearly as crowded as the beaches to the south. It is quite easy to find a place along the water most of the time. There are pit toilets. Small palapas are available. In the scrub behind the beach the residents have set up a small sand golf course.

The entrance to Punta Arena is .2 miles (.3 km) south of the Km 118 marker. The road in to the beach is rough but should be negotiable by any RV at very slow speeds. It is two miles (3 km) long, at .4 miles (.7 km) there is a Y where you go left for Playa los Naranjos and right for Playa Punta Arena.

PLAYA SANTISPAC

Price: Low

GPS Location: N 26° 45' 56.8", W 111° 53' 15.2"

CENTRAL GULF COAST

The farthest north beach on sheltered Bahía Coyote is very popular, partly because the entrance road is so short and easy. The fee here is slightly higher than most other beaches in the area.

The long beach offers beachside parking for many, but you will find that the beach sites are often very crowded together and full. There are flush toilets, a dump station, hot and cold showers, and a couple of restaurants. There is also a small muddy hot spring located a short walk to the west just below the highway and at the back of a grove of mangroves.

The entrance to Playa Santispac is midway between the Km 114 and Km 113 markers. The beach is visible from the road. While short and in good shape the entrance road is a little steep, exercise care when leaving the highway. There is a manned entrance station where the fee is collected.

POSADA CONCEPCIÓN/BAHÍA TORDILLO
Address: Apdo. 14, Mulejé, B.C.S., México
Price: Low

GPS Location: N 26° 45' 11.1", W 111° 53' 56.7"

Posada Concepción is really more subdivision than beachfront camping area, most of the people here live in houses or permanently installed trailers. There are a few spaces for transients, they are nowhere near the water but they do have hookups.

There are ten slots here with full hookups, electrical outlets have 15-amp plugs. The spaces are fine for large rigs. Nice restrooms have flush toilets and hot showers. This beach is well-protected, at low tide the water is very shallow and there are a few hot-water seeps in shallow water. There is also a tennis court.

The entrance to Posada Concepción is just north of the Km 111 marker.

PLAYA ESCONDIDA
Price: Inexpensive

GPS Location: N 26° 44' 42.4", W 111° 53' 44.7"

This small isolated beach is picture-perfect. There is a row of palapas along the water. Outhouses and cold water showers are on the hillside behind.

The road in to this beach is somewhat rough, we recommend it for rigs no longer than 30 feet and not for trailers. The entrance road is just south of Posada Concepción and is shared by the Eco Mundo kayaking operation. At first glance you'll think the road leads to the south side of the same bay occupied by Posada Concepción, but instead it leads .5 miles (.8 km) up over a low saddle to an unexpected beach, hence the name which means hidden beach.

PLAYA LOS COCOS
Price: Inexpensive

GPS Location: N 26° 44' 28.7", W 111° 54' 03.9"

Playa los Cocos is another beautiful beach with minimal facilities. There are palapas, pit toilets, and a dump station. Mangroves are at the rear.

The entrance is near the Km 110 marker. There is no sign and the entrance road is about .3 miles (.5 km) long. The campground can easily be seen from the highway because it runs very close.

PLAYA ENSENADA DEL BURRO
Price: Inexpensive

GPS Location: N 26° 43' 38.0", W 111° 54' 21.1"

This beach offers the standard pit toilets but also has a restaurant. There's even a small store across the highway. Parking is along the water where there are a number of palapas. Caravans often stay here.

The entrance to Playa Del Burro is at the Km 108 marker. You can easily see the beach from the highway.

PLAYA EL COYOTE
Price: Inexpensive

GPS Location: N 26° 42' 45.2", W 111° 54' 09.6"

Another good beach with few facilities. A tree or two provide shade on this beach and it is not quite as crowded as the spots farther north, perhaps because the road is slightly more difficult. It has bucket-flush toilets and a dump station. There is a hot spring along the rocks to the east. Several guides to the Baja have a picture on the cover of RVs parked on this beach, two palms right next to the water, often with RVs parked beneath, make an enticing shot from above.

The entrance road to El Coyote is near the Km 107 marker. After leaving the highway and driving down to the water turn right and proceed .5 miles (.8 km) along the water below the cliff to the camping area.

RESORT-HOTEL SAN BUENAVENTURA
Address: Km 93 Carr. Transp. Loreto - Mulegé,
                Playa Buenaventura, Mulegé, B.C.S., México
Telephone: (115) 3-04-08
Price: Low

GPS Location: N 26° 38' 34.4", W 111° 50' 43.5"

Playa Buenaventura has a very nice little hotel, restaurant/sports bar and trailer park, all under the same ownership. English is spoken. The trailer park has 15 slots along the beach with palapas but no hookups. Actually even a few more rigs can be accommodated. There is a flush toilet, hot showers, a launch ramp, and security with lights at night. The bar has U.S. television and there is a mini-market across the highway. Some caravans like this spot but individual campers seem to think the place is too expensive considering the wealth of nearby primitive camping beaches. This well-run operation necessarily has higher overhead than some of the shoestring camping areas on other beaches.

The entrance to San Buenaventura is near Km 93 on Mex 1. The main road is almost at beach level here. There's quite a bit of room out front making this a good turn-around spot if you have missed a turn-off to the north or south.

El Requesón

Price: Inexpensive

GPS Location: N 26° 38' 13.1", W 111° 49' 52.5"

This is the most picturesque of the Bahía Concepción beaches. The beach is a short sand spit which connects a small island to the mainland at low tide. Small, shallow bays border both sides of the spit. There are pit toilets but no other amenities. You can hike along the water to the south beyond Playa La Perla. Someone will come by to collect a small fee each evening.

The entrance to El Requesón is about a half-kilometer north of the Km 91 marker and is signed. The entrance road is rough but should present no problems for most RVs, it is about .2 miles (.3 km) long. You may find that it is easier to enter the road if you are approaching from the north so northbound travelers may drive on less than a mile and turn around in front of Playa Buenaventura.

Playa La Perla

Price: Inexpensive

GPS Location: N 26° 38' 03.6", W 111° 49' 27.1"

This beachside camping area offers pit toilets and many palapas. It is a small sandy cove with a lot of additional camping locations to the north and south of the cove. The cove itself is probably better for tent campers while rigs may prefer the adjoining areas.

The entrance road is between Km 90 and 91. If you enter this way the road is about .4 mile (.6 km) long. You can also use the entrance road to El Requesón, turn right as you reach the beach, and trundle slowly along the shoreline south to Playa La Perla. We find this entrance to be easier with larger rigs, there is less chance of scratching the side of your RV.

Playa Armenta

Price: Inexpensive

GPS Location: N 26° 37' 31.5", W 111° 48' 37.3"

This is an exposed location without a great beach, but it has palapas and pit toilets.

The entrance road is near Km 90. The entrance road is .5 miles long (9 km) and somewhat difficult for big rigs although we've seen 35-foot motorhomes in here.

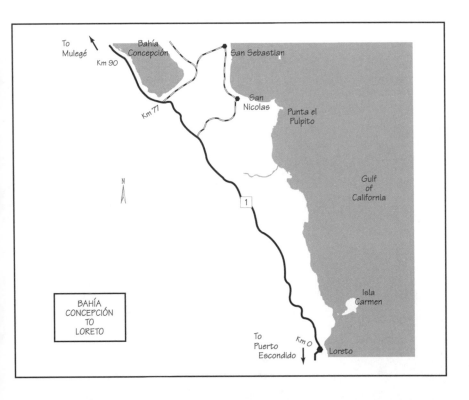

BAHÍA CONCEPCIÓN TO LORETO
71 Miles (115 Km), 2 Hours (from the northern end of the bay)

From Bahía Concepción to Loreto the kilometer markers continue to count down with zero at Loreto. After winding alongside Bahía Concepción for about 26 miles (42 km) the road climbs over a low saddle and then runs along a wide inland valley all the way south to Loreto. In some areas where water is available you'll see scattered ranchos in the valley. Off to the right are the Sierra de la Giganta. Prepare yourself, you'll soon be crossing them.

LORETO (LOH-RAY-TOE)
Population 7,200

Loreto is considered the oldest continuously occupied town on the Baja having been founded in 1697. This is theoretically true, however the town was virtually abandoned from the time of a major hurricane in 1829 until resettlement in the 1850's. The **Museo de los Misiones** has exhibits explaining the history of the area and also of the missions throughout the Baja. It is located next to the **Misión Nuestra Señora de Loreto**.

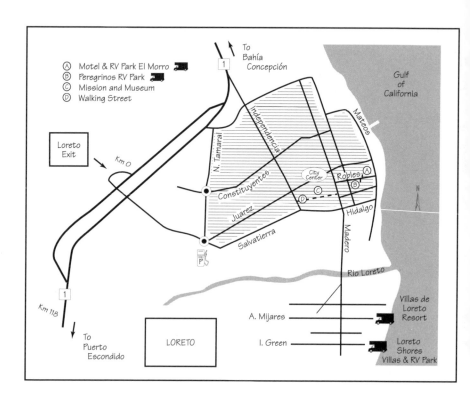

Today the town is part of a FONATUR development scheme like those in Cancún, Huatulco, Ixtapa, and Los Cabos (Cabo San Lucas and San José del Cabo). Most of the infrastructure was put in Nopoló, about 5 miles (8.2 km) south of Loreto. There you'll find an uncrowded but very nice golf course, a tennis center, the Loreto Inn, and a convention center. Even Bahía Escondido is part of the scheme, it is now supposed to be called Puerto Loreto. See the Puerto Escondido section below for more information.

Fishing and boating are popular activities in Loreto. You can arrange a trip in a panga or larger fishing cruiser. Just offshore from Loreto is Isla Carmen, the island has beaches and sheltered anchorages. Many experienced kayakers visit the island or you can arrange a panga for the trip.

Loreto Campgrounds

 LORETO SHORES VILLAS AND RV PARK

Address:	Apdo. 219, Loreto, C.P. 23880 B.C.S., México
Telephone:	(113) 5-06-29
E-mail:	shores@loretoweb.com.mx
Price:	Moderate

GPS Location: N 25° 59' 57.8", W 111° 20' 15.2"

This is the largest RV park in Loreto and a good place to stop for the night if you're traveling. It has plenty of room for big rigs on entry roads and inside the park. The spaces look a lot like those in the government parks, perhaps this was one of them. If so it has an unusually good waterfront location. Unfortunately the waterfront is now blocked by permanent structures. In fact, much of this campground has been used for permanents, the remaining free spaces seem to be managed as an afterthought.

There are about 35 pull-through spaces remaining here, all with 30-amp plugs, sewer, water and patios. The restrooms are clean and have hot water showers. A few small trees have been planted but will have to grow to provide much shade. The campground is fenced in the rear but the beach side is open.

Zero your odometer at the Loreto turn-off from Mex 1. This will take you toward the ocean through a traffic circle and then a stop light. Take the turn to the right at 1.4 miles (2.3 km) onto Francisco Madero at another light. You'll cross a dry arroyo and continue straight. When you are .8 miles (1.3 km) from the turn make a left turn onto Ildefonso Green, the RV park is directly ahead.

🚐 VILLAS DE LORETO RESORT

Address: Antonio Mijares y Playa, Apdo. 132, Loreto, C.P. 23880 B.C.S., México
Telephone: (113) 5-05-86
Internet: www.villasdeloreto.com
Price: Moderate

GPS Location: N 26° 00' 03.0", W 111° 20' 19.9"

This is a cute little hotel on the waterfront in Loreto, it has some RV slots in the rear. Eventually the trailer park may disappear as more permanent structures are built in the area, meanwhile this is probably the nicest RV park in Loreto.

There are about 11 sites with 15-amp plugs and water hookups and quite a bit of shade. There is a dump station. The restrooms are modern and very spiffy, they have hot showers of course. There's also a coin-operated laundry in the building. The resort has a swimming pool out front overlooking the water.

Zero your odometer at the Loreto turn-off from Mex 1. This will take you toward the ocean through a traffic circle and then a stop light. Take the turn to the right at 1.4 miles (2.3 km) onto Francisco Madero at another light. You'll cross a dry arroyo and continue straight. When you are .6 miles (1.22 km) from the turn make a left turn onto Antonio Mijares and you'll see the resort on the right as you reach the beach. Big rigs will want to enter the back entrance which is usually closed, just park outside while you walk in to register.

🚐 MOTEL & RV PARK EL MORO

Address: Rosendo Robles No. 8, Col. Centro, Loreto, C.P. 23880 B.C.S., México
Telephone and Fax: (113) 5-05-42
Price: Low

GPS Location: N 26° 00' 41.0", W 111° 20' 27.7"

THE LORETO PLAZA

The El Moro doesn't have a lot of extras in the way of facilities, just hookups and restrooms. There is also a motel on the property.

There are 12 spaces, all are large back-in slots with 30-amp plugs, sewer, and water. The restrooms are simple but clean and have hot water showers. Maneuvering room for both driving to the campground and parking would be tight for bigger rigs.

Zero your odometer at the Loreto turn-off from Mex 1. Drive straight into and through town until you reach the waterfront malecón at 1.6 miles (2.6 km). Turn left and take the second left turn on Rosendo Robles at odometer 1.7 miles (2.7 km). The RV park is on the left at odometer 1.8 miles (2.9 km).

PEREGRINOS RV PARK

Address: Rosendo Robles S/N, Colonia Centro,
              Loreto, C.P. 23880 B.C.S., México
Telephone: (113) 5-12-67
Price: Low

GPS Location: N 26° 00' 43.4", W 111° 20' 26.7"

Just across the road from the El Moro and a few feet closer to the ocean is a very small new RV park. It has already started to fill with permanently located units but a few spaces remain for tent campers and smaller RVs.

The RV park has 7 spaces, all are back-ins with 15-amp plugs, sewer and water. Showers with hot water and flush toilets are provided.

Zero your odometer at the Loreto turn-off from Mex 1. Drive straight into and through town until you reach the waterfront malecón at 1.6 miles (2.6 km). Turn left and take the second left turn on Rosendo Robles at odometer 1.7 miles (2.7 km). The RV park is on the right at odometer 1.8 miles (2.9 km).

LORETO TO PUERTO ESCONDIDO
16 Miles (26 Km), .5 Hour

Just south of the entrance road to Loreto is a road leading westward into the mountains to the **Misión San Francisco Javier**. This is the only mission on the Baja still standing that has not been rebuilt. The distance to the mission is 22 miles (35 km). See the *Backroad Adventures* section of this chapter for more information.

Five miles (8 km) south of the Loreto junction a road leads east to the **Nopoló resort area**. There's a hotel, a golf course, and tennis courts open to the public for reasonable fees.

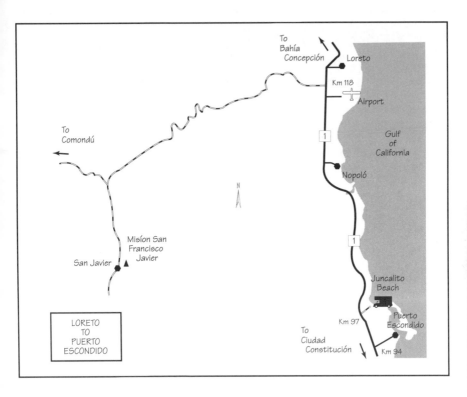

South of the Nopoló junction you'll see the golf course along the road, as well as two bridges used to cross water hazards.

Near Km 97 you'll see a road to the left which leads to the camping beach called Juncalito. See the listing below for more information.

You'll reach the junction for the short stub road eastward to Puerto Escondido 15 miles (24 km) south of the Loreto junction.

Loreto to Puerto Escondido Campground

JUNCALITO BEACH
    Price: Inexpensive

GPS Location: N 25° 49' 10.3", W 111° 18' 58.7"

This little beach has nothing in the way of amenities, not even pit toilets. However, it is a nice beach, close to the road, and excellent for self-contained campers. The road in is pretty good, better than a lot of the roads up at Bahía Concepción, and is only .7 mile (1.1 km) long.

The road to the beach is just north of the Km 97 marker, that's 1.7 miles (2.7 km) north of the road out to Puerto Escondido.

PUERTO ESCONDIDO (PWER-TOE ESS-KOHN-DEE-DOE)
Population 100

Long popular as a camping and yachting destination, Puerto Escondido is now a part of the FONATUR plan to turn the Loreto area into a world-class resort. You'll be amazed at the paved but deteriorating boulevards, quay, and abandoned half-built hotel sitting next to this beautiful hurricane hole. Yachts are thick in the bay but campers are nowhere to be seen, camping is not allowed at the port. There's a boat ramp here so fishermen like to use Puerto Escondido as a base for accessing the offshore waters and long stretch of coast to the south toward La Paz which has little road access. Kayakers put in here for the trips down the coast to La Paz.

Puerto Escondido Campground

TRIPUI RV PARK-HOTEL RESORT
    Address: Apdo. 100, Loreto, C.P. 23880 B.C.S., México
    Telephone: (113) 3-08-18
    Fax: (113) 3-08-28
    Price: Moderate

GPS Location: N 25° 48' 21.7", W 111° 19' 10.1"

CENTRAL GULF COAST

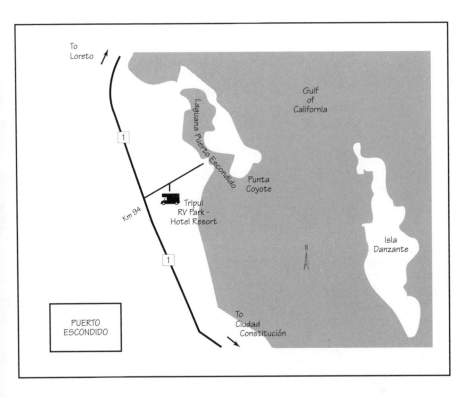

This RV park has lots of permanents and nice facilities, unfortunately traveling rigs are relegated to a somewhat barren gravel parking lot. Some small palm trees have been planted to help make the place more attractive. Still, full hookup campgrounds with lots of amenities are scarce in this area so the Tripui is well-used. Another reason the Tripui is popular is the boat-launch ramp a short distance away at the port.

There are 31 back-in spaces in a fenced gravel lot with 30 and 50-amp plugs, sewer, and water. Cement curbs separate the sites. The sites are short but no problem for big rigs since you can project far into the central area without really getting in anyone's way. The restrooms are fine, they have hot showers and flush toilets and are in good repair. This resort also has a lot of permanent rigs in a separate area, there's a small store, a gift shop, and a laundry as well as a nice pool area and a restaurant.

Take the Puerto Escondido cutoff from Mex 1 near Km 94 about 16 miles (26 km) south of Loreto. Drive .6 miles (1 km) on the paved road and you'll see the campground on the right. You'll first pass the transient camping area and then see the sign for the office. Big rigs may want to pull into the camping area if there appear to be empty spaces and then walk over to sign in.

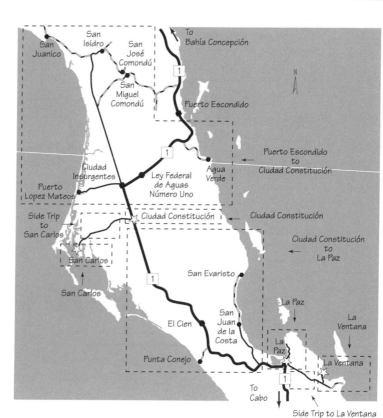

San Juanico
San Isidro
San José Comondú
San Miguel Comondú
San Juanico

To Bahía Concepción

1

Puerto Escondido

1

Puerto Escondido to Ciudad Constitución

Ciudad Insurgentes
Ley Federal de Aguas Número Uno
Agua Verde

Puerto Lopez Mateos

Side Trip to San Carlos

Ciudad Constitución

Ciudad Constitución

San Carlos

1

San Evaristo

Ciudad Constitución to La Paz

San Carlos

La Paz

La Ventana

El Cien

San Juan de la Costa

La Paz

La Ventana

Punta Conejo

La Ventana

1

To Cabo

Side Trip to La Ventana

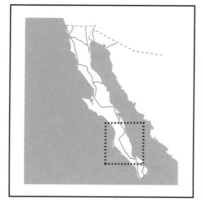

CHAPTER INDEX

Highlights	Page 139
Roads and Fuel Availability	Page 139
Sightseeing	Page 140
Beaches and Water Sports	Page 140
Fishing	Page 140
Backroad Adventures	Page 141
Puerto Escondido to Ciudad Constitución	Page 142
Ciudad Constitución	Page 142
Side Trip to Puerto San Carlos	Page 145
Puerto San Carlos	Page 145
Ciudad Constitución to La Paz	Page 147
La Paz	Page 148
Side Trip to La Ventana	Page 153
La Ventana	Page 153

SOUTH TO LA PAZ

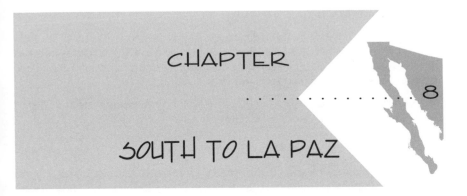

CHAPTER

· · · · · · · · · · · · 8

SOUTH TO LA PAZ

INTRODUCTION

This chapter of the book covers the peninsula from the point where the highway turns inland south of Loreto to the point where it again reaches the Gulf at Baja Sur's largest town, La Paz. Between the two is a huge farming area centered around Ciudad Constitución. Many folks just hurry through this section bound for points farther south, but if you want to slow down there are several side trips offering fishing, whale watching, and sightseeing possibilities

Highlights

La Paz is the largest city in Baja Sur and the one that feels the most like a mainland Mexican city. It is the best place to buy supplies south of Ensenada, many people spend the winter at one of the town's RV parks.

Roads and Fuel Availability

South of Loreto the road climbs to cross the Sierra la Giganta. On the far side you'll find a long and very gradual descent to the town of Ciudad Insurgentes. After a 90-degree left turn you'll drive for almost 50 miles (81 km) on an arrow-straight road through irrigated farming country. After that the road crosses dry rolling hills for another 90 miles (145 km) until it again reaches the east coast on the Gulf of California at the town of La Paz.

Kilometer markers on this section of the Baja count down from Loreto to Ciudad Insurgentes, a distance of 120 kilometers. Then they again count down until you reach La Paz, a distance of 239 kilometers.

Fuel is readily available in this section. Here are the locations, with types and distances between stations: **Loreto**, gas and diesel; **Ley Federal de Aguas Número**

Uno, gas and diesel, 62 miles (100 km), **Ciudad Insurgentes**, gas and diesel, 10 miles (16 km); **Ciudad Constitución**, gas and diesel, 14 miles (23 km); **El Cien**, gas and diesel, 69 miles (111 km), **El Centenario**, gas and diesel, 51 miles (82 km); **La Paz**, gas and diesel, 7 miles (11 km).

Sightseeing

During the months of January to March it is possible to visit the **gray whales** in Bahía Magdalena. Pangas go out to visit the whales from two different towns: San Carlos (which has a campground described below) and Puerto Lopez Mateos (see *Backroad Adventures* in this chapter).

You can visit the remote and scenic villages of **San José Comondú** and **San Miguel Comondú**, see *Backroad Adventures* below.

Beaches and Water Sports

Access to beaches in this section, except in the La Paz vicinity, requires taking side roads since the Transpeninsular does not run along the coast.

Bahía Magdalena is one of the three places on the Baja were gray whales can easily be seen in their nursery lagoons. The others, of course, are near Guerrero Negro and San Ignacio. Access to the bay is easiest at Puerto Adolfo Lopez Mateos and at Puerto San Carlos, paved roads lead to both of them. Puerto San Carlos has a full-hookup campground which is described in this chapter. The northern part of the bay is also an excellent kayaking and fishing location during months when access is not restricted due to the presence of the whales.

South of Bahía Magdalena are miles of Pacific Ocean beaches. Side roads lead from the highway, see *Backroad Adventures* below.

Ensenada de Aripes at La Paz doesn't have great beaches inside the protecting Peninsula el Mogote, but there are several good ones off the paved road that runs a few miles north to the ferry terminal at Pichilingue and beyond. They include Playas **Palmira**, **El Coromuel**, **Caimancito**, **El Tesoro**, **Pichilingue**, **Balandra** and **Tecolote**.

Southeast of La Paz Highway BCS 286 leads to **Bahía La Ventana**. There's a long sandy beach bordering the bay, this is a very popular windsurfing location. There's also a campground. See *La Ventana Side Trip* below.

Fishing

The waters of the northern half of **Magdalena Bay**, north of Puerto San Carlos, are good small-boat fishing waters when the whales are not present. Small car-top aluminum boats and kayaks work well. These are mangrove waters and offer bass, pargo, and corvina. Launch sites for larger boats are not available, you will be launching over the sand. Waters outside Bahía Magdalena are difficult to reach and hazardous because of strong surf and sand bars at the bay entrances.

La Paz has a lot more to offer. At one time this was a top destination for big game fish and it continues to be pretty good although not as good as farther south. Charter cruisers and pangas are readily available in La Paz, the best season for billfish is May through October.

Small aluminum boat fishermen around La Paz will find few fish, there is just too much fishing activity near town. Try heading north on the **coastal road toward San Evaristo** or southeast to **Ensenada Los Muertos**, both are described in the *Backroad Adventures* section of this chapter.

Backroad Adventures

See the ***Backroad Driving*** section of ***Chapter 2 - Details, Details, Details*** for essential information about driving off the main highway on the Baja and for a definition of road types used below.

From Km 63 Between Loreto and Ciudad Constitución - For a last visit to the Gulf of California before heading east you might try the road to **Agua Verde**. This small and isolated village sits on the shore of a bay and is a popular yachting destination. There are spots for primitive camping and the location is good for kayaking and sailboarding. The distance is 25 miles (40 km) on what is usually a Type 2 road.

From Km 0 at the Ciudad Insurgentes Junction - At the 90 degree turn of Mex 1 in Ciudad Insurgentes turn right and head north. Follow the paved road north for 1.5 miles (2.4 km), then turn left on another paved which will take you 21 miles (34 km) to **Puerto Lopez Mateos**. This is one of the easiest places to watch the gray whales from January to March. Panga operators offer whale-watching tours and boondocking is possible at several locations. Kayakers and fishermen also have access to the protected waters of northern Bahía Magdalena when whales are not present.

From Km 0 at the Ciudad In surgentes Junction - At the 90-degree turn of Mex 1 in Ciudad Insurgentes turn right and head north. Follow the paved road for 78 miles (126 km) to the oasis villages of **La Purísima** and **San Isidro**. Continue through these towns and take the right fork beyond on a Type 2 road that runs another 17.5 miles (28 km) to **San José Comondú** and neighboring **San Miguel Comondú**. These towns are small villages in verdant valleys, they are well worth the sightseeing trip. After passing through San Miguel Comondú you can follow another road 20 miles (33 km) back to the paved road north of Ciudad Insurgentes.

From Km 0 at the Ciudad Insurgentes Junction - At the 90-degree turn of Mex 1 in Ciudad Insurgentes turn right and head north. Follow the paved road for 68 miles (110 km) and then take the unpaved road left for 29 miles (47 km) to the coastal village of **San Juanico**. This unpaved road is usually a Type 2 road. An inexpensive camping area with no hookups is next to the excellent beach. This is a well-known surfing destination generally known as **Scorpion Bay**.

From Km 80 Between Ciudad Constitución and La Paz - A 10-mile (16 km) Type 2 road leads to the windswept coast at **El Conejo**. Punta Conejo is popular with surfers, it can also be good for experienced board-sailors and for surf fishing.

From Km 17 Between Ciudad Constitución and La Paz - This road leads up the coast from near La Paz. For the first 24 miles (39 km) to the mining town of **San Juan de la Costa** the road is paved. Just before reaching San Juan a fork leads right and a Type 2 road begins which leads another 34 miles (55 km) north to where the road becomes a rugged Type 3 road and continues another 16 miles (26 km) to **San Evaristo**. This is a very scenic road, there are a few places along it that are suitable for boondocking and the fishing offshore can be good.

From the Road to La Ventana - Follow the route described below from La Paz for the side trip to La Ventana. At mile 23 (km 37) do not take the left turn, continue instead straight on through San Juan de los Planes and then follow the highway as it takes a 90-degree left turn. You'll soon reach the end of the pavement at about mile 30 (km 48). From here a Type 2 road leads 6 miles (10 km) to **Ensenada los Muertos.** From Ensenada Los Muertos pangas can take you fishing out to Isla Cerralvo, about 8 miles out. There is room to boondock here and boardsailing is also popular. Before you reach Ensenada de los Muertos there is another cutoff going north that takes you to **Punta Arena de la Ventana**, another popular fishing and boondocking beach.

THE ROUTES, TOWNS, AND CAMPGROUNDS

PUERTO ESCONDIDO TO CIUDAD CONSTITUCIÓN
72 Miles (116 Km), 2 Hours

Five miles south of the junction for Puerto Escondido the highway begins to climb up into the Sierra Giganta.

At about Km 63 the road to Bahía Agua Verde goes left. See *Backroad Adventures* in this chapter for more information about this road.

Once the climb is over the road enters Arroyo Huatamote which leads out onto the gently sloping Magdalena Plain. The road is relatively straight and easy to drive as it gradually descends into irrigated farming country. You'll pass the gas station at Ley Federal de Aguas Número Uno and come to the Ciudad Insurgentes intersection where the highway turns 90 degrees left to head for Ciudad Constitución. If you turn right here you have access to Puerto Lopez Mateos, La Purísima, San José Comondú, San Miguel Comondú, and San Juanico. See the *Backroad Adventures* section of this chapter for more information about these destinations.

About 15 miles (24 km) after making the turn you'll enter Ciudad Constitución and see a Pemex station on the right side of the highway.

CIUDAD CONSTITUCIÓN (SEE-OOH-DAHD KOHN-STIH-TOO-SEE-OHN)
Population 45,000

This burgeoning farm town isn't found in most tourist guides. It has little to offer tourists but RV travelers will find services they can use. It has RV parks, supermarkets and automobile dealerships. Ciudad Constitución's location makes it a handy stop if you're headed north from beyond La Paz (only 130 easy miles (212 km) southeast) or need a base for whale watching in Bahía Magdalena to the west.

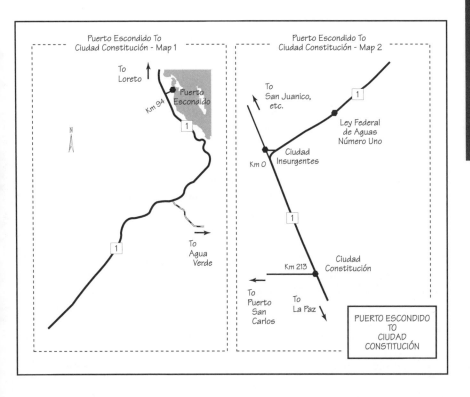

Ciudad Constitución Campgrounds

MANFRED'S RV TRAILER PARK
    Address: Apdo. 120, Cd. Constitución, B.C.S., México
    Telephone: (113) 2-11-03
    Price: Moderate

GPS Location: N 25° 02' 54.4", W 111° 40' 48.9"

This is a trailer park you just have to appreciate. The Austria-born owners are turning a dusty lot into a garden, at last count they had planted 1,600 shrubs and trees.

There are now 34 large pull-throughs with 15-amp plugs, sewer, and water and at least that many smaller back-in spaces with electricity and water. Two spotless restroom buildings have hot showers. There is a small swimming pool and even an Austrian restaurant with the food home-cooked by a lady who knows what she's doing.

The campground is very near the northwestern border of Ciudad Constitución and right on Mex 1 at about Km 212.

🚐 CAMPESTRE LA PILA BALNEARIO AND TRAILER PARK

Address: Apdo. 261, Ciudad Constitución, B.C.S., México
Telephone: (113) 2-05-82
Price: Low

GPS Location: N 25° 01' 02.0", W 111° 40' 37.1"

The La Pila is a balneario trailer park like El Palomar south of Ensenada. Winter travelers will probably not appreciate the pool quite as much as those passing this way during the really hot months.

There are 18 back-in spaces with 15-amp plugs and water. Sites are separated by grassy areas and the camping area is a very large lot surrounded by palm trees. The nicely landscaped pool area next to the camping area has the bathrooms and there are hot water showers. There is a dump station.

The turn-off from Mex 1 to the campground is near the south end of Ciudad Constitución at the point where the lateral streets begin. Turn west and follow the high tension electrical lines for .7 miles (1.1 km) and turn left into the campground at the sign. The campground is around to the left near the pools, the office in the large building on the right. There is plenty of room to maneuver.

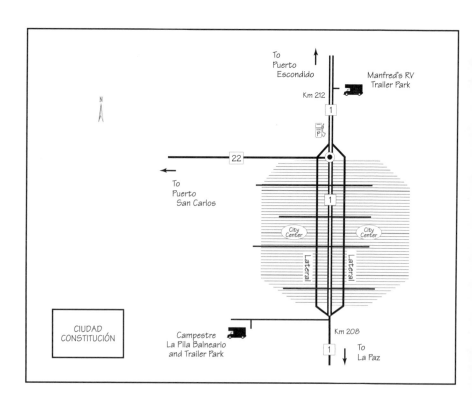

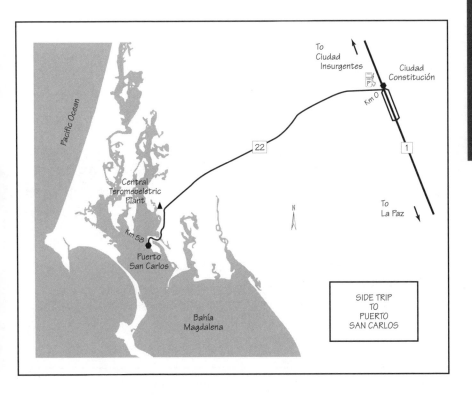

SIDE TRIP TO PUERTO SAN CARLOS
34 Miles (55 Km), .75 Hour

The road out to San Carlos heads west from the middle of Ciudad Constitución. This is a fine two-lane paved highway running across the very flat coastal plain. You'll know you're getting close when you spot the big electrical generation plant.

PUERTO SAN CARLOS (PWER-TOW SAHN KAR-LOHS)
Population 5,000

This little town serves as one of the only two deep-water ports on the west coast of the Baja, the other is Ensenada far to the north. Puerto San Carlos' port is primarily used for exporting the farm products of the plain to the east, and also for offloading fuel for the big electrical plant that is located there, one of three on the Baja. Puerto San Carlos also provides access to Bahía Magdalena, one of the three gray-whale watching locations on the Baja. The cannery is the largest building in town, the smell of fish processing tends to be noticeable almost everywhere.

Bahía Magdalena's protected waters are a good place to use your small boat, the fishing is excellent. It's also good kayaking and windsurfing water. There is a concrete launch ramp in town. Gray whales are present from January to March and during this season boating is limited to certain areas and boating permits are required. Panga operators offer whale-watching tours.

Puerto San Carlos has only small stores but does have several restaurants. During whale-watching season there are actually quite a few tourists in town.

Puerto San Carlos Campground

RV PARK NANCY
   Telephone: (113) 6-01-95
   Price: Moderate

GPS Location: N 24° 47' 27.6", W 112° 06' 37.4"

This is a small new RV park in a town that has needed such a facility for some time.

There are 8 back-in sites with 15-amp plugs and water, also a dump station. The lot where the RV park is located is small, maneuvering room is limited, but by backing

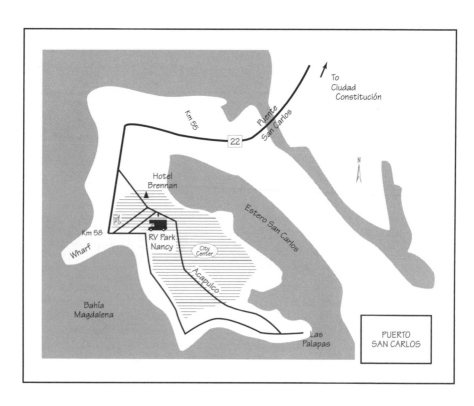

the short distance from the street rigs to 40 feet should fit. The restroom has a flush toilet and hot shower.

As you come in to San Carlos you will pass the huge power plant and then cross a slough onto the island. Watch for the sign for San Carlos. The left turn for the RV park is in another .1 mile (.2 km), there is a sign. The RV park is .4 mile (.6 km) down this road on the right.

CIUDAD CONSTITUCIÓN TO LA PAZ
130 Miles (210 Km), 3.75 Hours

The road south from Ciudad Constitución is flat and pretty much straight for 50 miles (82 km). You'll soon pass through the roadside town of El Cien, so named because it is 100 kilometers from La Paz. There's a Pemex station here with gas and diesel.

Fourteen miles (23 km) south of El Cien the road goes west for **Punta Conejo** which offers access to the coast. See this chapter's *Backroad Adventures* for more information about this road.

From El Cien the road crosses a region of hills and the highway is slower going, just exercise a little patience and soon you'll be in La Paz. As you finally begin to descend

GREEN ANGEL ASSISTING AN RVER

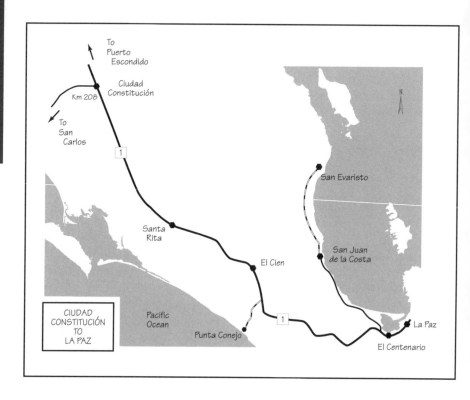

toward the coast you'll see La Paz ahead. Just before you reach the outlying town of El Centenario the road to **San Evaristo** goes left, this road is described in this chapter's *Backroad Adventures.*

LA PAZ (LAW PAHS)
Population 170,000

A favorite city on the Baja Peninsula, La Paz has lots of stores for supplies and a number of good campgrounds. Good, not fancy! This is not really a tourist town although it does have tourist amenities like hotels, good restaurants, beaches, and tour operators.

La Paz has been continuously occupied by Europeans only since 1811. Earlier settlement attempts, including one by Cortez in person, were not successful. The local Indians were not cooperative.

The city feels more like a larger mainland city than any other on the Baja. The waterfront **malecón** is good for strolling and you'll enjoy exploring the older part of town a few blocks back from the water. La Paz's best **beaches** are outside town toward and

A POPULAR RESTAURANT ON LA PAZ'S MALECÓN

past Pichilingue and are virtually empty except on weekends. There's a simple museum, the **Museum of Anthropology**, covering the area's early inhabitants. **Ferries** to the mainland cities of Topolobampo and Mazatlán dock at Pichilingue, see the *Ferries* section in the *Details, Details, Details* chapter.

La Paz Campgrounds

OASIS RV PARK

Address:	Km 15 Carr. Transp. al Norte, La Paz, B.C.S, México
Telephone:	(112) 4-60-90
Price:	Moderate

GPS Location: N 24° 06' 34.3", W 110° 24' 59.8"

This is a very small park located west of La Paz. It is in the small town of El Centenario and is located right on a rather marshy beach.

There are 24 back-in spaces, all with 15-amp plugs, sewer, and water. The restrooms are old but clean, they have tiled floors, white painted walls, and hot water showers. There is a nice swimming pool, a coin-operated laundry, and a restaurant/bar overlooking the beach. Some English is spoken and reservations are taken.

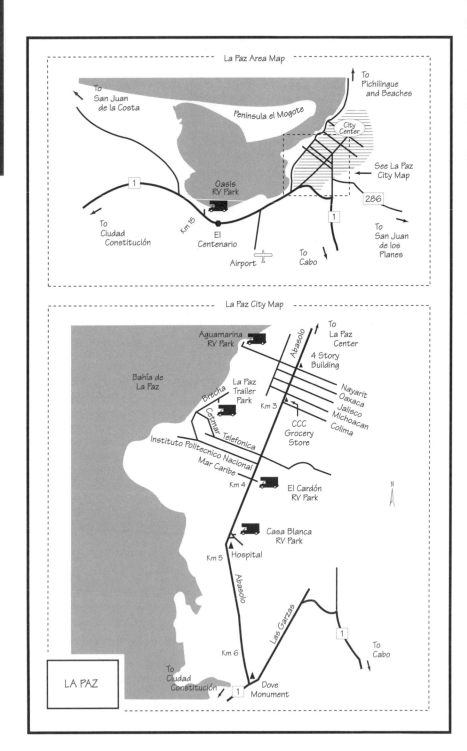

The campground is on the water side of Mex 1 half way between the Km 14 and Km 15 markers. It is in the town of El Centenario which is just west of La Paz.

CASA BLANCA RV PARK

Address: Carret. Al Norte Km 4.5, Esq. Av. Delfines, Apdo. 681, Fracc. Fidepaz, La Paz, C.P. 23094 B.C.S., México

Telephone and Fax: (112) 4-00-09

Price: Moderate

GPS Location: N 24° 07' 53.9", W 110° 20' 29.0"

The Casa Blanca is quite nice, very tidy, easy to find, and usually has lots of room.

There are 43 slots with electricity, sewer, and water. Some sites have 50-amp plugs, otheres are 15 amp. One is a pull-through, the others are all back-in spaces. The entire area is hard-packed sand and spaces are separated with low concrete curbs. The restrooms are plain but clean and have hot showers. The entire campground is surrounded by a high white concrete wall. It is good for security but seems to keep the temperature in the campground about 5 degrees higher than anywhere else in town. There is a swimming pool, a decent tennis court, and a palapa meeting/party room. There is often no one around to collect the fees, a siesta is taken from one to four in the afternoon, just pull in and park and someone will eventually show up.

LA PAZ'S CATHEDRAL AT THE DOWNTOWN ZÓCALO

The Casa Blanca is right off Abasolo. Zero your odometer at the dove statue (whale's tale) as you come into town, the campground is on the right at 1.2 miles (1.9 km).

EL CARDÓN RV PARK

Address:	Km 4 Transpeninsular, Apdo. 104, La Paz, C.P. 23000 B.C.S., México
Telephone:	(112) 2-12-61
Price:	Moderate

GPS Location: N 24° 08' 08.0", W 110° 20' 16.4"

The El Cardón is an older trailer park, but was being spiffed up a bit last time we visited. There is now an internet access operation located in the building out front, very handy.

There are about 60 usable spaces, most with 15-amp plugs, sewer, and water. Some also have patios and palapas for shade. Many are pull-throughs. The campground has two restroom blocks, one is fine with tile and hot water, the other is best ignored. Water at this campground is slightly salty but they do have a city water tap, ask about the location. This campground also has a swimming pool and a coin-operated laundry. There is a fence around the campground and a night watchman.

The El Cardón is right off Abasolo. Zero your odometer at the dove (whale's tail) statue and you'll see the campground on the right at 1.6 miles (2.6 km).

AQUAMARINA RV PARK

Address:	Nayarit Street # 10, Apdo. 133, La Paz, B.C.S, México
Telephone:	(112) 2-37-61
Fax:	(112) 5-62-28
Price:	Expensive

GPS Location: N 24° 09' 01.2", W 110° 20' 09.4"

We think this little campground is La Paz's nicest trailer park but you can make up your own mind. This is a well-kept park with flowering plants and lots of shade.

There are 19 back-in slots, all have 50 and 30-amp plugs, sewer, water, a patio and shade. Really big rigs might find this campground a little cramped. In the center of the park is a swimming pool and covered patio. Restrooms are well maintained and clean, they have hot water showers. The same owners have a dock in front of the campground where larger yachts tie up, there is a coin-operated laundry in the building they use as an office for both operations. English is spoken and reservations are recommended. This is the La Paz campground most likely to fill up.

The campground is located at the ocean end of Av. Nayarit, which is a dirt street off Absolo as it comes into La Paz. If you zero your odometer at the dove statue (some people see a whale's tail instead) Nayarit goes to the left at 2.5 miles (4 km). There is a small trailer pictogram sign marking the street and a four-story white building with balconies on the right opposite the turn. Follow Nayarit to the end, about .4 mile (.6 km) and you'll find the gate on your right at the beach. You'll pass another gate before reaching this one, it is the night gate and you won't be able to enter here during the day. This park has good security.

🚐 LA PAZ TRAILER PARK

Address:	Brecha California #1010, P.O. Box 482, La Paz, B.C.S., México
Telephone:	(112) 2-87-87
Fax:	(112) 2-99-38
Price:	Expensive

GPS Location: N 24° 08' 42.9", W 110° 20' 31.2"

This large park is a little off the beaten path which is good, less road noise. Unless it is filled by a caravan you can usually find a place to camp here even without reservations.

There are about 40 campsites, both pull-through and back-in. They have 30-amp plugs, sewer, and water. The sites are completely paved over and the few palms provide little shade but there should be plenty of room for slide-outs. The tiled restrooms are clean and modern and have hot showers. There is a swimming pool and coin-operated laundry. Reservations are accepted.

As you enter La Paz zero your odometer at the dove statue (whale's tail). At 1.7 miles (2.8 km) turn left on the first paved road after you pass the El Cardón Trailer Park, it has a stop light. This is Ave. Telefonica. Drive straight for .4 mile (.6 km) to a Y, take the right fork onto Cetmar and drive another block. Turn right and you will see the RV park on your right.

SIDE TRIP TO LA VENTANA
28 Miles (45 Km), .75 Hour

From La Paz you can follow a paved highway (BCS 286) southeast to the farming country in the vicinity of San Juan de los Planes. Just to the north along the coast of Bahía La Ventana is the town of La Ventana, a popular windsurfing destination. The campground located there is discussed below. There are also boondocking destinations along the coast to the east of Los Planes at Punta Arenas de la Ventana and Ensenada de los Muertos, see the *Backroad Adventures* section above for information about these.

From the boulevard called Calz. Forjadores de Sudcalifornia which is an extension of Mex 1 from the south in eastern La Paz follow the signs for Highway 286. The signs will say Los Planes. The two-lane paved highway climbs as it leaves town, it reaches a summit at 15 miles (24 km). Twenty-three miles (37 km) from La Paz you'll reach an intersection, turn left. This road is marked for La Ventana and El Sargento. You'll reach La Ventana in 5 miles (8 kilometers).

LA VENTANA (LAH VEHN-TAH-NAH)

This is a very small village stretched along the west shore of the bay. Actually, the towns of El Teso and El Sargento, both to the north, tend to merge together with La

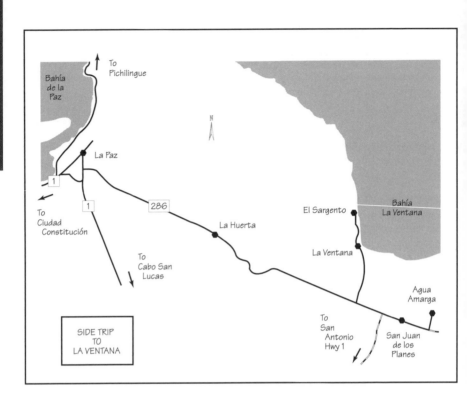

Ventana to form one town. Facilities in the towns are limited to a small store or two and a few restaurants.

La Ventana Campground

🚐 **PLAYAS MIRAMAR**
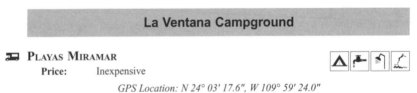
    Price: Inexpensive

GPS Location: N 24° 03' 17.6", W 109° 59' 24.0"

This campground is very popular with windsurfers, in fact, that's why it is here. Winter is the season with reliable winds from the north. Expect to find few RVs, it is usually filled with tents and vans.

The campground is a large flat sandy area directly adjoining the beach. You can park not twenty feet from the water. Watch for soft spots! Facilities consist of a couple of toilet blocks with flush toilets and cold water showers. There are a few water faucets

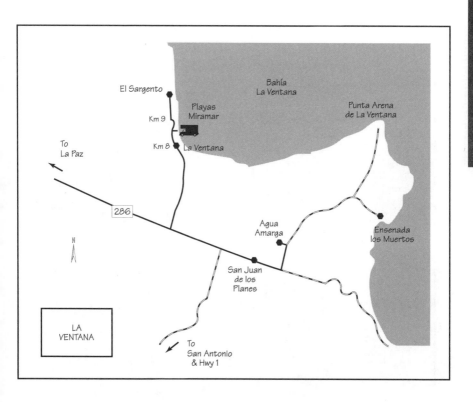

and also some scattered trees providing some shade. The entire area is fenced. There's a mini-super and a restaurant across the street.

As you enter La Ventana you can't miss the camping area and its chain-link fence on the right next to the beach.

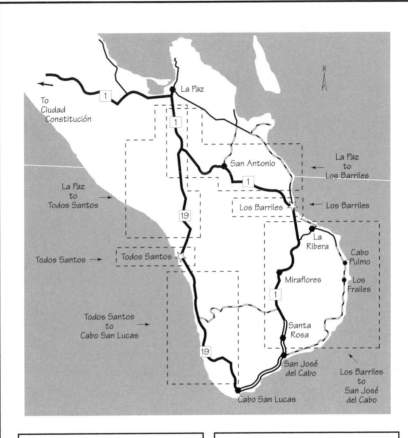

To
Ciudad
Constitución

La Paz

La Paz
to
Los Barriles

La Paz
to
Todos Santos

San Antonio

Los Barriles

Los Barriles

La
Ribera

Cabo
Pulmo

Todos Santos

Todos Santos

Miraflores

Los
Frailes

Todos Santos
to
Cabo San Lucas

Santa
Rosa

San José
del Cabo

Los Barriles
to
San José
del Cabo

Cabo San Lucas

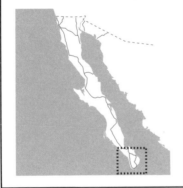

CHAPTER INDEX

Highlights . . . . Page 157
Roads and Fuel Availability . . . . Page 157
Sightseeing . . . . Page 158
Beaches and Water Sports . . . . . . Page 158
Fishing . . . . Page 158
Backroad Adventures . . . . Page 159
La Paz to Todos Santos . . . . Page 161
Todos Santos . . . . Page 161
Todos Santos to Cabo
   San Lucas . . . . Page 163
La Paz to Los Barriles . . . . Page 164
Los Barriles . . . . Page 165
Los Barriles to San José
   del Cabo . . . . Page 168

SOUTHERN LOOP

CHAPTER
· · · · · · · · · · · · 9
SOUTHERN LOOP

INTRODUCTION

This chapter of the book covers the area of the peninsula between La Paz and the Los Cabos area at the tip. The loop drive accesses both the west and east coasts, there are a good selection of destinations and activities.

Highlights

Todos Santos, near the west coast about half way between La Paz and the cape, has become something of an artist colony and day-trip destination for people who have flown in to Los Cabos. You'll find some good shopping and restaurants in the town.

Fishing fanatics congregate at **Los Barriles**. The combination of a decent campground and great fishing make this a place to stop or even base yourself for an extended stay.

Cabo Pulmo and **Los Frailes** offer some of the best diving, beach fishing, wind surfing and seaside boondocking on the whole peninsula.

Roads and Fuel Availability

South of La Paz there is a Y, you have a choice of traveling the west coast on Mex 19 or the eastern side of the peninsula on Mex 1. The Mex 19 route is a shorter and easier route to Los Cabos but the choice is yours, you'll probably drive the whole circle before you head back north.

The distance from La Paz to Cabo San Lucas via the western route is 99 miles (160 km). The kilometer markers on this highway, unlike all kilometers markers on Mex 1 in Baja Sur, run from north to south. They start with zero at the Y on Mex 1 at Km 185 and end with 124 in Cabo San Lucas.

The distance from La Paz to San José del Cabo in the Los Cabos area is 112 miles (181 km) via the eastern Mex 1 route. This is all two-lane blacktop except the last 6 miles (10 km) of 4-lane after you reach the main airport for the Los Cabos region just north of San José del Cabo. Kilometers on this section begin in Cabo San Lucas, they have reached 30 at San José del Cabo and 185 at the junction with Mex 19 south of La Paz and then 221 at La Paz.

Driving south on Mex 19 you'll find gas as follows, with types, and distances between stations: **La Paz**, gas and diesel; **Todos Santos**, gas and diesel, 48 miles (77 km); **Cabo San Lucas**, gas and diesel, 45 miles (73 km).

Driving south on Mex 1 you'll find gas as follows, with types and distances between stations: **La Paz**, gas and diesel; **San Antonio**, gas only, 36 miles (58 km); **Los Barriles**, gas and diesel, 28 miles (45 km); **Miraflores**, gas and diesel, 23 miles (37 km); **Santa Rosa**, gas and diesel, 22 miles (35 km); **San José del Cabo**, gas and diesel, 2 miles (3 km).

Sightseeing

Don't miss **Todos Santos** for excellent shopping and restaurants.

As you drive between San José del Cabo and Los Barriles you'll see a monument in the form of a big ball along the side of the road. This marks the **Tropic of Cancer**.

On Mex 1 just south of Los Barriles at Km 85 take the spur road about a mile and a half (2 km) out to **Santiago**. Once the site of a mission the little town now has a zoo that is fun to visit.

Beaches and Water Sports

There are excellent beaches for surfing along the west side of the peninsula. Access is probably easiest at the two campgrounds near Todos Santos: **San Pedrito** and **Los Cerritos**.

The east coast of the peninsula north of Los Cabos is accessible by dirt road, see the *Backroad Adventures* section below. **Cabo Pulmo** is home to one of the very few coral reefs on the whole west coast of the Americas and an excellent diving spot.

Fishing

Some of the best billfish fishing in the world is along the east coast of the peninsula. The reason is that deep water comes right close to shore. The fishing seasons are spring, summer and fall with May to July and October and November the best periods.

The area lacks formal ramps, La Paz and Cabo San Lucas are the closest. Boats are launched over the beach, there is a fairly sophisticated set-up for launching boat at Los Barriles using trucks.

Probably the best charter fishing is available at Los Barriles. There are both pangas and cabin boats available, good fishing waters are nearby, and campgrounds are handy.

If you are restricted to fishing from the beach you might want to try Los Frailes. An underwater canyon comes so close to shore here that billfish have actually been caught from the beach!

Backroad Adventures

See the *Backroad Driving* section of *Chapter 2 - Details, Details, Details* for essential information about driving off the main highway on the Baja and for a definition of road type classifications used below.

From Los Barriles - A road goes north along the coast. If you zero your odometer at Martin Verdugo's RV Park and drive north you will reach the small community of **Punta Pescadero** after 9 miles (15 km) and **El Cardonal** after 14 miles (23 km). In El Cardonal the El Cardonal Resort offers RV parking. This is normally a Type 2 road as far as the resort. The road continues north from El Cardonal to connect with the back road to La Paz at San Juan de los Planes, but the road north of El Cardonal is normally a Type 3 road.

From Km 93 Between San José del Cabo and Los Barriles - This is one of the more interesting back roads on the whole peninsula. Also one of the most heavily

SOUTHERN LOOP

BEACHSIDE CAMPING AT LOS CERRITOS

traveled, at least in the northern section. It follows the **eastern coastline of the peninsula** near the cape from San José del Cabo all the way north to La Ribera near Los Barriles. The better portion of the road is in the north so we'll describe it from north to south. On Mex 1 at Km 93 a paved road goes east toward La Ribera. Seven miles (11 km) from the junction another paved road goes south. Zero your odometer here at the turn. This road is gradually being upgraded, last time we checked the pavement ended at about 11 miles (17 km) from the turn. The Type 2 road continues to **Cabo Pulmo** (16 miles (26 km) from the turn), **Los Frailes** (21 miles (34 km) from the turn), and south all the way to San José del Cabo (55 miles (89 km) from the turn). The northern part of the road to Cabo Pulmo is usually Type 2, the southern portion usually Type 3. The condition of this road varies dramatically depending upon how much damage was done by erosion during the last rainy season and how much repair has been done. There are several places popular for boondocking along the road, particularly near Cabo Pulmo and Los Frailes.

From Km 71 Between San José del Cabo and Los Barriles - This is a road that passes across the lower elevations of the southern portion of the **Sierra de la Laguna**. If you are in the Los Cabos region and feel the need to do some exploring in your 4WD this is a possibility. The road is a Type 2 at the eastern end but becomes a Type 3 as it descends to Mex 19 near Km 71.

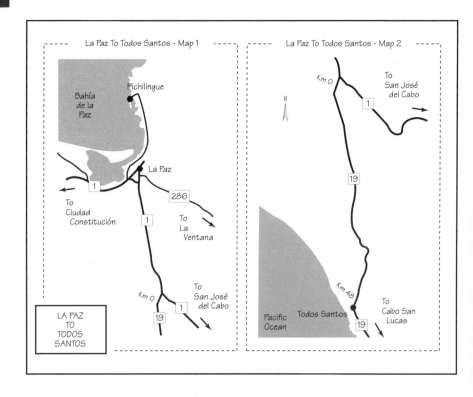

THE ROUTES, TOWNS, AND CAMPGROUNDS

LA PAZ TO TODOS SANTOS
48 Miles (77 Km), 1.50 Hours

Head out of town toward the south on Mex 1. In 19 miles (31 km) you'll come to a Y. Mex 1 continues straight, Mex 19 cuts off to the right. To get to Todos Santos we'll go right.

The green vegetation that appears as you approach Todos Santos is welcome after crossing miles of dry country. You'll enter the outskirts of town 29 miles (47 km) after turning right at the Y.

TODOS SANTOS (TOE-does SAHN-toes)
Population 3,000

Todos Santos is the Baja's art colony. This is an old mission and sugar cane town but today it is better known for the many Norteamericanos who have arrived in search of

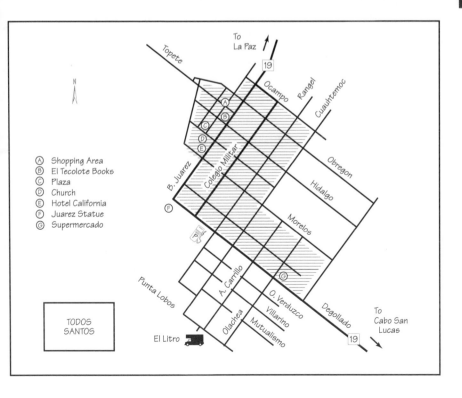

Ⓐ Shopping Area
Ⓑ El Tecolote Books
Ⓒ Plaza
Ⓓ Church
Ⓔ Hotel California
Ⓕ Juarez Statue
Ⓖ Supermercado

TODOS
SANTOS

a simple small-town ambiance. There are galleries, crafts stores, and restaurants, as well as a bookstore called El Tecolote. The town is only a mile or so from the coast, there are decent beaches near town but the one at the San Pedrito RV park is one of the best in the area. You're just south of the Tropic of Cancer in Todos Santos, that means you're in the Tropics!

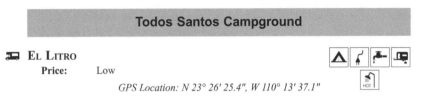

Todos Santos Campground

El Litro

    Price: Low

GPS Location: N 23° 26' 25.4", W 110° 13' 37.1"

This is a small campground on a dusty back road in the village of Todos Santos. The entrance road is a little tight but passable, once inside there's room for the largest rigs to maneuver. There's a definite small village Mexican ambiance to this campground.

The campground has 16 back-in spaces with 15-amp plugs, sewer, and water hook-ups. There is also a shaded area under a large tree for tent campers. Several of the spaces have patios, some are even shaded by palapas. A small building has two restrooms with flush toilets and hot water showers. The attendant is not always there but he'll be by in the evening to collect.

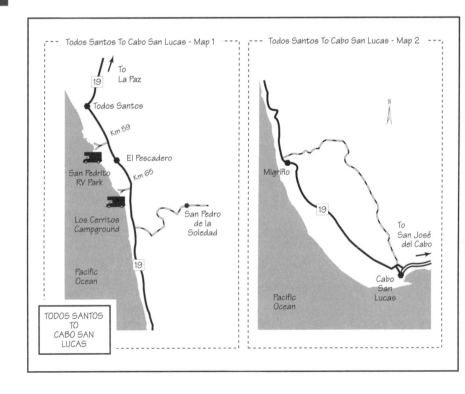

SOUTHERN LOOP

To find the campground turn west on Carrillo near the southern entrance to Todos Santos. The turn is marked by a campground sign. The campground is directly ahead .2 miles (.4 km) from the turn.

TODOS SANTOS TO CABO SAN LUCAS
45 Miles (73 Km), 1.25 Hours

Heading south from Todos Santos you'll find yourself much closer to the Pacific Ocean than you have been since San Quintín. Many small roads lead west to the beach. Two that you'll see lead to campgrounds, they're listed below. Seven miles (11 km) south of Todos Santos is the small farming town of El Pescadero. Watch for the restaurant with the tree growing through the roof.

As you get closer to Cabo the road turns inland. Before long you'll find yourself descending the last hill in to town. The main road doglegs to the left letting you bypass the chaotic streets of this fast-growing town with you RV. All of the RV parks are accessible from Mex 1 to the east of town, just see the following chapter for the details.

Todos Santos to Cabo San Lucas Campgrounds

SAN PEDRITO RV PARK

Address:	Apdo. 15, Todos Santos, B.C.S., México
Telephone:	(112) 7-99-09
Fax:	(112) 3-46-43
Price:	Moderate

GPS Location: N 23° 23' 29.3", W 110° 11' 17.2"

San Pedrito is located on a beautiful beach some 4 miles (6.5 km) south of Todos Santos. There's a sandy but decent road leading the 1.8 miles (2.9 km) from Mex 19 out to the campground. Once there you have a choice, there's an RV park with full hookups and a camping area next to the beach with no hookups. This is a popular surfing beach and many van and tent campers use the less expensive no-hookup area. The full-hookup area is just as popular with RVers.

The RV campground has 71 pull-through spaces with 15-amp plugs, sewer, and water. Exercise caution about straying off well-used roadways, this is a sandy area and there are soft spots. Restrooms for the RV area are clean and in good repair, they have hot showers. The San Pedrito has a restaurant/bar with satellite TV, a pool, and a laundry. There are even a few cabañas for rent. English is spoken and reservations are accepted.

The cutoff for the campground is near the Km 59 marker about 4 miles (6.5 km) south of Todos Santos. It is well marked with a large sign. The sandy road to the campground has a Y at 1.4 miles (2.3 km), go left. You'll reach the campground gate at 1.7 miles (2.7 km).

🚐 LOS CERRITOS CAMPGROUND

Price: Inexpensive

GPS Location: N 23° 20' 49.2", W 110° 09' 43.2"

This is another of the old government campgrounds. It is located just above a beautiful beach, a very popular surfing location.

Campers park either in the campground or in front above the beach. The front fence to the government campground is gone so there is little difference. The hookups other than sewer are non-functional anyway. There are no restrooms other than pit toilets.

The road out to the campground is .1 mile (.2 km) south of the Km 65 marker. The road is usually unmarked. It is a rough dusty road but can be traveled by any size rig. Driving toward the beach you'll reach a Y in 1.3 miles (2.1 km). The right fork takes you directly to a beach parking area, the left to the camping area in .3 miles (.5 km).

LA PAZ TO LOS BARRILES
64 Miles (103 Km), 2 Hours

Heading south from La Paz you'll come to a Y in the road after 19 miles (31 km). The left fork is Mex 1, that's the one we'll take. Soon the road begins climbing into the northern reaches of the Sierra Laguna.

Two towns soon appear. **El Triunfo**, 13 miles (21 km) from the Y is an old gold and silver mining town. The tall smokestack marks the smelter. A few miles farther on is **San Antonio**, a farming town that fills a valley. There is a gravel road, usually a badly washboarded Type 1, that connects this town with San Juan de los Planes and La Ventana to the north.

Near Km 110 there is a paved cutoff to the left that leads to a coastal road and central Los Barriles.

La Paz to Los Barriles Campground

🚐 RANCHO VERDE RV HAVEN

Address: 7975 Dahlberg Siding, Eureka,
                  MT 59917 USA (Reservations)
Telephone: (406) 882-4887 (U.S.)
Fax: (406) 882-4987 (U.S.)
Internet: www.rancho-verde.com
Price: Moderate

GPS Location: N 23° 45' 45.6", W 109° 58' 46.2"

This is a newer campground located in the mountains west of Los Barriles. The green high wooded country is a nice change from flat desert and sandy seashore.

There are 29 widely separated back-in spaces. Each one has water and sewer hookups, there is no electricity. The restrooms are in a simple palapa roof building but are

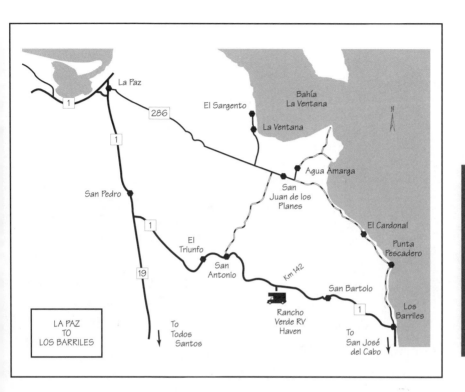

extremely clean and have hot water for showers. This is ranch country and there are miles of trails for hiking and bird-watching. Lots are for sale but you need not fear high pressure sales tactics. You may fall in love with the owner's open-air living area and RV shelter next to the campground.

Rancho Verde is located in the mountains about 20 miles (33 km) west of Los Barriles near San Bartolo. The entrance road is off Mex 1 near Km 142.

LOS BARRILES (LOES BAR-EEL-ACE)
Population 1,000

Los Barriles and nearby Buena Vista and La Ribera are enjoying a surge of RVer popularity as development overtakes the campgrounds farther south near Cabo. This is an excellent area for windsurfing. You'll find a number of restaurants, some small hotels, trailer parks, an airstrip, and a few shops in Los Barriles. Fishing is quite good because deep water is just offshore, campers keep their car-top boats on the beach. Trucks are used for launching boats, there is no ramp.

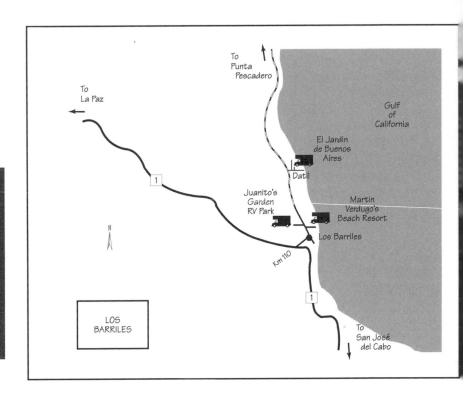

Los Barriles Campgrounds

🚐 MARTIN VERDUGO'S BEACH RESORT

Address: Apdo. 17, Los Barriles, C.P. 23501 B.C.S., México
Telephone: (114) 1-00-54
E-mail: martinv@lapaz.cromwell.com.mx
Price: Moderate

GPS Location: N 23° 40' 55.9", W 109° 41' 56.1"

The largest of the Los Barriles campgrounds is a very popular places. It's located on a beautiful beach although there are two large motel buildings between the camping area and the water. There is a swimming pool and a palapa bar overlooking the beach. The resort offers fishing expeditions on its own cruisers and room to keep your own small boat on the beach.

The campground has 65 RV spaces with 15 and 30-amp plugs, sewer, and water. The RVs seem a little crowded but plenty of big rigs find room. There are also 25 tent spaces with water and electric hookups. Restrooms are clean and modern, they have hot water showers. There is a coin-operated laundry, a library in the office, a restaurant atop one of the two hotel buildings, and of course the pool and palapa bar over-

VIEW FROM MARTIN VERDUGO'S BEACH RESORT

looking the beach. English is spoken and reservations are recommended. They require a $50 deposit.

Take the Los Barriles exit from Mex 1 between La Paz and Cabo San Lucas near the Km 110 marker. You'll reach a T in .3 miles (.5 km). Turn left and you'll see the RV park on the right in .2 miles (.3 km).

JUANITO'S GARDEN RV PARK

Address:	Apdo. 50, Los Barriles, C.P. 23501 B.C.S., México
Telephone and Fax:	(114) 1-00-24
E-mail:	hotellosbarriles@cabonet.net.mx
Price:	Moderate

GPS Location: N 23° 41' 00.7", W 109° 41' 56.9"

This smaller Los Barriles RV park is almost entirely filled with permanently-located units, but continues to be an acceptable alternative if you can get in.

The RV park has only three open spaces remaining, all with 30-amp plugs, sewer, and water. Restrooms are clean and modern and have hot water showers. There is a coin-operated laundry. A motel with the same management as the RV park is located on the property, it has a beautiful swimming pool that can be used by guests at the RV park. English is spoken and telephone reservations are recommended.

Take the Los Barriles exit from Mex 1 between La Paz and Cabo San Lucas near the Km 110 marker. You'll reach a T in .3 miles (.5 km). Turn left and you'll see the RV park on the left in .3 miles (.5 km).

EL JARDIN DE BUENOS AIRES
   Price: Low

GPS Location: N 23° 41' 54.5", W 109° 42' 05.3"

This is a new place gradually being built in a residential area to the north of the other Los Barriles campgrounds.

There are 10 sites with 30-amp plugs, sewer and water. There are currently no other facilities so the place is only suitable for self-contained rigs. Each site is separately fenced and has a patio. They are nice, the owner is aiming at folks who stay the season. He says he's planning more sites as well as bathrooms, a laundry, and a pool.

Take the Los Barriles exit from Mex 1 between La Paz and Cabo San Lucas near the Km 110 marker. You'll reach a T in .3 miles (.5 km). Turn left and drive 1.5 miles (2.4 km) and turn right on Datil. You will pass the end of the pavement and be on a sand and dirt road. Just after the turn you will see the campground on the left.

LOS BARRILES TO SAN JOSÉ DEL CABO
48 Miles (77 Km), 1.5 Hours

The road south from Los Barriles toward San José del Cabo does not follow the coast. To reach it you'll want to take the cutoff from Mex 1 to the left at Km 93. It leads northeastward to a small community on the coast known as **La Ribera**. There is a campground in this town that is described below. There is also a road running south along the coast, see *Backroad Adventures* above for more about this road.

Continuing south on Mex 1 you'll soon see a cutoff to the right near Km 85 for **Santiago**. It's a little over a mile off the road and has a Pemex, as well as a zoo. This was once a mission town but the mission is gone, now it's a ranching and farming town with a town square.

When you cross the **Tropic of Cancer** at latitude N 23° 27' near Km 81 you have entered the tropics. There's a monument in the shape of a globe, stop for a picture.

Miraflores, right from near Km 71, is known for its leathercrafts, there's a Pemex on the highway.

The road turns to four lanes near the international airport at Km 44, about 6 miles (10 km) north of San José del Cabo. You're about to enter Baja's tourist zone. See the next chapter for details.

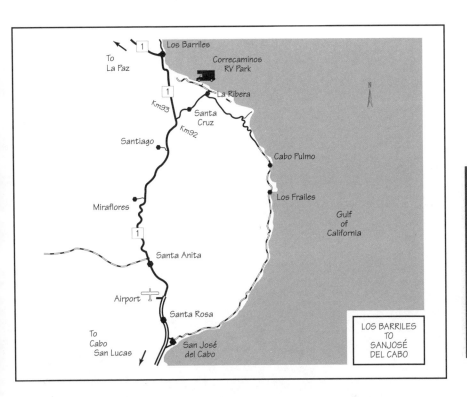

SOUTHERN LOOP

Los Barriles to San José del Cabo Campground

CORRECAMINOS RV PARK
    Price: Moderate

GPS Location: N 23° 36' 00.4", W 109° 35' 15.7"

If you are looking for an out of the way, slow-moving, friendly place to spend some time this is it. Located near the quiet little town of La Ribera, Correcaminos RV Park might seem like a little piece of paradise. The people we met there certainly think so.

Correcaminos is nothing fancy. There are 10 spaces with electricity, sewer and water. If you don't need hookups there's lots more space, including an area near the beach. The bathrooms are rustic and have hot water showers. There's also a washing machine. The wide beach is about a quarter-mile away along the sandy road that runs through the campground. Light boats can be launched across the sand.

To find the campground turn east on the paved road near Km 93 south of Los Barriles. The excellent road runs 7.3 miles (11.8 km) to the small village of La Ribera. Drive through town, and at the T just after the pavement ends and down a hill turn left. You'll see the campground entrance on the right .2 miles (.3 km) after the turn.

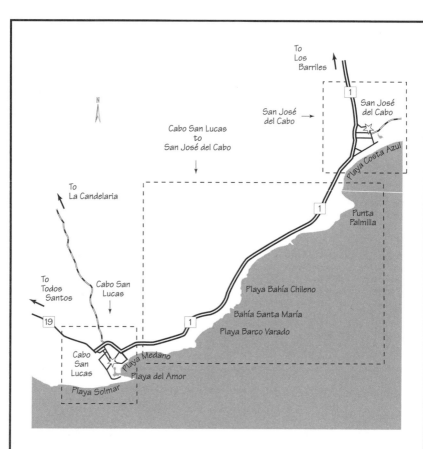

To
Los
Barriles

San José
del Cabo

1

San José
del Cabo

Cabo San Lucas
to
San José del Cabo

Playa Costa Azul

To
La Candelaria

1

Punta
Palmilla

To
Todos
Santos

Cabo San
Lucas

Playa Bahía Chileno

19

Bahía Santa María

1

Playa Barco Varado

Cabo
San
Lucas

Playa Medano

Playa del Amor

Playa Solmar

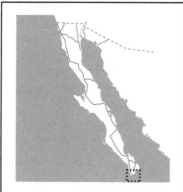

CHAPTER INDEX

Highlights .... Page 171
Roads and Fuel Availability .... Page 172
Sightseeing .... Page 172
Golf .... Page 172
Beaches and Water Sports .... Page 173
Fishing .... Page 173
Backroad Adventures .... Page 173
Cabo San Lucas .... Page 174
Cabo San Lucas to San José
  del Cabo .... Page 176
San José del Cabo .... Page 179

LOS CABOS

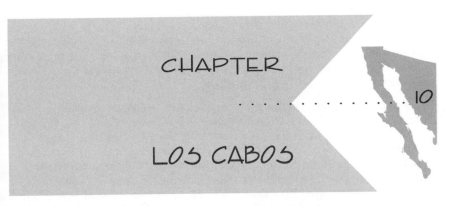

CHAPTER

· · · · · · · · · · · · · 10

LOS CABOS

INTRODUCTION

For many campers headed down the peninsula for the first time Los Cabos (The Capes) is the end of the rainbow, the ultimate destination. While Los Cabos is a world-class resort and very popular destination for tourists flying out from the U.S. and Canada you will probably find that you've seen a fine selection of much more desirable stops during your trip south. The truth is that Los Cabos is hectic and oriented toward folks looking for a few days of fun in the sun.

Many old-timers decry the growth and avoid Los Cabos at all costs. That reaction to the Los Cabos area is probably a little extreme. Los Cabos has lots to offer and a good number of decent RV parks provide excellent accommodations. The number of RV parks in the Los Cabos area seems to be declining, however, as land values increase.

The Los Cabos area really covers two major towns: Cabo San Lucas and San José del Cabo which is located about 20 miles (33 km) east. San José del Cabo is the older town and is more relaxed and comfortable. Cabo San Lucas, on the other hand, is chock full of hotels, restaurants, shops, and activity. The area between the two is known as the Cabo Corridor. Most campgrounds are located in the Cabo Corridor just to the east of Cabo San Lucas.

Highlights

Los Cabos is probably best known for its **deep-sea fishing**. This is one of the world's premier fly-in resort areas as well as a cruise ship port so it also offers lots of excellent **restaurants**, **shopping**, and **golf**. It's much different than the much quieter country to the north, if you judiciously indulge in the entertainment offerings you'll find the area to be a lot of fun.

Roads and Fuel Availablilty

The primary road on this section of the peninsula is the four-lane free highway between Cabo San Lucas and the Los Cabos International Airport which is located about six miles (10 km) north of San José del Cabo. The distance between Cabo San Lucas and San José del Cabo is 18 miles (29 km). The road is marked with kilometer posts, they start in Cabo San Lucas and have reached 30 by the time you reach San José del Cabo. This road was upgraded to four lanes less than ten years ago and when this was done the kilometer posts moved, some addresses along the road reflect the old numbers. Our directions to campgrounds use the new mileposts, the ones in place during February 2000.

Fuel is readily available in the area. There is a Pemex station near the intersection of the road that circles Cabo San Lucas and Mex 1. It has gas and diesel. There is another in the northern outskirts of Cabo San Lucas along Mex 19. Eastward along the Cabo Corridor toward San José del Cabo there is a Pemex station right along the road on the north side near Km 23. At the north side of San José del Cabo near the intersection with Calle Zaragoza there is a Pemex station and finally, about 2.2 miles (3.5 km) north in the suburb of Santa Rosa there is another on the east side of Mex 1. All of these stations sell both gas and diesel except the one near Km 23 which does not have diesel.

Sightseeing

Probably the most popular excursion from Cabo San Lucas is the boat ride out to see **Los Arcos** at **Finisterra** (Land's End), perhaps with a stop at **Playa del Amor** (Lover's Beach). This trip really does offer the chance for some spectacular photos. You may see sea lions on the rocks.

A popular stop for visitors is the **glass factory** in Cabo San Lucas.

San José del Cabo's **Boulevard Mijares** is a good place to do some shopping for Mexican folk art and souvenirs. It's much quieter than similar places in Cabo San Lucas, and just as good.

There are some spectacular **hotels** in Los Cabos. You might want to visit the **Hotel Presidente Inter-Continental Los Cabos** along the beach in San José del Cabo; **Hotel La Jolla** just west of the Brisa del Mar RV Park; **Hotel Palmilla** near Km 27 along the Cabo Corridor; the **Cabo Real** resort area including the Hotel Westin Regina, the Hotel Melia, and the Hotel Casa del Mar, all between Km 39 and Km 24 of the Cabo Corridor; **Hotel Cabo San Lucas** near Km 15 of the Cabo Corridor; **Hotel Twin Dolphin** near Km 11 of the Cabo Corridor; **Cabo del Sol** resort area near Km 10 of the Cabo Corridor (great views of Land's End); the **Hotel Finisterra** perched on the ridge west of the marina in Cabo San Lucas (the bar is good for whalewatching); or the **Hacienda Beach Resort** or **Melia San Lucas** along Playa El Medano looking out toward Land's End.

Golf

Los Cabos now has no less than six golf courses with more to come. Most of these are world-class, with prices to match. The most economical is the 9-hole **San Jose Campo del Golf** located between downtown San José del Cabo and the beach hotel strip. Others are the **Palmilla Golf Course, Cabo Real Golf Course, Cabo del Sol Golf Course, Cabo San Lucas Country Club and Golf Course**, and the **El Dorado**.

Beaches and Water Sports

The best known beach in Los Cabos must be **Playa del Amor** (Lover's Beach). It is a small beach out on the Lands End cape that is hemmed in by rocks. Snorkeling is excellent here. Access is via water taxis and tour boats from the Cabo San Lucas harbor. Just offshore (to the east) is a 3,000-foot underwater canyon that is the most popular scuba location in the area, unique sandfalls down the underwater cliffs are the attraction.

The most populous swimming beach near Cabo San Lucas is called **Playa Medano**. It stretches east from the harbor mouth. The beach on the western side of Land's End is called **Playa Solmar**, the water is considered dangerous and access is difficult so the beach doesn't get much use.

Between Cabo San Lucas and San José del Cabo, along the Cabo Corridor, there are quite a few beaches although many are difficult to access because hotels, condos, and housing developments overlook them. Access routes of one kind or another are usually available since under the law access can not be cut off. Easiest access is to **Playa Barco Varado** (Shipwreck Beach) near Km 9, **Bahía Santa María** near Km 13, and **Playa Bahía Chileno** near Km 15.

The **Playa Costa Azul** is a long beautiful beach stretching from the lagoon at San José del Cabo westward for several miles. The Brisa del Mar RV Park is located on this beach.

A popular **scuba diving** spot offshore (also a popular fishing spot) is the **Gorda Banks** with a depth of 110 feet. The location has lots of fish, sometimes whales, and also black coral.

Fishing

Fishing for large game fish is the thing to do in Los Cabos. The possible catch includes marlin, sailfish, dorado, and tuna. The months for the best fishing are May to July and October to December. Catch-and-release fishing is popular here, no one wants to see the fishing decline as it inevitably would if everyone kept all the fish caught. It is easy to arrange charter fishing trips in cruisers or pangas.

Backroad Adventures

See the *Backroad Driving* section of *Chapter 2 - Details, Details, Details* for essential information about driving off the main highway on the Baja and for a definition of road types used below.

From Km 1.7 of the Cabo San Lucas Ring Road - The small village of **La Candelaria**, located in the foothills of the Sierra Laguna north of Cabo is becoming a popular destination for tours from Cabo. The town is known for its handicrafts (pot-

CABO SAN LUCAS FISHING CRUISER

tery, baskets, and simple furniture) and for its "white magic" witches, actually traditional curanderos or healers with a knowledge of local herbs. You can drive there yourself from a turnoff on the road that runs around the east side of Cabo San Lucas some 1.1 miles (1.7 km) north of its intersection with Mex 1. This road (normally a Type 2) leads about 25 miles (40 km) north to the village. From there a rough normally Type 3 road leads on to Mex 19 north of Cabo.

🚗 **From very near the central shopping district in San José del Cabo -** A dirt road goes east to the beachside village of La Playa. The road continues beyond and leads all the way up the coast to **Los Frailes**, **Cabo Pulmo**, and **La Ribera**. It is described in more detail in the previous chapter under *Backroad Adventures*. This is usually a Type 3 road south of Los Frailes and then Type 2 to the north but conditions vary a lot.

THE ROUTES, TOWNS, AND CAMPGROUNDS

CABO SAN LUCAS (KAH-BOW SAHN LOO-KAHS)
Population 25,000

Cabo San Lucas is the major resort town in the Los Cabos area. It is filled with fly-in visitors and often also with cruise ship passengers wandering the streets during their short visits.

The town is centered around the **harbor**. The harbor itself is surrounded by modern hotels and shops, they almost cut it off from the streets of town which stretch off to the north. These streets become less touristy and more Mexican as you progress northward, there is a large population here attracted in recent years by the tourism industry.

In the harbor area you can arrange for a boat trip. Many people come to Los Cabos primarily for the fishing and this is where most of the charter boats are based. You can also find water taxis or tour boats to take you out to see **Finisterra (Lands End)** or visit **Playa Amor (Lover's Beach)**. There's always a lot of activity in the harbor and you can stroll along taking it in.

In the streets immediately north of the harbor you'll find most of the **restaurants and tourist-oriented shops** in town. This is actually a pretty good place to shop for Mexican gifts and art. There are also some supermarkets in the area.

The closest beach to Cabo San Lucas is **Playa Medano**. It is on the far side of the harbor. Driving access is actually best from Mex 1 near the point where Mex 19 joins it just east of town.

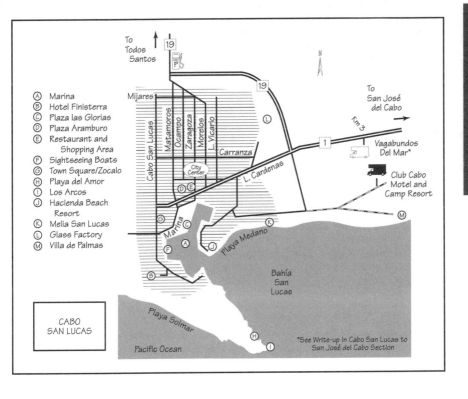

Ⓐ Marina
Ⓑ Hotel Finisterra
Ⓒ Plaza las Glorias
Ⓓ Plaza Aramburo
Ⓔ Restaurant and
      Shopping Area
Ⓕ Sightseeing Boats
Ⓖ Town Square/Zocalo
Ⓗ Playa del Amor
Ⓘ Los Arcos
Ⓙ Hacienda Beach
      Resort
Ⓚ Melia San Lucas
Ⓛ Glass Factory
Ⓜ Villa de Palmas

To Todos Santos

19

19

To San José del Cabo

N

Km 3

1

Mijares

Matamoros
Ocampo
Zaragoza
Morelos
L. Vicario

Cabo San Lucas

Carranza

City Center

L. Cardenas

Vagabundos Del Mar*

Club Cabo Motel and Camp Resort

Marina

Playa Medano

Bahía San Lucas

Playa Solmar

Pacific Ocean

CABO SAN LUCAS

*See Write-up in Cabo San Lucas to San José del Cabo Section

LOS CABOS

Cabo San Lucas Campground

CLUB CABO MOTEL AND CAMP RESORT

Address:	Apdo. 463, Cabo San Lucas, B.C.S, México
Telephone and Fax:	(114) 3-33-48
Internet:	mexonline.com/clubcabo
E-mail:	clubcabo@cabonet.net.mx
Price:	Expensive

GPS Location: N 22° 54' 00.3", W 109° 53' 42.6"

This campground is different than the others in Cabo. It somehow seems more European than Mexican. It is a combination motel and campground and is slightly off the beaten track.

There are 10 campsites, most have 15-amp plugs, sewer, and water. These are all back-in sites. There isn't room for really big rigs, 24 feet is about the maximum length motorhome that can easily enter and park. The bathroom and shower building has a flush toilet and good hot shower. There is a very nice pool and hot tub, coin-operated laundry, hammock lounge area with color TV, barbecue, and kitchen clean-up station. English is spoken and reservations are recommended.

The Club Cabo is located right behind the Vagabundos campground. To get to it you must take a roundabout route. Start from Mex 1 about two miles (3 km) east of downtown Cabo San Lucas where Mex 19 and Mex 1 intersect. Go south from this intersection for .3 miles (.5 km) until it dead-ends. Turn left and drive .2 miles (.3 km) to a Y, the Villa de Palmas is right, go left for Club Cabo. You are now on a small dusty road, in .6 mile (1 km) you'll see the Club Cabo on the left.

CABO SAN LUCAS TO SAN JOSÉ DEL CABO
20 Miles (32 Km), .5 Hour

Mex 1 starts in Cabo San Lucas so kilometer markers count up as you drive eastward and then turn north in San José del Cabo. The area between the two towns is known as the "Cabo Corridor" or simply as "The Corridor". From Cabo San Lucas all the way to the Los Cabos International Airport north of San José del Cabo the highway is four lanes wide and heavily traveled.

Three of the campgrounds in this section are located near the western end of the Cabo Corridor. Vagabundos del Mar is near Km 3 on the south side of the road, El Arco is near Km 5 on the north side of the road, and Villa Serena is near Km 7 on the south side of the road.

As the highway approaches San José del Cabo you'll see the Brisa del Mar RV park on the right side of the highway near Km 30, then it turns north to pass just west of central San José del Cabo. There are several stop lights along this section of the highway. You can turn right along Paseo San José if you are in a tow car or small rig to reach the shopping district south of the central plaza.

Frequent busses run both ways along the Cabo Corridor. They are inexpensive and convenient, and they are the best way to visit the central area of either Cabo San Lucas or San José del Cabo. During the high season it can be difficult to find convenient parking in either of these towns.

Cabo San Lucas to San José del Cabo Campgrounds

🚐 **VAGABUNDOS DEL MAR RV PARK**

Address:	Apdo. 197, Cabo San Lucas, B.C.S., México
Telephone:	(114) 3-02-90 (Mex), 800 474-Baja
	or (707) 374-5511 (U.S.)
Fax:	(114) 3-05-11
Price:	Expensive

GPS Location: N 22° 54' 03.1", W 109° 53' 49.4"

The Vagabundos park probably has the nicest facilities in Cabo. However, it has no view and is not on the beach. It is more convenient to town than most other parks.

There are 85 spaces with 15 or 30-amp plugs, sewer, water, and patios. Many are filled with permanently-located rigs. The roads are paved and the parking spaces are gravel. The restrooms are clean and modern and have hot water showers. There's a

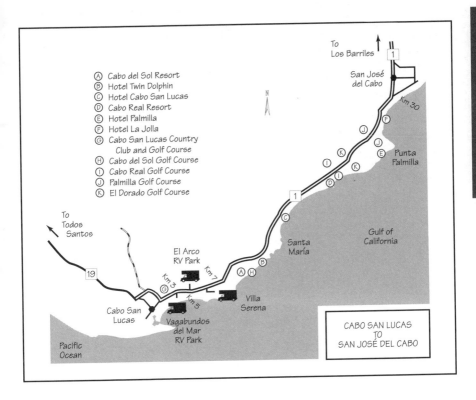

LOS CABOS

swimming pool with a palapa bar and restaurant, a laundry, vehicle washing facilities, and a fence all the way around. English is spoken and reservations are recommended.

The campground is right at the Km 3 marker on Mex 1 east of Cabo San Lucas. It is on the south side of the road.

EL ARCO RV PARK

Address: Km 5.5, Carr. a San Jose del Cabo,
                 Cabo San Lucas, B.C.S., México
Telephone: (114) 3-16-86
Fax: (114) 3-39-98
Price: Expensive

GPS Location: N 22° 54' 18.9, W 109° 52' 29.7"

This is a large park located on a hillside overlooking Cabo San Lucas. Many permanents and the bar/restaurant have an outstanding view, but the sites available for travelers really don't have any view at all.

There are 90 camping slots, all have 15-amp plugs, sewer, water, and patios. They are arranged around a semi-circular brick driveway or in an area farther up the hill. They are all back-ins. The restrooms are clean and have hot showers. There is a restaurant/bar, swimming pool, and a self-service laundry. English is spoken and reservations are recommended.

The campground is located just east of Cabo San Lucas with the entrance road on the north side of Mex 1 at Km 5.2.

VILLA SERENA

Address: Km 7.5 Carretera Transpeninsular Benito Juárez,
                 Cabo San Lucas, C.P. 23410 B.C.S., México
Telephone
or Fax: (114) 3-05-09
Price: Expensive

GPS Location: N 22° 54' 21.9", W 109° 51' 47.7"

This is a new campground with lots of room for big rigs. The facilities are good, but because the place is brand new there is little in the way of landscaping. In fact, there is no shade at all on this large sandy lot. Some trees have been planted but it will take them a while to grow to the point where they are of some use. The campground sits near the highway which is far above the water at this location. Some of the upper sites have a water view. This should be the last campground in the area to fill up.

The campground has 56 very large back-in spaces. Each has electricity, sewer, and water hookups. The plugs are the small 15-amp variety although the breakers are 40 amp. There's a new and very nice facilities building with restrooms with flush toilets and hot showers, a self-service laundry with washers and dryers, and a lounge area. Nearby is the Restaurant Bar Villa Serena, a nice place.

The entrance road goes south from near the Km 7 marker between Cabo San Lucas and San José del Cabo.

LOS CABOS

SAN JOSÉ DEL CABO (SAHN HO-SAY DELL KAH-BOH)
Population 25,000

San José is the older of the two Los Cabos towns. A Jesuit mission was founded here in 1730 but the estuary to the east had been used by ships as a watering stop far before that. Today San José is the center of business and government for the cape area.

We find the streets of San José much more pleasant to wander than those of Cabo San Lucas. Boulevard Mijares running south from the plaza is the center of the action for Norteamericanos, there are many restaurants and shops along it. If you walk westward on the streets between the plaza and Mex 1 you'll find a much more authentic Mexican town, and it has been around longer than Cabo San Lucas so it has more character.

South of the downtown area is a golf course built by FONATUR when the Los Cabos scheme was just getting off the ground. South of that are the hotels along Playa Costa Azul. East of town is the Estero San José, a swampy lagoon with a walking path along the western border. You can follow a dusty road along the northern border of the estero to reach the small village of La Playa. On the beach in front of this little place you'll find lots of pangas available for charter, San José doesn't have a marina, this is the substitute.

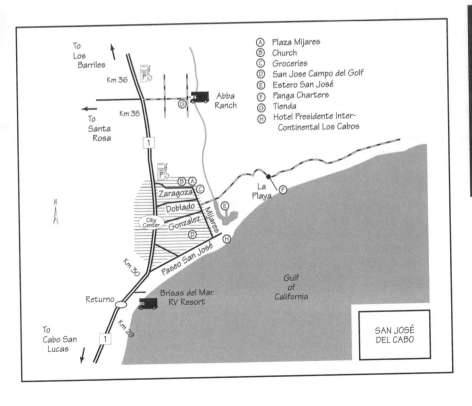

A   Plaza Mijares
B   Church
C   Groceries
D   San Jose Campo del Golf
E   Estero San José
F   Panga Charters
G   Tienda
H   Hotel Presidente Inter-
     Continental Los Cabos

SAN JOSÉ DEL CABO

LOS CABOS

San José del Cabo Campgrounds

BRISA DEL MAR RV RESORT

Address: Apdo. 45, San José del Cabo,
C.P. 23400 B.C.S., México
Telephone: (114) 2-29-35
Internet: www.brisadelmar.com/rvresort/
Price: Front row - Very expensive, Other - Expensive

GPS Location: N 23° 02' 16.2", W 109° 42' 31.5"

The Brisa del Mar is the only beachfront campground left in the Cape region. This is a large popular campground with decent facilities, it is much closer to San José del Cabo than to Cabo San Lucas. The beach is very nice.

This is a large campground, the sites along the beach are pull-in or back-in, the others are mostly pull-throughs. All have 30-amp plugs and water, the beach sites don't have sewer. The sites back from the beach also have patios and some shade. Restrooms are OK but not outstanding, they have hot water showers. There is a bar and restaurant, a pool, and a laundry. There are also some game areas and equipment rentals as well as a small store. English is spoken and reservations are accepted and strongly advised during the winter.

BEACH CAMPING AT THE BRISA DEL MAR

LOS CABOS

You'll see the campground just south of Mex 1 between the Km 29 and Km 30 markers just west of San José del Cabo. Access heading east is easy, just turn in. If you are heading west on this divided highway you'll have to go another .2 miles west (.3 km) to a returno and come back to get into the park. There is plenty of room at the turn-around for big rigs.

🚐 **ABBA RANCH**

Address: P.O. Box 206, San José del Cabo,
                     C.P. 23400 BCS, México
Telephone: (114) 14 23 715
Price: Low

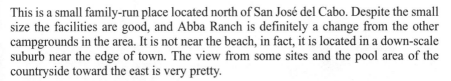

GPS Location: N 23° 05' 23.2", W 109° 42' 05.2"

This is a small family-run place located north of San José del Cabo. Despite the small size the facilities are good, and Abba Ranch is definitely a change from the other campgrounds in the area. It is not near the beach, in fact, it is located in a down-scale suburb near the edge of town. The view from some sites and the pool area of the countryside toward the east is very pretty.

There are 14 back-in spaces for rigs to about 35 feet. Spaces have 15-amp plugs, sewer and water. Restrooms are modern and have flush toilets and hot water showers and there is a nice swimming pool. The campground is walled and has lots of trees for shade. There is no swimming or work on Saturdays for religious reasons. The owner will cook vegetarian meals when ordered ahead and also bakes and sells excellent bread.

This campground is located north of San José del Cabo between town and the airport. From town drive north about 1.8 miles (2.9 km). Watch for the sign for Santa Rosa about .1 miles (.2 km) north of the Km 35 marker. The turn for Santa Rosa is at a stop light and points left, instead turn right on a dirt road. Drive about two blocks eastward, the campground is directly ahead.

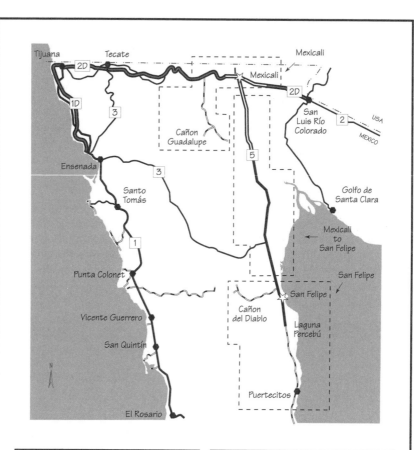

Tijuana

Tecate

2D

Mexicali

Mexicali

Mexicali

1D

3

2D

San
Luis Río
Colorado

2

USA

MEXICO

Ensenada

Cañon
Guadalupe

3

Santo
Tomás

3

5

Golfo de
Santa Clara

Mexicali
to
San Felipe

Punta Colonet

1

San Felipe

San Felipe

Vicente Guerrero

Cañon
del Diablo

San Felipe

Laguna
Percebú

San Quintín

N

Puertecitos

El Rosario

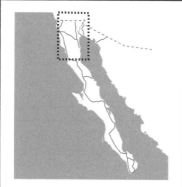

CHAPTER INDEX

Highlights .... Page 183
Roads and Fuel Availability .... Page 183
Beaches and Water Sports .... Page 184
Fishing .... Page 184
Backroad Adventures .... Page 184
Mexicali .... Page 185
Mexicali to San Felipe .... Page 186
San Felipe .... Page 188

SAN FELIPE

CHAPTER

· · · · · · · · · · · · · · · · II

SAN FELIPE

INTRODUCTION

Many folks think San Felipe offers the best combination of easily accessible sand, sun, and laid-back Mexican ambiance of any of the destinations close to the border. It's an excellent introduction to Mexican RVing.

Highlights

The **drive south to San Felipe** across the driest of Baja's deserts is an experience itself. If you've not been in to Mexico before you'll probably have the chance to experience your first **army checkpoint**, there's usually at least one along this road.

Once you reach San Felipe the prime attraction is beautiful sandy beaches, lots of good places to park your RV, and a friendly little town to enjoy.

Roads and Fuel Availabilty

The road south from Mexicali to San Felipe is paved all the way. Kilometer markers count up as you drive south. The highway starts as four lanes and then, about 24 miles (39 km) south of Mexicali, narrows to two. It is generally in fine condition and you can easily maintain the speeds shown on the speed-limit signs, usually 80 kph. The distance to San Felipe is 122 miles (197 km).

There are lots of Pemex stations in Mexicali offering both gas and diesel. Between Mexicali and San Felipe there are three more stations, at Km 32, Km 105, and Km 142. The first and last have diesel but not the middle one. As a practical matter, most people gas up north of the border so they won't need to worry about fuel until they reach San Felipe. In San Felipe there are two Pemexes, both sell gasoline but only one sells diesel. In the past diesel has also been available at the marina.

Beaches and Water Sports

San Felipe's malecón (waterfront promenade) borders **Playa San Felipe**. Like other beaches in the north end of the Gulf of California when the tide goes out here it *really* goes out. Locals use pickups and special trailers to launch and retrieve their pangas across the wide hard-packed sand flats. When the tide is in, however, this is a great beach.

North of town is **Playa Las Almejas** (Clam Beach). It's eight miles long and starts about 5 miles (8 km) north of town. Many of the boondocking campgrounds, and also the El Dorado Ranch campground, are on this beach.

South of town a popular beach is **Laguna Percebú**. It's a great place to collect sand dollars. The beach is located about 18 miles (29 km) south of town and has a small restaurant. Watch for the sign pointing left from the road to Puertecitos.

Fishing

Fishing is not nearly as good here as it once was. Over fishing, much of it by big commercial boats, decimated fishing in the northern gulf during the late sixties. Things have recovered somewhat, charter pangas are available.

Backroad Adventures

See the *Backroad Driving* section of *Chapter 2 - Details, Details, Details* for essential information about driving off the main highways on the Baja and for a definition of road type classifications used below.

The back country around San Felipe is extremely popular with folks who have dune buggies and other vehicles capable of traveling across soft sand. If you have a high-flotation vehicle you'll have a great time following the many tracks in the area. It is best to stay on established tracks to minimize damage to the desert.

From Km 178 Between San Felipe and Mexicali - One possibility is the road to the **Cañon del Diablo**. Access is via the road that heads for the Sierra San Pedro Mártir past El Cachanilla RV Park. This road goes out past the El Dorado homesites and then continues across the dry lakebed of the Laguna Diablo and then right up to the mountains. The canyon is green and has water, an oasis of sorts. It is possible to park and hike up into the Sierra from here. This is real backroad exploration on a Type 3 road, take all the precautions we recommend in the *Backroad Driving* section of *Details, Details, Details* and discuss your plans with someone with good local knowledge before attempting this drive.

From San Felipe - The road to **Puertecitos** leads 47 miles (76 km) south from San Felipe. At one time this road was paved, now the pavement is so broken up that a dirt road would be faster. Consider it a Type 2 road. In Puertecitos there is a hot springs at the tide line on the outer side of the peninsula. There is sometimes a fee for use. Puertecitos has a launching ramp useable at high water and fishing is better than in San Felipe. A Type 2 road continues south from Puertecitos along the coast to **Ensenada San Francisquito** and then inland to meet Mex 1 south of Cataviña after

81 miles (131 km). The government says that some day this route will be paved providing a second access route leading south.

From Km 28 on Mex 2D West of Mexicali - While not strictly in the San Felipe area **Cañon Guadalupe** is a popular camping destination also near Mexicali. Access to the canyon and the campground there requires driving a Type 2 road with soft sandy spots 35 miles (56 km) south across the desert to the campground. Once there you will find no hookups but campsites have tubs with hot water fed by springs. You should make reservations, get directions, and check road conditions by calling 949 673-2670. There is also a web site: www.guadalupe-canyon.com.

THE ROUTES, TOWNS, AND CAMPGROUNDS

MEXICALI (MECK-SEE-KAL-EE)
Population 800,000

This large border city is the capital of Baja California. The big business here is farming, the Colorado river irrigates thousands of surrounding acres growing produce,

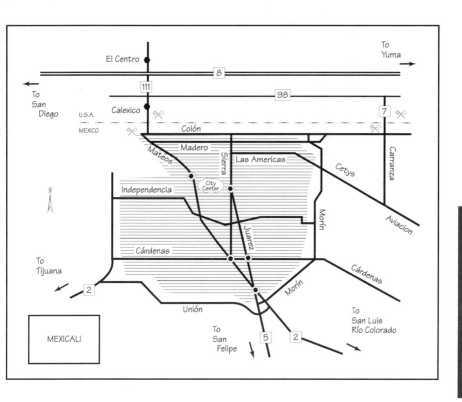

primarily for markets north of the border. Mexicali is a sprawling low-rise town. There are two border crossings, one at the center of town and another about 7 miles to the east. Neither crossing is usually particularly busy and even the traffic through town from the central crossing isn't bad since the route follows a major boulevard south.

Most RVers probably think of Mexicali as a barrier to get around rather than as a place to stop. On the outskirts of town you'll find some of the large Mexican supermarkets, if you didn't stock up north of the border these offer a much better selection than anything in San Felipe. There's even a Costco.

MEXICALI TO SAN FELIPE
122 Miles (197 Km), 4 Hours (including border crossing)

From either border crossing the route to San Felipe is well signposted. Mex 5 heads south from an intersection with the east-west Mex 2 at a point in the southern suburbs of Mexicali near a Costco store.

For the first 24 miles (39 km) the road has four lanes and is bordered by scattered homes and business. Watch the speed limit signs, they require you to drive much

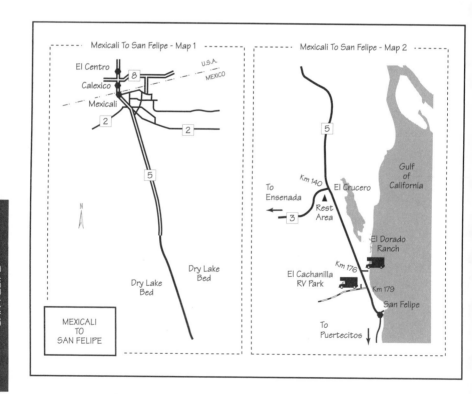

slower than the speed you will feel is safe.

The highway passes a Pemex station at Km 32 and then skirts the western edge of the Rio Hardy, a small river that drains into the Colorado to the east. Soon the highway makes a 12-mile (19 km) crossing of the dry Laguna Salada, at one time this area flooded with Colorado River water.

Once south of the Laguna the highway runs through very dry desert country. There's another Pemex with only gas at Km 105. Mex 3 from Ensenada joins the highway at a crossroads known as El Crucero at Km 140. There is another Pemex station south of the intersection with gas and diesel.

Often there are army checkpoints along the highway near El Crucero where soldiers may search your rig. See the *Drugs, Guns, and Roadblocks* section of the *Details, Details, Details* chapter.

Finally, near Km 175 the highway nears the ocean although you really can't see it from the highway. Many small roads lead eastward to campos along the water. Many offer camping, usually little more than boondocking sites. You'll have a selection of these almost all the way in to San Felipe which the road reaches at about Km 189.

Mexicali to San Felipe Campgrounds

EL DORADO RANCH

Res.:	P.O. Box 3088, Englewood, CO 80155
Telephone:	(303) 790-1749 or (800) 404-2599
	(U.S.A.), (657) 7-00-10
Fax:	(657) 7-00-09
Internet:	www.eldoradoranch.com
E-mail:	email@eldoradoranch.com
Price:	Very Expensive

GPS Location: N 31° 08' 09.4", W 114° 54' 37.1"

The El Dorado Ranch is a land development a few miles north of San Felipe along the coast. The area to be developed is huge, the project complex, and the promotion very active. Most importantly, to us anyway, there is a nice new RV park incorporated into the project.

There are 100 sites with 15 and 30-amp plugs, sewer, and water. All are on packed sand and separated by rows of painted white rocks. There are no patios and no shade but lots of room for large rigs. There is a very nice swimming pool pavilion with bar, a pool that is kept at bath temperature, and hot tubs that are even hotter. The campground has modern restrooms with flush toilets and hot showers. There's also a restaurant, a store, beautiful tennis courts, horse-back riding, desert tours, and lifestyle (sales) presentations.

The El Dorado Ranch is located about 8 miles (13 km) north of San Felipe. Take the well-marked road toward the beach between the 176 and 177 Km markers. There's also a second campground that has been developed as part of this project, El Cachanilla, we talk about it below.

SAN FELIPE

You should be warned that while this is a great RV park it is also a membership-type real estate development. They have a friendly but active sales force. The park often offers promotional escorted RV tours south to the campground, this is an excellent way to make your first trip into Mexico. Call the reservation number for details.

El Cachanilla RV park

Res.:	P.O. Box 3088, Englewood, CO 80155
Telephone:	(303) 790-1749 or (800) 404-2599 (U.S.A.), (657) 7-00-10
Fax:	(657) 7-00-09
Internet:	www.eldoradoranch.com
E-mail:	email@eldoradoranch.com
Price:	Expensive

GPS Location: N 31° 06' 54.0", W 114° 54' 21.6"

This campground is also part of the El Dorado Ranch. It is located in the desert away from the ocean, but is a good facility.

The latest word is that there are 130 sites here, 50 have full hookups and 80 are dry, hookups have been increased since our last visit. Some sites have covered patios and picnic tables. There are modern restrooms with flush toilets and hot showers, also a club house and a self-service laundry.

To reach the campground turn toward the mountains near the Km 179 marker, this is about a mile closer to town than the El Dorado Ranch cutoff and is well signed. The campground is on the right a short distance up the side road.

SAN FELIPE (SAHN FAY-LEE-PAY)
Population 15,000, Elevation sea level

Although San Felipe is a Baja town its location in the far northeast portion of the peninsula means that it is not normally part of a visit to the peninsula's destinations farther south. That doesn't mean that this isn't a popular place, like Puerto Peñasco this town is full of Americans looking for easily accessible sun and sand. The majority of them seem to be RVers.

In many ways San Felipe and Puerto Peñasco are very similar. Both are small towns at the north end of the Gulf of California pretty much devoted to RV tourism. Both are probably on the cusp of a development boom, both need a golf course or two to really become big-time tourist resort areas. It is beginning to look like the folks in Puerto Peñasco will get their golf course first and that's fine, San Felipe can retain its dusty, small-town, no-big-money charm for a while longer.

Most of the action in San Felipe is found along its **malecón** (waterfront promenade) and the street one block inland - Mar de Cortez. Overlooking the malecón and the strip of sandy beach that fronts it is Cerro El Machorro, a tall rock with a shrine to the Virgin de Guadalupe at its top. This is a great place for photos. The bay in front of town goes dry at low tide, the panga fishermen who use the beach launch and retrieve their boats by driving out on the solid sand. Several of the campgrounds are located along the southern extension of Mar de Cortez so strolling in to central San Felipe is very easy. The town has a selection of decent restaurants and small shops as well as two Pemex stations.

Most of the important streets in town are paved and the rest present no driving problems. Watch for stop signs, however. They are in unexpected places. Sometimes the smallest dusty side street has priority over a main arterial.

It seems like San Felipe always has some kind of celebration in the works. The **San Felipe 250** is a big off-road race at the end of March. Just before the off-road race is the **Mid-Winter West Hobie Cat Regatta**. Like many Mexican ports San Felipe celebrates **Carnival** (Mardi Gras) at the appropriate time in late February or early March. **Spring Break** is big here, just as on the rest of the peninsula, it happens during the third and fourth weeks of March. **Semana Santa**, the week up to and including Easter, is a big Mexican beach holiday and San Felipe is very popular as it hosts a number of sporting events. During the summer the town celebrates **Día de la Marina** on June 1. And in November there's the **Shrimp Festival**, one of the biggest celebrations of the year in San Felipe.

GULF OF CALIFORNIA VIEW FROM DOWNTOWN SAN FELIPE

SAN FELIPE

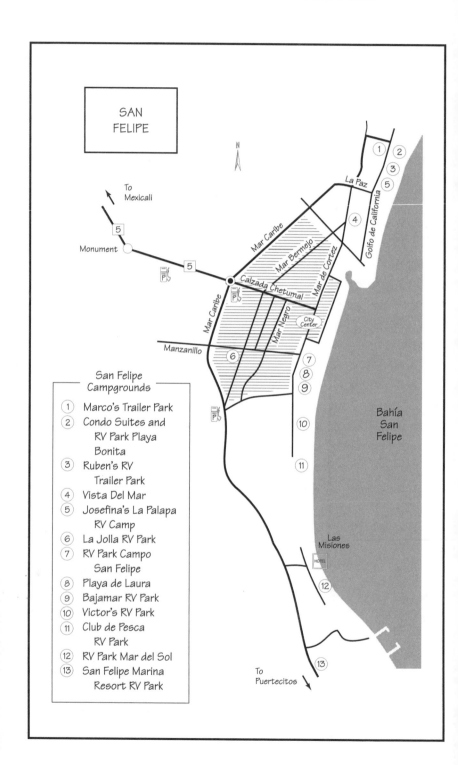

SAN
FELIPE

To
Mexicali

Monument

San Felipe
Campgrounds

1. Marco's Trailer Park
2. Condo Suites and
   RV Park Playa
   Bonita
3. Ruben's RV
   Trailer Park
4. Vista Del Mar
5. Josefina's La Palapa
   RV Camp
6. La Jolla RV Park
7. RV Park Campo
   San Felipe
8. Playa de Laura
9. Bajamar RV Park
10. Victor's RV Park
11. Club de Pesca
    RV Park
12. RV Park Mar del Sol
13. San Felipe Marina
    Resort RV Park

La Paz

Golfo de California

Mar Caribe

Mar Bermejo

Mar de Cortez

Calzada Chetumal

Mar Caribe

Mar Negro

City
Center

Manzanillo

Bahía
San
Felipe

Las
Misiones

HOTEL

To
Puertecitos

San Felipe Campgrounds

⊞ MARCO'S TRAILER PARK

Address: Av. Golfo de California 788, San Felipe, B.C., México
Telephone: (657) 7-18-75
Price: Moderate

GPS Location: N 31° 02' 08.6", W 114° 49' 42.5"

Marco's isn't on the water and all San Felipe campers seem to want to be in a campground next to the beach, even if they're parked so far back that they never see the water. Nonetheless Marco's succeeds in staying relatively full, perhaps because it is *almost* next to the beach.

There are 20 back-in spaces arranged around the perimeter of the campground. There is lots of room in the middle of the campground but large rigs have some difficulty parking because the lot slopes and the leveled parking pads aren't very long. Each space has 15-amp plugs, sewer, water, and a nice little covered patio. There is even a little shrubbery to separate the sites, unusual in San Felipe. The restrooms are old but clean and in good repair, they have hot water showers. There is a small meeting room with a library and a sun deck on top.

From the glorieta (traffic circle) at the entrance to town take the road that leads northeast. This is Mar Caribe Norte and is the road to the left as you come from Mexicali. It will curve to the right at .8 miles (1.3 km) and come to a T at 1 mile (1.6 km). Turn left and you'll see the entrance to the campground on the left in one block.

⊞ CONDO SUITES AND RV PARK PLAYA BONITA

Address: 475 E. Badillo Street, Covina,
                Cal. 91723 U.S.A. (Reservations)
Telephone: (657) 7-12-15 (Mex), (818) 967-8977 (USA)
Price: Expensive

GPS Location: N 31° 02' 08.6", W 114° 49' 42.5"

This is another beachfront campground at the north end of town. Someday the campground may be replaced by condo suites, but so far only one building has been completed and it cohabits peacefully with the RVs and trailers.

There are 36 camping spaces in this campground. Ten are large back-in spaces with 30-amp plugs, sewer and water. Another 26 spaces are suitable only for vans, tents or small trailers. Most of these smaller spaces have electricity, sewer, and water. All spaces have paved patios with palapa-style roofs and picnic tables. The restrooms are older and rustic, the showers were barely warm when we visited. There's a nice beach out front.

From the glorieta (traffic circle) at the entrance to town take the road that leads northeast. This is Mar Caribe Norte and is the road to the left as you come from Mexicali. It will curve to the right at .8 miles (1.3 km) and come to a T at 1 mile (1.6 km). Turn left and you'll see the entrance to the campground on the right across from Marco's.

🚍 Ruben's RV Trailer Park

Address: Apdo. 59, San Felipe, C.P. 21850 B.C., México
Telephone: (657) 7-14-42
Price: Moderate

GPS Location: N 31° 02' 03.6", W 114° 49' 43.0"

Ruben's is well known in San Felipe for its two-story patios. These are very popular with tenters during the Mexican holidays, it is easy to enclose the patio below and use the roof for added room. Some people think the two-story patios give the crowded campground the atmosphere of a parking garage but Ruben's remains a popular beach-front campground. There's always a lot of activity at this place, maybe too much.

There are 45 camping spaces, all with 15-amp plugs, sewer and water. Most spaces are small and maneuvering room is scarce. The restrooms are adequate and have hot water showers. There is also a well-liked bar/restaurant. The campground has a boat ramp and also a special rig for launching boats at low tide.

From the glorieta (traffic circle) at the entrance to town take the road that leads north-east. This is Mar Caribe Norte and is the road to the left as you come from Mexicali. It will curve to the right at .8 miles (1.3 km) and come to a T at 1 mile (1.6 km). Turn left and you'll almost immediately see the two entrances to Ruben's on the right.

🚍 Vista del Mar

Address: 601 Ave. de Cortez, San Felipe, B.C., México
Price: Low

GPS Location: N 31° 01' 49.7", W 114° 49' 51.2"

The Vista del Mar is another campground suffering from a location far from the water. The facility is really very good, but often virtually empty.

There are 21 back-in spaces arranged on both sides of a sloping lot with a view of the ocean and hills to the north of town. Each space has 15 and 30-amp plugs, sewer, and water. Large rigs will have trouble parking because the level parking pad is not very long. The entire campground is paved, much of it with attractive reddish bricks. Each campsite has a tile-roofed patio with a table and barbecue. The restrooms are spic-and-span and have hot water showers. At the upper end of the campground is a group barbecue area.

From the glorieta (traffic circle) at the entrance to town take the road that leads north-east. This is Mar Caribe Norte and is the road to the left as you come from Mexicali. It will curve to the right at .8 miles (1.3 km). You must take the turn to the right at .9 miles (1.4 km) just before the fenced sports field, the campground is a short way up the hill on the left.

🚍 Josefina's La Palapa RV Camp

Price: Big rigs - Moderate, Small rigs - Low

GPS Location: N 31° 01' 52.5", W 114° 49' 41.6"

SAN FELIPE

This little trailer park is located right next to the much better known Ruben's. At first glance it even looks like Rubens, it has some of the same two-story palapas. It's much quieter, however.

There are 22 spaces in this park. Six are along the front next to the beach. Most spaces are really van-size or short-trailer-size but a few will take large rigs. The camping slots have 15 or 30-amp plugs, sewer, water, and paved patios with a roof serviced by a ladder. You can use them for the view or pitch a tent up there. The bathrooms are old and need maintenance, they have hot water showers.

From the glorieta (traffic circle) at the entrance to town take the road that leads northeast. This is Mar Caribe Norte and is the road to the left as you come from Mexicali. It will curve to the right at .8 miles (1.3 km) and come to a T at 1 mile (1.6 km). Turn left and the campground will be on the right almost immediately, the sign is very small.

▄ LA JOLLA RV PARK

Address:	300 Mar Bermejo, San Felipe, B.C., México
Res.:	P.O. Box 9019, Calexico, CA 92232
Telephone:	(657) 7-12-22
Price:	Moderate

GPS Location: N 31° 01' 11.0", W 114° 50' 28.6"

The La Jolla isn't on the beach and suffers as a result. It is a friendly, well-run place and has spaces available when the campgrounds on the beach are full. If you want a quieter atmosphere you might give this place a try.

There are 55 campsites, each with 15-amp plugs, sewer, water, and covered patios. These are pull-through spaces. Unfortunately they are closely spaced and may not have room for modern slide-outs. The restrooms are in a simple cement block building with an unfinished interior but are in good condition and have hot water showers that are metered and cost a quarter. The La Jolla has a nice new swimming pool and hot tub. English is spoken.

As you enter town zero your odometer at the glorieta (traffic circle). Turn right toward the airport and drive .4 miles (6 km) to a stop sign at Manzanillo. Turn left and drive about .2 miles (.3 km) and you'll see the La Jolla on the right.

▄ RV PARK CAMPO SAN FELIPE

Address:	Ave. Mar de Cortez #301, San Felipe, B.C., México
Mail:	P.O. Box 952, Calexico, CA 92232
Telephone:	(657) 7-10-12
Price:	First row - Expensive, Second and third row - Moderate

GPS Location: N 31° 01' 04.7", W 114° 50' 08.6"

You'll find the San Felipe to be very much like the Playa de Laura next door but in much better condition. It has the distinction of being the closest campground to central San Felipe.

The campsites are arranged in several rows parallel to the beach, the closer to the beach you are the more you pay. Thirty-four sites have 30-amp plugs, sewer, water, and covered patios with tables. Most are pull-throughs. Another 5 are small and have sewer and water only. The restrooms are clean and in good repair, they have hot water showers. There is a handy telephone next to the office. English is spoken.

As you enter town zero your odometer at the glorieta (traffic circle). Turn right toward the airport and drive .8 miles (1.3 km) to the Pemex. Turn left here and drive down the hill toward the beach. You'll come to a T at 1.2 miles (1.9 km). Turn left and almost immediately you'll see the Campo San Felipe on the right in .2 miles (.4 km).

⛌ Playa de Laura

Address: P.O. Box 549, Calexico, CA 92232 (U.S.)
Phone: 657-7-11-28
Price: Along beach - Expensive, Back rows - Moderate

GPS Location: N 31° 01' 03.4", W 114° 50' 06.3"

This older RV park doesn't seem to have been kept up to quite the same standards as the ones on either side. Still, it has a good location and is quite popular.

Forty-three campsites are arranged in rows running parallel to the beach. The front row is really packed and limits beach access by campers in the rows farther from the beach. Pricing varies with beach slots much more expensive than those farther back. Each camping space has 15-amp plugs, water and a covered patio with table and barbecue. Many have sewer hookups. Most of the spaces are pull-throughs. Restrooms are older and need maintenance, they have hot water showers.

As you enter town zero your odometer at the glorieta (traffic circle). Turn right toward the airport and drive .8 miles (1.3 km) to the Pemex. Turn left here and drive down the hill toward the beach. You'll come to a T at 1.2 miles (1.9 km). Turn left and almost immediately you'll see the Playa de Laura on the right in .2 miles (.3 km).

⛌ Bajamar RV Park

Address: Av. Mar de Cortez s/n, San Felipe, B.C., México
Telephone: (65) 53-23-63 (Res.)
Fax: (65) 63-13-60 (Res.)
Price: Along Beach - Expensive, Others - Moderate

GPS Location: N 31° 01' 05.8", W 114° 50' 10.5"

The Bajamar is the newest of the downtown San Felipe campgrounds. Rather than having rows of sites on sand, this campground has large back-in spaces off paved access roads. It's on a nice beach and you have convenient strolling access to central San Felipe.

There are 60 full-service spaces with 30-amp breakers (15-amp plugs however), sewer, and water. The central access roads are paved with curbs and the parking pads are gravel with patios, some have sun shades. This campground has left the waterfront open so that it can be enjoyed by all of the residents, there is a large patio with a palapa there and some small tables with umbrellas on the sand. The Bajamar has a much less crowded feel than the other campgrounds in this area. The campground has no apparent permanents yet. Restrooms are new and clean and have hot water showers. There is a self-service laundry, and a playground.

As you enter town zero your odometer at the glorieta (traffic circle). Turn right toward the airport and drive .8 miles (1.3 km) to the Pemex. Turn left here and drive down the hill toward the beach. You'll come to a T at 1.2 miles (1.9 km). Turn left and almost immediately you'll see the Bajamar on the right.

■ VICTOR'S RV PARK

Address:	P.O. Box 1227, Calexico, CA (Res.)
Telephone:	(657) 7-10-56
Price:	Moderate

GPS Location: N 31° 00' 48.6", W 114° 50' 11.7"

This 50-space campground is older with a lot of permanently located or long-term rigs. A few slots are available for daily rent. It is jointly run with the El Cortez Motel located just next door so the facilities are really pretty good for such a small park.

Victor's parking slots have 30-amp plugs, sewer, and water. Each space has a covered patio. The restrooms are clean and showers have hot water. The campground has a meeting room near the front next to the beach and the motel next door has a swimming pool and restaurant for the use of campground residents. There is also a laundry. This campground is fully fenced, even along the beach, and usually has an attendant.

WATCHING THE MOON RISE OVER SAN FELIPE

SAN FELIPE

As you enter town zero your odometer at the glorieta (traffic circle). Turn right toward the airport and drive .8 miles (1.3 km) to the Pemex. Turn left here and drive down the hill toward the beach. You'll come to a T at 1.2 miles (1.9 km). Turn right and almost immediately you'll see Victor's on your left.

CLUB DE PESCA RV PARK

Address:	P.O. Box 3090, Calexico, CA 92232
Telephone:	(657) 7-11-80
Fax:	(657) 7-18-88
E-mail:	clubdepesca@canela.sanfelipe.com.mx
Price:	Along beach - Expensive, Off beach - Moderate

GPS Location: N 31° 00' 47.7", W 114° 50' 08.4"

This is an old San Felipe favorite. The campground has many permanents, but also some choice slots for smaller rigs along the ocean and others toward the rear of the park.

There are 32 slots along the beach with 30-amp plugs and water but no sewer hook-ups. These spaces are paved and have palapas. We've seen rigs to 34 feet in them but usually only shorter rigs park here. At the rear of the park are 22 slots with 15-amp plugs, sewer, and water. Larger rigs fit here better. Restrooms are neat and clean and have hot water showers. There is a small grocery store and a room with a ping-pong table next to the beach dividing the beachside sites.

As you enter town zero your odometer at the glorieta (traffic circle). Turn right toward the airport and drive .8 miles (1.3 km) to the Pemex. Turn left here and drive down the hill toward the beach. You'll come to a T at 1.2 miles (1.9 km). Turn right and you'll find the Club de Pesca at the end of the road.

RV PARK MAR DEL SOL

Address:	Av. Misión de Loreto No. 130, San Felipe, B.C., México
Res.:	Baja California Tours, Inc., 7734 Hersihel Ave., Suite "O", La Jolla, Ca 92037
Telephone:	(657) 7-10-88 (Mex), (619) 454-7166 or (800) 336-5454 (U.S. Res.)
Price:	Expensive

GPS Location: N 30° 59' 52.3", W 114° 49' 59.2"

The Mar del Sol is another very nice but rather expensive trailer park located a short distance south of San Felipe. It is affiliated with the very nice Hotel Las Misiones next door. There's a beautiful beach out front.

The campground has 85 spaces with 30-amp plugs, sewer and water. These are back-in sites but are large with lots of room for bigger rigs. There are another 30 spaces with no utility hookups, these cost a lot less. The restrooms are individual rooms for toilets and showers, they are tiled, clean, and in good repair. The showers have hot water. The campground has a swimming pool overlooking the beach, a palapa and meeting room for get-togethers, and a laundry. The nearest restaurant is in the Hotel Las Misiones next door and there's a handy public telephone by the office.

SAN FELIPE

To find the Mar del Sol zero your odometer as you reach the glorieta (traffic circle) at the entrance to town. Turn 90 degrees right toward the airport and head south. At 2 miles (3.2 km) turn left on the well-marked road to the Hotel Las Misiones and the RV Park Mar del Sol. The road winds down a short hill to a T, turn right and you will find the campground at the end of the street.

SAN FELIPE MARINA RESORT RV PARK

Address: Km 4.5 Carr. San Felipe-Aeropuerto, San Felipe, C.P. 21850 B.C., México
Telephone: (567) 7-14-55, (800) 291-5397 (U.S. Reservations)
Fax: (657) 7-15-66
Internet: www.sanfelipe.com.mx/sfmarina/index.htm
E-mail: snmarina@telnor.net
Price: Expensive

GPS Location: N 30° 59' 18.3", W 114° 49' 40.4"

This campground may have the nicest facilities you will find in Mexico. It is only a few years old and is affiliated with a resort hotel below the campground on the beach. The campground itself is not next to the beach, it is set on a hillside above and has a great view.

There are 143 large back-in spaces with lots of room for bigger rigs. They have 50-amp and 30-amp plugs, sewer, water, and satellite TV. The campsites are all paved and have patios but no shade. The central facilities building has clean modern restrooms (an understatement) with hot showers, a beautiful pool and a lounge area. There is also a laundry in the building. The hotel has two more pools, tennis courts, and a restaurant. The campground and hotel are gated and have tight 24-hour security.

To find the San Felipe zero your odometer as you reach the glorieta (traffic circle) at the entrance to town. Turn 90 degrees right toward the airport and head south. At 2.9 miles (4.7 km) you'll see the campground on the left.

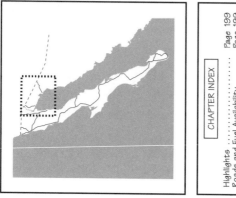

CHAPTER INDEX

Highlights . . . . Page 199
Roads and Fuel Availability . . . . Page 199
Sightseeing . . . . Page 200
Golf . . . . Page 200
Beaches and Water Sports . . . . Page 201
Fishing . . . . Page 201
Backroad Adventures . . . .
Sonoyta, Sonora and
  Lukeville, Arizona . . . . Page 202
Lukeville/Sonoyta Crossing to
  Puerto Peñasco . . . . Page 203
Puerto Peñasco . . . . Page 205
San Luis Río Colorado and
  San Luis, Arizona . . . . Page 212
San Luis Río Colorado to
  Golfo de Santa Clara . . . . Page 212
Golfo de Santa Clara . . . . Page 213

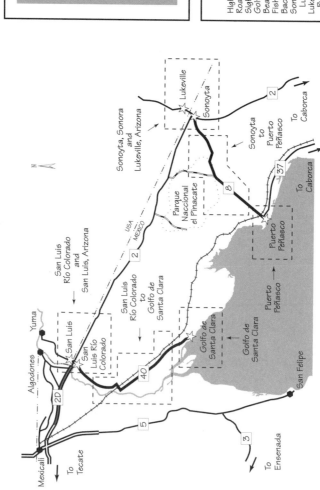

PUERTO PEÑASCO AND GOLFO

PUERTO PEÑASCO (ROCKY POINT) AND GOLFO DE SANTA CLARA

INTRODUCTION

Two of the easiest places for RVers to visit in Mexico are Puerto Peñasco and Golfo de Santa Clara. They are both easy drives from easy border crossings on quiet roads. Of the two, Puerto Peñasco (often called Rocky Point), has more to offer. There are hundreds of campsites and services designed for folks from north of the border. Golfo de Santa Clara on the other hand has only a handful of sites and virtually no services. Golfo is an authentic little Mexican fishing town.

Highlights

The attraction of these towns is that they are the only beach towns easily available to residents of Arizona. Here you can camp just a few feet from the water. The quality of some of these parks compares favorable with those north of the border. You don't need to worry at all about being able to speak Spanish or use pesos. It's almost like you're still in the U.S.

Roads and Fuel Availability

The road from the Lukeville/Sonoyta crossing leads 62 miles (100 km) south to Puerto Peñasco. The route passes through the outskirts of Sonoyta, but this is a quiet little town and driving through is no problem. You can wait until you reach Puerto Peñasco if you want to change money or shop.

From the junction in Sonoyta where Mex 8 intersects Mex 2 the road is marked with kilometer posts, they count up from 0 at the junction to 95 as you enter Puerto Peñasco.

Gas is available in Lukeville if you wish to gas up before heading south, we recommend that you do this if you have not visited a Mexican gas station before. There is a Pemex station along the road as you drive through Sonoyta, there is not another one until you reach Puerto Peñasco.

If you are bound for Golfo de Santa Clara you will want to cross in San Luis Río Colorado. This crossing is about 26 miles (42 km) south of Yuma, AZ. Follow signs for Golfo de Santa Clara once you cross the border, they'll lead you through the small border town and onto Hwy. 40, a two-lane paved highway. The distance to Golfo is about 71 miles (114 km). Both gas and diesel are available north of the border, in San Luis, and at a Pemex station in Golfo.

Sightseeing

You will want to visit **Puerto Peñasco's old town on Rocky Point**. You'll find a selection of restaurants and several stores selling Mexican handicrafts.

Another interesting place to visit while visiting Puerto Peñasco is **CEDO**, also known as the **Desert and Ocean Studies Center**. It's located a few miles east of town in the Las Conchas housing development. It's a learning and research center with the skeleton of a fin whale and other exhibits.

Golf

Right now there are no golf courses in Puerto Peñasco but they are coming. Everyone knows that this town needs a golf course if it is to draw more than weekenders and RVers so it will happen, probably sooner rather than later. Plans are in the works for several courses; and locals think that the financing and infrastructure needed for a first-class waterfront course will soon fall into place.

Beaches and Water Sports

Puerto Peñasco has beaches both northwest and east of the rocky point that gives the town its name. The sandy beaches near town are sometimes interrupted by outcrops of the basalt lava rock that makes up the point.

East of the point is **Playa Miramar**. It is rocky at the western end but sandy to the east. Many of the campgrounds line this beach, there are boat-launching ramps at some of them.

Northwest of the point is a long sandy beach that begins as **Playa Bonita** and then becomes **Sandy Beach** as it curves westward to the gringo village of Cholla Bay. There are also campgrounds along this beach. At the western end, accessible off the road to Cholla Bay, are areas used for boondocking, watch for soft sand. ATV use is popular on Sandy Beach and in the dunes to the north.

In Golfo de Santa Clara the good beach is about a mile south of town. That is where the out-of-town campgrounds are located. Access is via a mile-long sand road. The sand on this road can be soft, check locally about the condition of the road before trying to take a big rig out to the beach area. Tides in this section of the Gulf of California can have as much as 25 feet between high and low water. When the tide is in there is a nice sand beach, when the tide is out there are miles of mud flats.

Fishing

While the fishing in the far northern Gulf of California can't compare with the fishing farther south in the gulf, Puerto Peñasco does have a healthy sports fishing fleet. You can easily charter a panga or cruiser for a day of fishing. These aren't really big fish waters but there is something to catch all year long.

Backroad Adventures

See the *Backroad Driving* section of *Chapter 2 - Details, Details, Details* for essential information about driving off the main highway on the Baja and for a definition of road types used below.

Km 73 Between Sonoyta and Puerto Peñasco - Riserva De La Biosfera De El Pinacate y Gran Desierto De Altar is an infrequently visited but interesting destination located west of the highway. It's an austere desert region filled with volcanic craters, lava fields, and sand dunes. The last eruption was in 1935. Permits are required to visit the park, you can get them at the ranger station near the entrance. There are also entrances from Mex 2 between Sonoyta and San Luis Río Colorado. Some of

SHOPPING IN DOWNTOWN ROCKY POINT

the roads in the park are Type 2, others Type 3. The reserve has two very basic camping areas with no hookups.

THE ROUTES, TOWNS, AND CAMPGROUNDS

Sonoyta, Sonora and Lukeville, Arizona

These small towns are located on opposite sides of the border about a mile from each other. During the week the crossing here is a pleasant experience because it tends to be very quiet. Sometimes, but not always, weekends are much busier. Lukeville has a gas station and a motel with a good RV park in the back. Organ Pipe National Monument with another good campground is located just a few miles to the north. The crossing here is open 24 hours, it issues vehicle permits for those bound for points to the east and insurance is available in Lukeville.

After crossing the border the route curves through the edge of quiet Sonoyta and Mex 8 heads southwest toward Puerto Peñasco. Gas and diesel are available at the Pemex here but most folks have already gassed up in the U.S. and don't even stop.

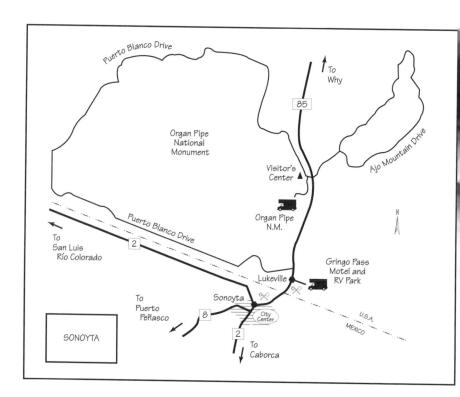

Sonoyta and Lukeville Campgrounds

ORGAN PIPE N.M.
  Price: Moderate

GPS Location: N 31° 56' 28.3", W 112° 48' 39.8"

This national monument campground is an excellent place to stay on the U.S. side of the border before or after your crossing. It is only a few miles north of the border crossing at Sonoyta, the desert flora here is spectacular. This is the north end of the range for the organ pipe cactus, known as the pithahaya dulce on the Baja.

The campground has over 200 sites. They are all pull-throughs but due to their length are only suitable for rigs to 35 feet. There are no hookups. The restrooms have flush toilets but no showers. There is a dump station and water fill. The entrance road for the campground passes an information center, when we visited the fees were being collected there although there is also a fee station at the campground for busier seasons. There are excellent hiking trails from the campground and nearby, also some interesting drives.

The turn-off for this campground is at Mile 75 of Highway 85, north of the crossing at Lukeville/Sonoyta.

GRINGO PASS MOTEL AND RV PARK
  Address: P.O. Box 266, Hwy. 85, Lukeville, AZ 85341
  Telephone: (602) 254-9284
  Price: Low

GPS Location: N 31° 52' 54.2", W 112° 49' 04.4"

If you find that you have reached the border crossing at Lukeville/Sonoyta too late in the day to drive on to Puerto Peñasco before dark you can stay in this conveniently located RV park and go on in the morning.

The Gringo Pass Motel has a large number of sites out back. There are a variety of site types, some back-in and some pull-through. The sites have full hookups with 50 and 15-amp plugs. Sites have picnic tables and there is a swimming pool. Restrooms have hot showers and some sites have shade.

The motel is located just north of the border crossing on the east side of the road. There's a Chevron station, a grocery store, an insurance office, and a restaurant on the west side.

LUKEVILLE/SONOYTA CROSSING TO PUERTO PEÑASCO
62 Miles (100 Km), 1.25 Hours

After crossing the border the road leads to an intersection with Mex 2 just 2 miles (3 km) from the crossing. Turn left, drive past the Pemex, and turn right in just a quarter-mile to follow Mex 8 south toward Puerto Peñasco.

Within a minute or so you'll be driving across the desert. There is little traffic other than folks headed to or returning from Puerto Peñasco.

As you approach Puerto Peñasco you'll begin to see a few scattered RV parks. A major new intersection is near Km 90, the road to Caborca is to the left, the new Laguna del Mar land development to the right, Puerto Peñasco is straight ahead. At Km 95 you'll pass under the "Welcome to Rocky Point" sign.

Lukeville/Sonoyta Crossing to Puerto Peñasco Campgrounds

HACIENDA DE MARCOS

Res.:	P.O. Box 379, Lukeville, AZ 85341
Telephone:	(638) 5-10-30
Price:	Moderate

GPS Location: N 31° 25' 36.2", W 113° 28' 09.1"

This new campground is located north of town on the road to Sonoyta. If you are looking for a small friendly place you should stop in here.

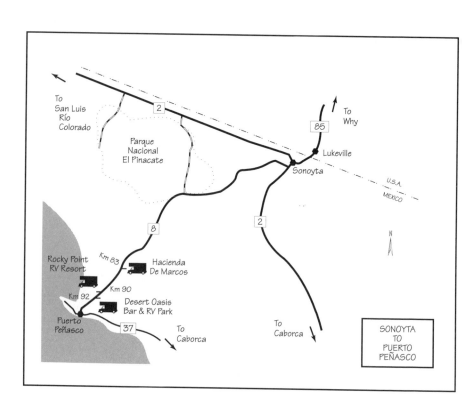

The campground has 9 back-in spaces with full hookups (50 and 30-amp plugs) and another 32 or so with water and sewer only. There's a laundry and restrooms are modern and clean with flush toilets and hot water showers. The owner/managers are from north of the border.

The Hacienda De Marcos is located on the east side of Mex 8 some 7.5 miles (12 km) north of Puerto Peñasco.

ROCKY POINT RV RESORT

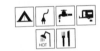

Address:	Carr. Sonoyta-Peñasco Km 91.5, Puerto Peñasco, Son., México
Price:	Low

GPS Location: N 31° 22' 05.4", W 113° 30' 28.8"

The campground is located right in the middle of barren desert north of Puerto Peñasco. There are 28 large pull-through spaces, each with 15-amp plugs, sewer, water and satellite TV hookups. The restrooms are clean with hot showers. There is a recreation room and a self-service laundry.

You'll find the campground on the west side of Mex 8 some 2.7 miles (4.4 km) north of Puerto Peñasco.

DESERT OASIS BAR AND RV PARK

Address:	Carr. Sonoyta-Peñasco Km 91, Puerto Peñasco, Son., México
Telephone:	(638) 5-29-61
Price:	Moderate

GPS Location: N 31° 21' 51.8", W 113° 30' 27.6"

This is a modern campground that was in use but still under construction when we visited. There's a nice bar/restaurant here and the facility was being used as a checkpoint for an off-road race. The facilities are nice and this might be a good place to stay if you don't mind being a bit removed from the water and town.

The campground has 50 back-in spaces with full hookups. Power outlets are 30-amp and parking is on gravel. The restrooms have hot showers and flush toilets. There is no shade in the RV park.

The park is located at Km 91 which is 2.5 miles (4 km) north of Puerto Peñasco.

PUERTO PEÑASCO (PWEHR-TOE PEN-YAHS-KOE)
Population 13,000

Many Mexico travel guides ignore Puerto Peñasco as if it weren't even part of Mexico. This attitude is understandable, the town really does have a great deal of American influence. To ignore Puerto Peñasco in a camping guide to Mexico would be something of a crime, however. RVers virtually own this town, hordes of them fill RV parks

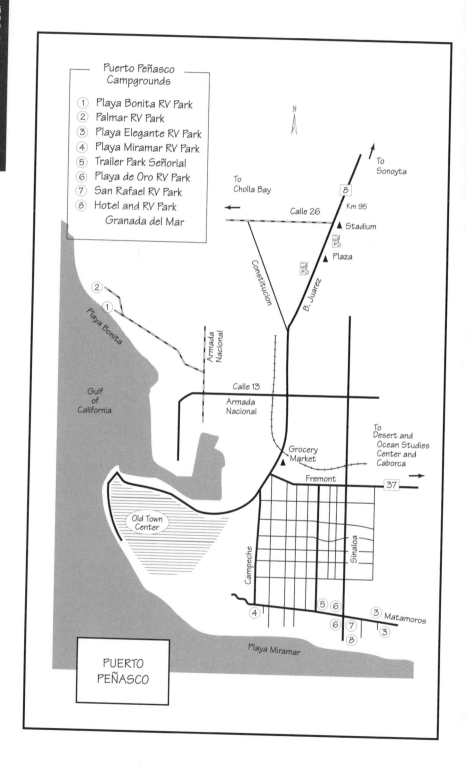

Puerto Peñasco
Campgrounds

1. Playa Bonita RV Park
2. Palmar RV Park
3. Playa Elegante RV Park
4. Playa Miramar RV Park
5. Trailer Park Señorial
6. Playa de Oro RV Park
7. San Rafael RV Park
8. Hotel and RV Park
   Granada del Mar

N

To Sonoyta

To Cholla Bay

8   Km 95

Calle 26

Stadium

Plaza

Constitucion

B. Juarez

Playa Bonita

Armada Nacional

Calle 13

Armada Nacional

Gulf of California

To Desert and Ocean Studies Center and Caborca

Grocery Market

Fremont

37

Old Town Center

Campeche

Sinaloa

5 6

6 7

8

3 Matamoros

3

4

Playa Miramar

PUERTO PEÑASCO

and boondock in the vicinity. On weekends and holidays Puerto Peñasco is even more popular. After all, it is only a little over an hour's driving time south of the Arizona border, it is located in a free zone requiring no governmental paperwork, and there are beaches, desert, fishing, and Mexican crafts and food. Don't forget to pick up Mexican auto insurance, however.

Americans often call the town Rocky Point, you'll see why when you see the location of the old town. The road to Rocky Point was built by the American government during World War II when it was thought that it might be necessary to bring in supplies this way if the west coast was blockaded by Japanese submarines. That never happened, but the road, now paved and in good shape, makes the town easy to reach. Puerto Peñasco is also a fishing port, not everything here is tourist oriented. Campgrounds are located in three areas: most are along the beach to the east of the old town, two others are along the beach to the northwest. Some campgrounds are also starting to appear along the main highway north of town. Boondockers congregate farther west toward La Choya on Sandy Beach and north of La Choya. There is lots of talk of major tourist developments in Rocky Point in the next few years, perhaps even with a golf course. Supplies of all kinds are available, but no large supermarkets have appeared yet.

Puerto Peñasco Campgrounds

PLAYA BONITA RV PARK

Address: 147 Balboa Blvd., Apdo. 34, Puerto Peñasco, Son. México
Telephone: (638) 3-25-96 or 800 569-2586 (U.S. Res)
Price: Moderate

GPS Location: N 31° 19' 06.4", W 113° 33' 15.9"

This is the larger of two trailer parks located northwest of town on Playa Bonita. The Playa Bonita RV Park is affiliated with a nice hotel next door.

There are 300 spaces in this huge campground. All are back-in slots with 30-amp plugs, sewer, water, and satellite TV connections. Restrooms are modern and clean and have hot water. The campground has a small recreation room with a TV, a self-service laundry, and the affiliated hotel next door has a restaurant. The beach out front is beautiful.

As you enter town you will pass two Pemexes, the first on the left and then one on the right. A half mile (.8 km) after the second Pemex is a cross road marked with many large green signs over the road. Turn right here on Calle 13. Proceed across the railroad tracks and drive for .3 mile (.5 km), turn right on sandy Armada Nacional. The turn is marked with a sign for the campground. Drive up this road for .9 miles (1.5 km) to the gate of the trailer park.

PUERTO PEÑASCO AND GOLFO

PALMAR RV PARK

Address: 348 Balboa Blvd, Apdo. 24,
              Puerto Peñasco, C.P. 83550 Sonora, México
Telephone: (638) 3-66-33
Price: Moderate

GPS Location: N 31° 19' 12.7", W 113° 33' 49.1"

This is the second trailer park on Playa Bonita. It's a large, well-run park with only one disadvantage, no electricity.

The campground has about 150 generously-sized spaces, 100 of these have sewer and water hookups. The restrooms are modern and clean, they have hot water showers that cost a dollar. There is also a meeting room. The beach in front is very nice.

To reach the campground follow the instructions for finding the Playa Bonita given above. Just before you reach the Playa Bonita gate you will see a sign pointing right to a road running around the Playa Bonita. Follow this another .5 mile (.8 km) to the Palmar.

PLAYA ELEGANTE RV PARK

Address: 91 Matamoros Ave., Puerto Peñasco, Son., México
Res.:   P.O. Box 56, Lukeville, AZ 85341
Telephone: (638) 3-37-12
Fax: (638) 3-60-71
E-mail: elegante@infotech.net.mx
Price: Moderate

GPS Location: N 31° 17' 45.5", W 113° 31' 54.2"

The Playa Elegante is the farthest-east trailer park in the look-alike group clustered along Calle Matamoros on the oceanfront east of the old town. It is a large beach-fronting campground with easy access. There is another section of the campground located a short distance away, not along the water.

The campground has 350 spaces. They are all back-in slots with 30-amp plugs, sewer, water, and satellite TV hookups. None of the spaces has a patio or shade, they all have a gravel parking surface. The bathrooms are in the main building which also houses a self-service laundry and meeting room. The bathrooms are modern and clean and have metered hot showers, they cost a quarter. There is a sun deck on the top of the main building, the beach is better for sun but the deck offers a good view. This campground also has a boat ramp.

To reach the campground when approaching Puerto Peñasco from the north on Mex 8 zero your odometer as you pass the airport. At 1.3 miles (2.1 km) you'll enter Puerto Peñasco, at 2 miles (3.2 km) you'll see the town square on the left, at 3.1 miles (5 km) you'll cross Armada Nacional Avenue/Hidalgo which is marked with cluster of green overhead signs. At a stoplight at 3.5 miles (5.6 km) Fremont Boulevard cuts off to the left, this is Son. 37 to Caborca. Continuing straight and bear left at the Y at 3.6 miles (5.8 km) and at 4.1 miles (6.6 km) you'll reach Matamoros Ave. which runs east and west along the beach. Turn left here and pass a series of campgrounds and finally reach the right turn for the Playa Elegante at 4.7 miles (7.6 km). The campground is just down the road toward the water and to the left, the entrance is obvious.

BEACH FRONT CAMPGROUND AT PLAYA BONITA

If you are approaching from Caborca on Son. 37 watch carefully as you enter town. You'll see a paved road with wide shoulders on the left that is well marked with campground signs. This is Sinaloa, if you turn here you'll soon reach the beach and can make a left and then a right to reach the Playa Elegante. The other Calle Matamoros campgrounds are to the right stretching westward along the beach.

PLAYA MIRAMAR RV PARK

Address:	27 Matamoros Ave., Apdo. 2, Puerto Peñasco, C.P. 83550 Sonora, México
Res.:	P.O. Box 456, Lukeville, AZ 85341
Telephone:	(638) 3-25-87
Fax:	(638) 3-23-51
Price:	Moderate

GPS Location: N 31° 17' 52.4", W 113° 32' 25.2"

This is the last (or first) of the three big RV parks between Ave. Matamoros (Calle 1) and the beach. The Playa Miramar has 146 spaces, all are back-in with 30-amp electricity, sewer, water and satellite TV. The restrooms are very clean and have hot water for showers that are metered and cost a quarter. There is a recreation room, and a laundry. This campground is close to the base of the big rock that gives Rocky Point it's name, as a result there is no sandy beach, instead the shoreline is made up of bowling ball-sized black rocks. English is spoken.

If you follow the instructions given above for reaching the Playa Elegante Trailer Park the Playa Miramar is the first trailer park you'll see after turning onto Matamoros. It is on the right.

TRAILER PARK SEÑORIAL

Address: Apdo. 76, Puerto Peñasco, 83550 Son., Mexico (same as Playa de Oro)
Telephone: (638) 3-35-30
Price: Moderate

GPS Location: N 31° 17' 50.6", W 113° 32' 10.7"

The Trailer Park Señorial is located just across the street and slightly west of the Playa de Oro and has the same owners. It is a smaller park and has a swimming pool to make up for the fact that it is not on the beach. Many of the spaces are filled with rigs that appear to be permanently located.

The campground has 65 spaces. All are back-in slots with 30-amp plugs, water, and sewer. The parking pads are cement but there are no patios or shade. The bathrooms are clean and in good repair, the showers are hot and require a $.25 payment. The swimming pool sits at the upper end of the campground and is quite nice. There's also a laundry.

To find the campground follow the instructions given for the Playa Elegante above. After turning left onto Matamoros proceed .3 miles (.5 km), you'll see the entrance on the left.

PLAYA DE ORO RV PARK

Address: 60 Matamoros Ave., Apdo. 76, Puerto Peñasco, C.P. 83550 Son., Mexico
Telephone: (638) 3-26-68
Price: Moderate

GPS Location: N 31° 17' 51.6", W 113° 32' 06.7"

This huge campground is one of the oldest ones in Puerto Peñasco. It bills itself as the only full service RV park in Rocky Point. This is somewhat true, the campground does have many amenities, but also is showing it's age in some ways.

There are now 350 spaces at the Playa de Oro. They are located south of Matamoros Ave. along and back from the beach and also extending well inland to the north of Matamoros. The sites have 30-amp electricity, sewer, and water. They have gravel surfaces, no shade, and no patios. The bathrooms are older but clean, the showers require a quarter for 4 to 5 minutes and the hot water was intermittent when we visited. The campground has a small, simple restaurant, a mini-mart, a self-service laundry, and a boat ramp. There is also a large long-term storage yard for those wishing to leave a trailer or boat when they go back north.

To find the campground follow the instructions given for the Playa Elegante above. After turning left onto Matamoros proceed .4 miles (.6 km), you'll see the Playa de Oro entrance on the right.

🚐 SAN RAFAEL RV PARK

Address:	Apdo. 58, Puerto Peñasco, C.P. 83550 Son., México
Telephone:	(638) 3-50-44, (638) 3-26-81
Price:	Expensive

GPS Location: N 31° 17' 48.7", W 113° 31' 58.0"

This is a smaller campground with no beachfront sites even though it is south of Calle Matamoros.

The campground has 53 slots, all have 30-amp plugs, sewer, and water. These are gravel-surfaced back-in spaces without patios or shade. The campground has clean modern restrooms with hot showers, a TV room, a self-service laundry, and English is spoken.

To find the campground follow the instructions given for the Playa Elegante above. After turning left onto Matamoros proceed .5 miles (.8 km), you'll see the San Rafael entrance on the right.

🚐 HOTEL AND RV PARK GRANADA DEL MAR

Address:	41 Durango Ave., Puerto Peñasco, Son., México
Res.:	P.O. Box 30806, Tucson, AZ 8575
Telephone:	(638) 3-27-42
Price:	Moderate

GPS Location: N 31° 17' 46.8", W 113° 32' 01.5"

The Granada del Mar is a new trailer park in Puerto Peñasco, it occupies the beach in front of the San Rafael and also some of the beach in front of the Playa de Oro. The trailer park is an addition to a hotel that has occupied the site for some time.

The campground has 40 back-in spaces, they all have 30-amp plugs, sewer, and water. These spaces have the customary Puerto Peñasco gravel surface with no patio or shade. About a third are beachfront sites. The small bathroom cubicles are new and clean and have hot water. There is a bar/disco on the water to the west of the hotel building that serves some food and is popular with the younger folks from this park and also the Playa de Oro next door.

To find the campground follow the instructions given for the Playa Elegante above. After turning left onto Matamoros proceed .5 miles (.8 km), you'll see the San Rafael entrance on the right. Turn right down the street just before the San Rafael, the Granada is at the end of the street next to the water.

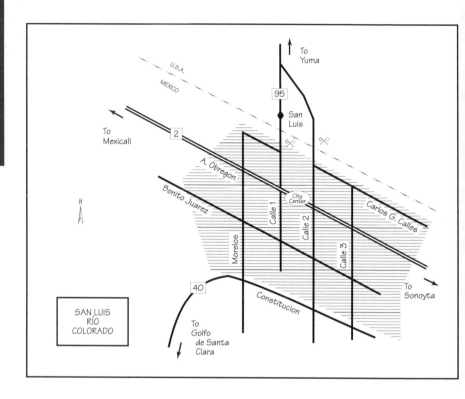

SAN LUIS RÍO COLORADO, SONORA AND SAN LUIS, ARIZONA

This small town, tucked right up against the line directly south of Yuma, is the best place to cross if you are headed toward Golfo de Santa Clara. It is open 24 hours and has a much better reputation with RVers than Algodones, the crossing nearest to Yuma. Besides, the route to Golfo is much shorter and quicker than if you cross in Algodones.

Yuma probably has more campgrounds than any similar sized city anywhere in the U.S. so we won't pick one as the best place to stay before heading south. You should be aware that most of these campgrounds are filled with snowbirds for the entire season so get a reservation ahead of time if you plan to spend the night.

SAN LUIS RÍO COLORADO TO GOLFO DE SANTA CLARA
71 Miles (114 Km), 2 Hours

The road to Golfo de Santa Clara is Highway 40. Watch for signs in San Luis Río Colorado, the way is well-signed. This it a two-lane paved road, much of it through

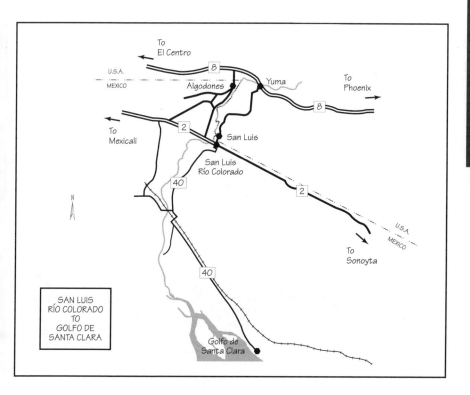

farming country. You may share the road with a few tractors and overloaded trucks during the first half of your drive.

GOLFO DE SANTA CLARA (GOLF-OH DAY SAHN-TAW CLAW-RAH)
Population 1,500

If you are looking for a piece of the real outback Mexico with no tourist glitz Golfo de Santa Clara is the place for you. This is a small fishing village surrounded by miles and miles of sand. Most tourist guides don't even mention the town but it is becoming something of a popular camping destination. Recently a camping club took over the best campground in town, however, so your choices of campgrounds are limited if you are not a member. The beach south of town stretches for miles and ATVs are welcome.

Golfo de Santa Clara is built entirely on sand. This means that driving can be challenging. The streets in town aren't much of a problem, they are packed and if you are careful you aren't likely to get stuck, even with a big rig. The road out of town toward the campgrounds located a mile south on the beach is another story. This road is

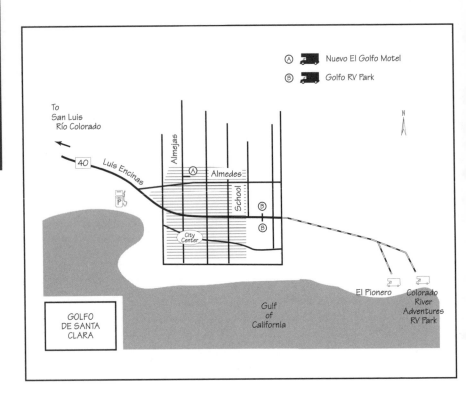

usually passable and big rigs, even fifth-wheels and 40-foot motorhomes can make it to the campgrounds if they do not slow and stop in the loose sand. Momentum is everything so stay to the part of the road that seems best and forge ahead. You might be smart to stop in town before starting down this road and see if other traffic is having problems, you can see almost the entire mile of soft sandy road straight ahead.

The busiest day of the year for Golfo is June 1, **Día de la Marina**, lots of people come down from Mexicali and San Luis for the party.

Golfo de Santa Clara Campgrounds

NUEVO EL GOLFO MOTEL

Address: Av. Almejas y 1ra., Golfo de Santa Clara, Son. Mexico
Telephone: (653) 8-02-21
Price: Low

GPS Location: N 31° 41' 20.0", W 114° 29' 58.6"

There are two campgrounds in town. These campgrounds have a big advantage, they can be reached without driving the sand road a mile south to where the other Santa

Clara campgrounds are located. This can be important if the sand happens to be soft.

There are three back-in slots behind the motel. They have full hookups with 30-amp plugs. The motel has toilets built for the camping area but no showers. They may let you use one of the showers at the motel. There's a laundry next door.

The motel is well signed so it is easy to find. Zero your odometer at the Pemex as you enter town. The left turn for the motel is at .1 mile (.2 km) on Almejas.

GOLFO RV PARK
  Telephone: (653) 8-02-21
  Price: Low

GPS Location: N 31° 41' 08.3", W 114° 29' 52.8"

This second campground in town is some distance from the motel but has the same owners.

There are 26 back-in slots with 30-amp plugs, sewer, and water on a gravel lot. There are no restroom facilities. When we visited a manager was living on site.

To find the RV park zero your odometer as you come to the Pemex at the entrance to town. Continue straight on the pavement for .2 miles (.3 km), the park is on both sides of the road and you reach it just before you reach the end of the pavement.

Other Camping Possibilities

There is an RV park about a mile south of town on the beach. We stayed there several years ago, it had a great location but terrible facilities. The new operator has improved the facilities so this is probably the best place in Golfo. It is operated by Colorado River Adventures, a camping club with 5 campgrounds along the lower Colorado River. You must be a member to stay there. They are affiliated with Coast to Coast so members of that organization may also find a spot. Call 760 663-4941 to check.

Also out the road to the south is El Pionero. This place has a restaurant and places to park with no hookups except perhaps some very low amperage electricity. On weekends and holidays it can be very popular with folks from San Luis Río Colorado and Mexicali. During the week, however, it is usually very quiet and a decent place to stay.

INDEX

Abba Ranch, 181
Agua Caliente District, 48
Agua Verde, 141
Algodones, 26
Alisitos K-58 Surf Point Camping, 56
Aquamarina RV Park, 152
Army checkpoints, 183
Avenida Constitución, 48
Avenida Revolución, 48

Backroad Adventures, 47, 76, 92, 115,
    141, 159, 173, 184, 201
Backroad Driving, 19
Bahía Concepción, 16, 113, 115, 125
Bahía de los Angeles, 15, 90, 92, 104
Bahía Falsa, 77
Bahía La Ventana, 140
Bahía las Animas, 93
Bahía Magdalena, 90, 140, 145
Bahía San Francisquito, 93
Bahía San Quintín, 74
Bahía San Rafael, 93
Bahía Tortugas, 93
Baja Country Club, 47
Baja gas gap, 75, 90
Baja Seasons Beach Resort, 57
Bajamar Ocean Front Golf Resort, 47
Bajamar RV Park, 194
Ballet Folklórico, 48
Balneario El Palomar, 79
Banditos, 33
Bank machines, 23
Beaches, 47, 76, 91, 114, 140, 158,
    173, 184
Benito Juárez Trailer Park, 101
Boat permits, 25

Boondock, 16
Border crossings, 25, 203, 212
Boulevard Mijares, 172
Breakdowns, 37
Bribes, 32
Brisa del Mar RV Resort, 180
Brisa Marina RV Park, 106
Butane, 31

Cabo Pulmo, 158, 160, 174
Cabo San Lucas, 16, 163, 174
Caleta San Lucas, 120
Caliente Greyhound Track, 48
California gray whales, 16, 90, 100, 140
California Trailer Park and Motel, 59
Camalú, 78
Camp Archelon, 107
Camp Gecko, 106
Campestre La Pila Balneario and Trailer
    Park, 144
Campgrounds in Mexico, 20
Campo Playa RV Park, 61
Cañon del Diablo, 184
Cañon Guadalupe, 185
Caravans, 22
Casa Blanca RV Park, 151
Cash and Credit Cards, 23
Cash machines, 23
Cataviña, 15, 90, 95, 96
Cave Art Museum, 16
Cave Art, 91, 94, 114, 115
CEDO, 200
Centro Cultural Tijuana, 48
Cerro Pedregoso, 98
Chapter Key, 6
Chula Vista RV Resort, 49

Chula Vista, 48
Cielito Lindo Motel and RV Park, 82
Ciudad Constitución, 17, 142
Club Cabo Motel and Camp Resort, 176
Club Campestre Campo de Golf Tijuana, 47, 48
Club Campestre de Mexicali, 47
Club de Pesca RV Park, 196
Colorado River Adventures, 215
Condo Suites and RV Park Playa Bonita, 191
Corona Beach Park, 65
Correcaminos RV Park, 169
Crossing the border, 24
Cuesta del Infierno, 118
Cuota, 50

Daggett's Beach Camping, 107
Debit cards, 23
Department of Fisheries, 25
Desert Oasis Bar and RV Park, 205
Diesel, 28
Discover Baja Travel Club, 25
Distance table, 21
Diving, 158, 173
Drinking water, 26
Driving, 31
Drugs, 27

Eagle statue, 98
El Arco RV Park, 178
El Arco, 109
El Cachanilla RV Park, 188
El Cardón RV Park, 152
El Cardonal Resort, 159
El Conejo, 141
El Dorado Ranch, 187
El Faro Beach Motel and Trailer Park, 64
El Jardin de Buenos Aires, 168
El Litro, 162
El Mármol, 90, 92, 96
El Pabellón RV Park, 84
El Pinacate, 201
El Pionero, 215
El Requesón, 130
El Rosario, 17, 74, 85
El Tomatal, 93, 98

El Triunfo, 164
Electricity, 37
Ensenada Los Muertos, 141, 142
Ensenada, 15, 45, 46, 60
Eréndira, 77
Estero Beach Hotel/Resort, 64
Estero Beach, 60

Ferries, 17, 28, 149
Finisterra, 172, 175
Fishing permits, 25
Fishing, 16, 28, 45, 47, 76, 91, 114, 115, 132, 140, 158, 173, 184, 201
FONATUR, 132
Frontón Palacio Jai Alai de Tijuana, 48
Fuel, 28, 45, 74, 90, 113, 139, 158, 172, 183, 199

Gas, 28
Golf, 16, 46, 114, 135, 172, 200
Golfo de Santa Clara, 24, 213
Golfo RV Park, 215
GPS, 43
Gran Desierto De Altar, 201
Green Angels, 90
Gringo Pass Motel and RV Park, 203
Groceries, 30
Guadeloupe Valley, 46
Guerrero Negro, 16, 90, 100
Guillermo's Hotel and RV Park, 105
Gulf of California, 16
Guns, 27

Hacienda De Marcos, 204
Hacienda Santa Verónica, 68
Hotel and RV Park Granada del Mar, 211
Hotel Joker, 63
Hotel Serenidad, 124

Inspection stations, 27
Insurance, 24
Internet, 30
Itinerary, 14

Josefina's La Palapa RV Camp, 192
Juanito's Garden RV Park, 167
Juncalito Beach, 136

Kayaking, 16, 91, 115, 132
Key to Symbols, 42
King's Coronita RV & Trailer Park, 59

L.A. Bay Junction, 98
La Bufadora, 60, 61
La Candelaria, 173
La Espinita Restaurant, 101
La Jolla Beach Camp, 66
La Jolla RV Park, 193
La Paz Trailer Park, 153
La Paz, 16, 148
La Playa, 174
La Posada de Don Vicente, 102
La Purísima, 141
La Reforma District, 48
La Ribera, 168, 174
La Trinidad canyon, 115
La Ventana, 153
Laguna Chapala, 98
Laguna Hanson, 47
Laguna Manuela, 93, 98
Laguna Ojo de Liebre, 90
Laguna Percebú, 184
Laguna Salada, 187
Laguna San Ignacio, 90, 94, 110
Land's End, 172, 175
Las Palmas RV Park, 119
Las Tres Vírgines, 117
Lázaro Cárdenas, 78
Libramiento, 50
Lomas del Mar, 66
Loreto Shores Villas and RV Park, 132
Loreto, 16, 113, 131
Los Arcos, 172
Los Barriles, 158, 165
Los Cerritos Campground, 164
Los Cerritos, 158
Los Frailes, 158, 161
Los Mochis, 17
Los Naranjos, 127
Lover's Beach. 175
LP Gas, 31
Lukeville, 202, 203

Malarrimo RV Park, 101
Malibu Beach Sur RV Park, 80
Manfred's RV Trailer Park, 143

Map Legend, 41
Marco's Trailer Park, 191
Martin Verdugo's Beach Resort, 166
MasterCard, 24
Meling Ranch, 77
Mesón de Don Pepe, 80
Mexicali, 26, 185
Migración, 15
Miraflores, 168
Misión el Rosario, 75, 77
Misión Nuestra Señora de Loreto, 131
Misión San Borja, 91, 93, 98
Misión San Fernando
    Velicatá, 91, 92, 95
Misión San Francisco Javier, 116, 135
Misión San Vicente Ferrer, 75
Misión Santa Gertrudis, 93
Misión Santa Maria, 91
Misión Santa Rosalía, 122
Misión Santo Domingo, 75
Misíon Santo Tomás de Aquino, 75
Mission church of San Ignacio, 110
Mission Santo Tomás de Aquino, 74, 75
Missions, 16
Mona Lisa RV Park, 65
Mordida, 32
Motel & RV Park El Moro, 133
Motel Kaadekamán, 109
Motel Sinai RV Park, 86
Mulegé, 16, 114, 122
Museo de los Misiones, 131
Museum of Anthropology, 149

Nopoló resort area, 135
Nuevo El Golfo Motel, 214

Oasis Resort, 52
Oasis RV Park, 149
Ojo de Liebre Lagoon
    Campground, 103
Ojo de Liebre, 108
Old Mill Trailer Park, 83
Old Pier (Muelle Viejo) Motel and RV
    Park, 84
Organ Pipe N.M., 203
Otay Mesa, 25

Palmar RV Park, 208

Parque Nacional Constitución
   de 1857, 47
Parque Nacional San Pedro
   Mártir, 74, 75, 77
Parque Natural Desierto Central Trailer
   Park, 96
Peregrinos RV Park, 134
Pets, 30
Picacho Diablo, 75
Pichilingue, 140
Playa Amor, 175
Playa Armenta, 130
Playa Bonita RV Park, 207
Playa Bonita, 200
Playa de Laura, 194
Playa de Oro RV Park, 210
Playa del Amor, 172, 173
Playa el Coyote, 129
Playa Elegante RV Park, 208
Playa Encantada, 54
Playa Ensenada Del Burro, 129
Playa Escondida, 128
Playa La Gringa, 107
Playa La Perla, 130
Playa Las Alejas, 184
Playa Los Cocos, 128
Playa Medano, 173, 175
Playa Miramar RV Park, 209
Playa Miramar, 200
Playa Pabellón, 76
Playa Saldamando, 58
Playa San Felipe, 184
Playa Santa María, 76
Playa Santispac, 127
Playa Solmar, 173
Playas Miramar, 154
Popotla Mobile Home Park, 56
Posada Concepción, 128
Posada Don Diego Trailer Park, 81
Potrero Regional Park, 67
Price Categories for RV Parks, 42
Propane, 31
Puertecitos, 92, 184
Puerto Escondido, 136
Puerto Lopez Mateos, 141
Puerto Nuevo, 46, 54
Puerto Peñasco, 24, 205
Puerto San Carlos, 145

Puerto San Isidro, 77
Puerto Santo Tomás, 77
Punta Arena de la Ventana, 142
Punta Arena, 127
Punta Banda, 61
Punta Chivato, 114, 121
Punta Colonet, 78
Punta Conejo, 147
Punta Pescadero, 159
Punta Prieta RV Park at the L.A. Bay
   Junction, 99

Ramona Beach Motel and RV Park, 59
Rancho La Trinidad, 115
Rancho Mal Paso RV Park, 56
Rancho Santa Inez, 97
Rancho Sordo Mudo, 70
Rancho Tecate Resort and Country
   Club, 47
Rancho Verde RV Haven, 164
Real del Mar Golf Resort, 47
Resort-Hotel San Buenaventura, 129
Rice and Beans Oasis, 110
Road type classifications, 20
Roadblocks, 27
Roads, 31, 45, 74, 90, 113, 139, 158,
   172, 183, 199
Rock-art sites, 110
Rocky Point RV Resort, 206
Rocky Point, 207
Rosarito Cora RV Park, 51
Rosarito, 46, 53
Ruben's RV Trailer Park, 192
Rupestrian art, 91
RV Camacho, 121
RV Park Campo San Felipe, 193
RV Park El Padrino, 110
RV Park Mar del Sol, 196
RV Park Nancy, 146
RV Park San Lucas Cove, 121

Safety, 32
Salsipuedes Camping, 57
San Agustín RV Park, 96
San Antonio, 164
San Diego Metro KOA, 50
San Evaristo, 141, 142
San Felipe Marina Resort RV Park, 197

San Felipe, 188
San Francisco de la Sierra, 109
San Francisco, 94
San Ignacio, 16, 17, 91, 110
San Isidro, 141
San José Comondú, 140, 141
San José de Magdalena, 115
San José del Cabo, 179
San Juan de la Costa, 141, 148
San Juanico, 141
San Louis Río Colorado, 26, 212
San Miguel Comondú, 140, 141
San Nicolas, 116
San Pedrito RV Park, 163
San Pedrito, 158
San Quintín, 15, 75, 78, 81
San Rafael RV Park, 211
San Sebastian, 116
San Vicente, 78
San Ysidro, 25, 48
Sandy Beach, 200
Santa Rosalía, 16, 114, 118
Santa Rosalillita, 93, 98
Santiago, 158, 168
Santo Tomás Valley, 74
Santo Tomás, 78
Scammon's Lagoon, 16
Security, 32
Sierra de la Giganta, 16
Sierra de la Laguna, 16, 17, 160
Sierra San Francisco, 109
Sightseeing, 46, 75, 90, 114, 140, 158,
    172, 200
Sonora free zone, 24
Sonoyta, 26, 202
State border, 98
Superclorination, 26
Surfing, 47, 58, 76, 77, 91

Tecate KOA, Rancho Ojai, 68
Tecate, 26, 67
Telephones, 33
Temporary vehicle permits, 24
The Orchard RV Park, 123
Tijuana Trolley, 48
Tijuana, 15, 25, 48
Time zones, 99
Todos Santos, 17, 158, 161

Toll Road, 50
Topolobampo, 17
Tourist card, 24
Tourist Permits, 15
Traffic cops, 32
Trailer Park Martin Quezada Ruíz, 111
Trailer Park Señorial, 210
Travel Clubs, 25
Travel Library, 35
Traveler's checks, 23
Tripui RV Park-Hotel Resort, 136
Tropic of Cancer, 158, 168
Type 1 road defined, 20
Type 2 road defined, 20
Type 3 road defined, 20

Units of measurement, 36

Vagabundos del Mar RV Park, 177
Vagabundos del Mar, 25
Vehicle Permits, 15
Vehicle preparation, 37
Vicente Guerrero, 78
Victor's RV Park, 195
Villa de San Miguel, 58
Villa Maria Isabel Recreational
    Park, 124
Villa Serena, 178
Villa Vitta Hotel Resort, 106
Villarino Campamento Turistico, 66
Villas de Loreto Resort, 133
Visa, 24
Vista del Mar, 192
Vizcaíno, 109
Vizcaíno Desert, 108

Water Sports, 47, 76, 91, 114, 140, 158,
    173, 184, 200
Water treatment, 26
Water, 38
Weather, 38
Whale watching, 60
Wineries, 46

Zona Río Tijuana, 48

ABOUT THE AUTHORS

Several years ago Terri and Mike Church decided to travel full-time. Their savings wouldn't cover hotels and restaurants for anything like the length of time they wanted to be on the road. On the other hand living out of a backpack wasn't a particularly attractive idea either. RVs turned out to be the perfect compromise.

In their time on the road the Churches have toured the continental U.S., Europe, Alaska, and Mexico in one type of RV or other. During the course of their travels they noticed that few guidebooks were available with the essential day-to-day information that camping travelers need when they are in unfamiliar surroundings. *Traveler's Guide to European Camping, Traveler's Guide to Mexican Camping, Traveler's Guide to Alaskan Camping, RV Adventures in the Pacific Northwest,* and *Traveler's Guide To Camping Mexico's Baja* are designed to be the guidebooks that the authors tried to find when they first traveled to these places.

Terri and Mike now have a base of operations in the Seattle, Washington area but they continue to spend at least nine months of each year traveling. The entire first edition of the Europe book and most of the Mexico, Alaska, Northwest, and Baja books were written and formatted for printing using laptop computers while on the road.

Traveler's Guide To Alaskan Camping
6" x 9" Paperback, 416 Pages, Over 100 Maps
ISBN 0-9652968-2-2

Alaska, the dream trip of a lifetime! Be prepared for something spectacular. Alaska is one-fifth the size of the entire United States, it has 17 of the 20 highest peaks in the U.S., 33,904 miles of shoreline, and has more active glaciers and ice fields than the rest of the inhabited world.

In addition to some of the most magnificent scenery the world has to offer, Alaska is chock full of an amazing variety of wildlife. You are likely to see bald eagles, Dall sheep, moose, bison, brown bears, caribou, beavers, black bears, a wide variety of marine birds and waterfowl, whales, porpoises, sea lions, sea otters, and more. Some of these animals may even pay you a visit at your campsite.

Alaska is an outdoor enthusiast's paradise. Fishing, hiking, canoeing, rafting, hunting, and wildlife viewing are only a few of the many activities which will keep you outside during the long summer days.

Traveler's Guide To Alaskan Camping makes this dream trip to Alaska as easy as camping in the "lower 48". It provides details on:

- ❑ Over 400 campgrounds throughout Alaska and on the roads north in Canada with full campground descriptions and maps showing the exact location of each campground.
- ❑ Complete coverage of the routes north, including the Alaska Highway, the Cassiar Highway, and the Alaska Marine Highway.
- ❑ RV rental information for both Alaska and Canada.
- ❑ Things to do and see throughout your trip, including suggested fishing holes, hiking trails, canoe trips, wildlife viewing opportunities, and much more.

Traveler's Guide To European Camping
6" x 9" Paperback, 448 Pages, Over 250 Maps
ISBN 0-9652968-3-0

Does the map on the side of your camping rig show you've visited most of the 48 contiguous states, Alaska, or even Mexico? You've shopped the biggest mall in America, wintered in the Florida Keys, camped in the desert outside Quartzsite, Arizona, seen the color in the Northeast in the fall? What next?

If you're looking for a new camping experience, try Europe. *Traveler's Guide To European Camping* makes touring the European continent as easy and as affordable as traveling in North America. The guide gives you complete information for planning your trip as well as cost data and specific instructions on how to ship your camping vehicle from North America to Europe, buy a camping vehicle in Europe, or rent a camping vehicle in Europe.

The guide covers almost 250 campgrounds including several in each important European city. Both driving directions and maps are provided to make finding the campgrounds in these foreign cities as easy as finding those in America. The book features campgrounds in:

* Paris	* Munich	* The Romantic Road
* London	* Madrid	* The Loire Valley
* Rome	* Athens	* The Swiss Alps
* Lisbon	* Istanbul	* The Greek Islands
* Amsterdam	* Oslo	* And Many More!

In addition to planning and campground information, *Traveler's Guide To European Camping* gives you invaluable details about the history and sights you will encounter. This information will help you plan your itinerary and enjoy yourself when you are on the road.

Go for a week, a month, or a year. Europe could fill your vacations or RVing seasons for years to come!

Traveler's Guide To Mexican Camping
6" x 9" Paperback, 416 Pages, Over 200 Maps
ISBN 0-9652968-1-4

How would you like to spend your winter camped near crystal-clear blue water on a white sand beach? Mexico has many world–famous beach resorts, and they all have campgrounds. Try Cancun, Acapulco, Ixtapa, Mazatlan, or Puerto Vallarta. If you are looking for a beach, but not a resort town, Mexico has miles and miles of beautiful, empty beaches and many of them also offer camping opportunities.

If beaches aren't your thing, don't despair. The interior of Mexico is full of attractions. Many North Americans are drawn to the superior climate and cultural attractions of Guadalajara, Lake Chapala, San Miguel de Allende, Alamos, Guanajuato, and Cuernavaca.

Visit Mexico City, the largest city in the world. Or see the Pre-Columbian Mesoamerican archeological sites scattered throughout the country. There are so many sites you may even discover one yourself!

Traveler's Guide To Mexican Camping will give you all the information you need to cross the border and travel Mexico like a veteran. The book features:

- ❑ Complete descriptions of over 200 campgrounds, accompanied by maps and detailed driving instructions for each campground listed. You'll know the exact location of virtually every campground in Mexico.

- ❑ Coverage of the entire Mexico mainland and the Baja Peninsula.

- ❑ Four possible itineraries including the Baja Peninsula, the Grand Coastal Tour, Colonial Mexico, and Down the West Coast.

- ❑ Border Crossing Information including maps of the major border crossing cities.

- ❑ Descriptions of sights to see and things to do in every city covered by the guide.

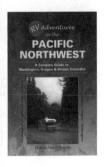

RV Adventures in the Pacific Northwest
6" x 9" Paperback, 224 Pages, Over 75 Maps
ISBN 0-9652968-4-9

There are many reasons why the Pacific Northwest is considered an RVers paradise. It offers everything an RV vacationer could desire; seashores, snow-topped mountains, old-growth forests, visitor-friendly cities, and national parks. In fact, the Pacific Northwest is one of the most popular RVing destinations in North America.

RV Adventures in the Pacific Northwest provides exciting and interesting 1-week itineraries from the Northwest gateway cities of Seattle, Portland, and Vancouver. Maps and written descriptions guide you along scenic easy-to-negotiate tours. Each day's drive is to an interesting destination. The book includes descriptions of the local attractions and activities as well as maps showing good local RV campgrounds.

So come and join us for a tour of the Northwest. Go for a week or spend the entire summer, the choice is yours. Here are a few of the well known destinations we'll visit:

* The Olympic Peninsula	* Mount Rainier
* Mount St. Helens	* The North Cascades
* The Oregon Coast	* The Oregon Trail
* The Columbia Gorge	* Hell's Canyon
* Victoria	* Vancouver Island
* Banff and Lake Louise	* And Lots More!!

To order complete the following and send to:

Rolling Homes Press
P.O. Box 2099
Kirkland, WA 98083-2099

Name_____

Address_____

City_____State_____Zip_____

Telephone_____

Description	Qty	Price	Subtotal
Traveler's Guide To Alaskan Camping	____	$19.95	_____
Traveler's Guide To Mexican Camping	____	$19.95	_____
Traveler's Guide To Camping Mexico's Baja	____	$12.95	_____
Traveler's Guide To European Camping	____	$19.95	_____
RV Adventures in the Pacific Northwest	____	$14.95	_____

Subtract - Multiple Title Discounts

3 Book Set (3 Different Titles Shown Above)	**-10.00**	_____
4 Book Set (4 Different Titles Shown Above)	**-15.00**	_____
5 Book Set (5 Different Titles Shown Above)	**-20.00**	_____

Method of Payment
- ❑ Check
- ❑ Visa
- ❑ Mastercard

Order total: _____

Shipping: 4.00 *

Total: _____

Credit Card # _____ Exp. date _____

Signature _____

To order by phone call toll free from the U.S. or Canada 1-888-265-6555
Outside the U.S. or Canada call (425) 822-7846
Have your VISA or MC ready

U.S. Dollars or MC/VISA only for non-U.S. orders

Rolling Homes Press is not responsible for taxes or duty on books shipped
outside the U.S.

*$4 shipping regardless of quantity ordered for all orders sent to the same address

Visit our web site at **www.rollinghomes.com**